Introduction to Ethnographic Research

This work is dedicated to humanistic teachers everywhere who go beyond instruction and into the hearts of their students.

Sara Miller McCune founded SAGE Publishing in 1965 to support the dissemination of usable knowledge and educate a global community. SAGE publishes more than 1000 journals and over 800 new books each year, spanning a wide range of subject areas. Our growing selection of library products includes archives, data, case studies and video. SAGE remains majority owned by our founder and after her lifetime will become owned by a charitable trust that secures the company's continued independence.

Los Angeles | London | New Delhi | Singapore | Washington DC | Melbourne

Introduction to Ethnographic Research

A Guide for Anthropology

Kimberly Kirner
California State University, Northridge

Jan Mills
Greater Albany Public Schools

Los Angeles | London | New Delhi
Singapore | Washington DC | Melbourne

FOR INFORMATION:

SAGE Publications, Inc.
2455 Teller Road
Thousand Oaks, California 91320
E-mail: order@sagepub.com

SAGE Publications Ltd.
1 Oliver's Yard
55 City Road
London, EC1Y 1SP
United Kingdom

SAGE Publications India Pvt. Ltd.
B 1/I 1 Mohan Cooperative Industrial Area
Mathura Road, New Delhi 110 044
India

SAGE Publications Asia-Pacific Pte. Ltd.
18 Cross Street #10-10/11/12
China Square Central
Singapore 048423

Printed in the United States of America

Library of Congress Cataloging-in-Publication Data

Names: Kirner, Kimberly, author. | Mills, Jan, author.

Title: Introduction to ethnographic research : a guide for anthropology / Kimberly Kirner, California State University Northridge, Jan Mills, Greater Albany Public Schools.

Description: Los Angeles : SAGE, [2020] | Includes bibliographical references and index.

Identifiers: LCCN 2019020593 | ISBN 9781544334011 (paperback)

Subjects: LCSH: Ethnology—Research—Methodology. | Anthropology–Research.

Classification: LCC GN345 .K57 2020 | DDC 305.8/00723–dc23

LC record available at https://lccn.loc.gov/2019020593

SUSTAINABLE FORESTRY INITIATIVE

Certified Chain of Custody
Promoting Sustainable Forestry
www.sfiprogram.org
SFI-01268

SFI label applies to text stock

Acquisitions Editor: Josh Perigo
Content Development Editor: Alissa Nance
Editorial Assistant: Noelle Cumberbatch
Marketing Manager: Zina Craft
Production Editor: Veronica Stapleton Hooper
Copy Editor: Laureen Gleason
Typesetter: Hurix Digital
Proofreader: Dennis W. Webb
Indexer: Jeanne R. Busemeyer
Cover Designer: Scott Van Atta

This book is printed on acid-free paper.

19 20 21 22 23 10 9 8 7 6 5 4 3 2 1

Brief Contents

Detailed Contents

Preface

We are a mother–daughter duo who are passionate about teaching, especially for students who come underprepared and under-resourced. We deeply believe in the ability of all students to learn and grow, and in the capacity for education to be transformational for individuals and entire communities. Our central tenet is that methodological skill is a cornerstone for social change work. Students trained in qualitative methodology gain more than new knowledge and skills: They develop critical thinking and analysis skills, they learn the power of storytelling, and they begin to "own" their own stories and a role they can play in serving their own or others' communities. While methodology is so often thought of as a dry, academic set of skills for students to master, to us, it is part of the foundation for empowering students as future academics, advocates, and activists. It builds on the informal and intuitive ways students already come to know their social worlds, and it offers formalized ways to merge the objective and subjective, to reflect deeply and carefully, and to become recognized as legitimate producers of knowledge.

While we are critical of this process of legitimacy, believing in multiple intelligences and learning styles, multiple backgrounds and competencies, and multiple ways of knowing as equally legitimate, we recognize that power and authority are embedded in formalized systems of education and knowledge production. Our goal, therefore, is to open such formalized education in methodology in inclusive, accessible ways to students who may be entering such an endeavor from an underserved or underrepresented social space. We were once those students: a young mother working on her bachelor's degree as her oldest daughter finished high school. Indeed, we completed our doctorates in the same decade! We were, together, the first in our families to achieve the terminal degree in our fields, and we came to that place through state university systems. We conquered our own poverty through our educations, and we have dedicated our lives since to serving similar communities through our teaching and research. We have lived the transformative power of education, personally and professionally, and we hope that this will also be the path for many students who encounter this book and then bring their new capacities back to their families and communities.

Connecting the Workbook and the Textbook

Students who are beginning to learn about the research process often struggle not with *how* to acquire data but rather with how to articulate *what* their project is and *why* their project matters. Most students in anthropology, sociology, psychology, or other social science fields can, relatively early on, learn to ask questions in an interview or to make a survey—even if it feels uncomfortable at first. However, students frequently feel a bit lost in how to understand the comprehensive process of research—from design to write-up. Creating a design that works, analyzing data in meaningful ways, and describing their findings to others are at the heart of the challenge. This text was created to help you—the student learning qualitative methods for the first time—understand *and be able to execute* the entire process of research design. The first time will be awkward as you try many new things, but the only way to get good at something is to practice, so be brave and leap in!

This textbook is part of a textbook–workbook combination, which is meant as a basic introduction to qualitative and mixed methods research for undergraduate students. Instructors have the option to use both texts or either one. Your instructor might use the textbook and design their own activities for you to complete, or they might use the workbook and assign a variety of readings connected to the activities they assign you. In both the workbook and the textbook, you'll notice we orient you to learning objectives, which tell you what you'll learn in each chapter. In the textbook, we review concepts (including providing definitions of key terms) and provide many examples to help you understand these concepts. We also provide visual diagrams to help you understand some of the concepts and processes and a study guide to orient you to the key terms and information. In each chapter, we also provide a brief case study, based on an interview, of an example of an ethnographic research project conducted by a mid- or late-career cultural anthropologist. The reference to the case study provides the student (and instructor) with material to draw from for scholarly reading, but the interview offers a conversation with the anthropologist, in their own words, describing their decisions in their research project, what they learned over time as a researcher, and the advice they'd give to student researchers. We conclude our chapters with reflection questions that bring together the case study interview and the students' own experiences and interests.

In the workbook, we begin with learning objectives that are more experiential and skill (process) oriented, and we start each chapter by asking students to reflect on their own lives and experiences related to the chapter's topic. We then offer scaffolded, detailed activities to teach the chapter's topic step by step. Each activity begins with a brief orienting "background" that links the activity to the core concepts in the textbook (an extensive, detailed discussion of these concepts is available in the corresponding textbook chapter). These activities include detailed instructions and examples and non-examples (so that students know what a good and a poor response look like). At the end of each chapter, there is a *culminating activity* that allows you to comprehensively demonstrate what you've learned for that topic. Finally, the workbook offers multiple *culminating experiences* that demonstrate your new methodological skills across chapters in an integrated fashion. This process is designed to take you from A to Z in qualitative research design, beginning with selecting a topic for focus, trying various methods to answer your research question, and concluding with one or more projects that demonstrate what you've learned (and help you take your project from exploratory to a thesis-worthy design).

You might notice a few things about our textbook–workbook combination that are different from most of the textbooks you've had as a student:

- *Conversational tone:* This book is meant to be as comfortable an introduction to methodology as possible. Think of it as a conversation between us, the authors (a professor of cultural anthropology and a master teacher, both qualitative methodologists), and you, the beginning researcher.

- *Sticking to the basics of each method, but covering a range of methods:* This book was written for beginners, so we stick to the basics as we cover design and each method. Rather than go deeply into any one method, we cover what you need to get started for many methods. You will need more practice after this in order to work as a professional researcher, but this is a good starting point that covers most of the research-based work available to college graduates.

- *Bridge to application:* While the methods and research design process we discuss are relevant to academic anthropology, the examples often draw on applied dimensions of the social sciences—because this is where the majority of the jobs are and because the majority of students will not acquire a doctoral degree.

- *A wide range of examples, especially thesis-level examples:* We offer primarily examples that students would encounter in BA- or MA-level thesis projects or those they might encounter in application/practice after they graduate.

For the student wishing to go on to graduate school, or the graduate student who has newly embarked in the social sciences and for whom this is a preliminary introduction to or a helpful reminder of the basics—you will want a number of books on methods. No one book is sufficient on its own: You'll want one or a few introductory books like this, one or two that link method and theory more explicitly, at least one more advanced and comprehensive book, at least one or more books specifically on ethnographic writing, and one or more that specifically address specialized methods you plan to use for your thesis. If you plan to train as an applied or practicing anthropologist, you will also want to get one or more applied anthropology methods textbooks that teach you how to adjust qualitative methods for more rapid, focused research. Our textbook offers a brief list of suggested readings at the end of each chapter related to that chapter's topic, which is a good start to identify other books you may wish to invest in if you plan to pursue a graduate education. If you plan to enter another field using qualitative methodology, such as education or social work, you will (likewise) want to augment any methods training with books that bridge general qualitative methods and your specific field. But this is a good way to start, so let's get going!

Ancillaries

SAGE Instructor Resources support teaching by making it easy to integrate quality content and create a rich learning environment for students. Go to **study.sagepub.com/kirner** to access the companion site.

- Editable, chapter-specific **PowerPoint®** slides offer complete flexibility for creating a multimedia presentation for the course.

- **Class activities** for individual or group projects reinforce active learning.

Doing Ethnographic Research is a new companion workbook designed to accompany this textbook. The workbook aligns active learning and critical thinking applications with the 12 chapters, offering hands-on materials that prepare students to be effective researchers.

Acknowledgments

Kimberly Kirner: In all my work, I first give thanks to and for my parents, one of whom is the coauthor of this book! My parents modeled for me a strong work ethic and a passion for making a difference in the world, and this has shaped my entire career. Second, I would like to thank my advisers and key professors from University of California, Riverside, who shaped my development as an anthropologist across my entire student career. Gene (E. N.) Anderson was always an engaged, supportive adviser, from the time he took me on at the beginning of my bachelor's work, through my honors thesis, and eventually as my doctoral adviser. Gene is a brilliant scholar who has never lost his excitement for learning, doing fieldwork, or writing; I can never aspire to his prolific level of reading and publication, but I like to think I picked up his never-ending thrill of pursuing new knowledge. His works and guidance, so often in hours-long conversations at his office throughout my entire student career, developed my passion for ethnoecology and cultural ecology, as well as allowed me to have a very individualized space for processing theory. My other doctoral committee members, David Kronenfeld and Maria Cruz-Torres, were also instrumental in my development, each providing a different piece to the methodological and theoretical puzzle my work demands. David's research and coursework formed my training in cognitive anthropology, and his guidance and insights continue to shape my work. Maria was a model for me as a female anthropologist conducting doctoral work in a male-dominated subculture. Her work and classes in political ecology built my understanding of the integration of political and economic systems in the lives of communities and their places, but more than this, her caring support and the courage she showed in her own research helped me know I could also walk such a path.

Jan Mills: Thank you to my daughters, Kimberly and Brooke, who taught me so very much about providing for children's needs and how differently those may be expressed. I want to thank my father for teaching me the importance of freedom and giving back to the world; my mother, who taught me the importance of family and independence; and my sister Jackie for sharing the sacred journey. Also, thanks to the children, families, and staff of Rialto Unified School District, who taught me the importance of community. Finally, thanks to Helen Howard for her unending belief in my capabilities and Diane Williams, who was my supervisor so long ago and who trusted me to creatively teach "outside the box," thereby allowing me to reach so many students from diverse backgrounds.

Collectively, we would like to thank our students, who have taught us how to teach, even as we have taught them.

We would also like to thank the anthropologists who so generously provided us with their time, their willingness to reflect on their fieldwork experiences (and even mistakes!), and the insights that they pass on to beginning researchers. Thank you to E. N. (Gene) Anderson, Maria Cruz-Torres, David Kronenfeld, Sabina Magliocco, Yolanda Moses, Suzanne Scheld, and Carlos Vélez-Ibáñez.

SAGE would like to thank the following reviewers:

Carol Chetkovich, *Mills College*

Kimberly Dark, *California State University, San Marcos*

Sarah Daynes, *University of North Carolina, Greensboro*

Susan I. Dummer, *Georgetown College*

Patricia Gagne, *University of Louisville*

Anastasia Hudgins, *University of Pennsylvania*

Lisa R. Merriweather, *University of North Carolina at Charlotte*

Robert A. Rubinstein, *Syracuse University*

Armando L. Trujillo, *University of Texas at San Antonio*

About the Authors

Kimberly Kirner: I grew up fascinated with other cultures and nature, so I suppose it was inevitable that I would eventually become a cultural anthropologist. Yet I initially began my BS in biomedical sciences, intending to become a surgeon. While volunteering in a hospice program for terminally ill women with no surviving family, I realized I was much more interested in my patients' stories and the impact of social systems on the human experience than I was in my patients as medical cases. I found anthropology to offer the most compelling union of social and natural sciences and switched majors. I then continued in anthropology for the rest of my student career, eventually receiving my doctorate in cultural anthropology from University of California, Riverside in 2007.

As an applied anthropologist, my research primarily focuses on using anthropological approaches, theories, and methods to work toward solving environmental problems and related issues in human well-being and health. More specifically, my research is in the application of cognitive anthropology (decision-making studies, cultural model theory, and ethnoscience) to critical policy and systems studies and to community-based or grassroots efforts at improving the lives of human and other-than-human beings. I am interested in the relationships between cultural knowledge systems and worldview, identity and community, and behavior. My research has focused on the ethnoecology of the American West and contemporary Pagans (contextualized by American political and economic systems) and issues of cultural competency for minority religious practitioners in the American healthcare system. In addition to my academic work, I work as a practicing anthropologist in organizational capacity building, program design, and program evaluation, particularly for organizations focused on mental health and social services. When not working, I can be found riding my horses, hiking, creating visual art, and reading works by mystics.

Jan Mills: As a child, I didn't sit still but was constantly outside exploring the rural environments in which I lived. My second favorite place to be was in school, learning with fascination about the natural world around us. I became a mother at the tender age of twenty, and my learning then took a back seat to parenting, which became my new focus of learning. From community college to a four-year university and over a decade of time, I finally achieved my BA in sociology, with a heavy concentration in psychology and child development right up until my last semester, when I finally had to choose one discipline for my BA. Being aware of my talent and intuitive skills for working with children, I immediately went into the teacher credential program at California State University, San Bernardino and received such a strong education in instruction that twenty-five years later, teachers are still learning what I learned long ago.

I finished my doctorate in education at Oregon State University in 2010, having begun while working as a teacher in a first-grade classroom in a public school. My doctoral research focused on how, in my role as a teacher, I could co-create a more functional learning environment for the whole group by helping develop students' individual capacities to self-regulate their behavioral choices (helping develop their executive functioning skills). In the role of observing participant using an ethnographic self-study approach, I conducted research on classroom management covering an entire school year, seeking to identify the most effective interventions for a large group of highly disruptive primary students with high needs. My ongoing research focuses on the dysfunctional behaviors that have increased in the classroom over the past decades, increasing in both severity and in sheer numbers of students. Though there have been periods of time when I've left the classroom to do administrative work in education, I've always felt pulled back to the elementary classroom, where children need me most. My personal interests include backpacking and hiking, reading for pleasure about current work in quantum physics, and sustaining a positive relationship with an Energy greater than myself.

CHAPTER 1

Introduction
The Basics of Research Design

Orientation

The first step to doing research is design. In order to do research well, we have to generate a research question, identify the assumptions that are grounded in our work, and then create a plan for collecting and analyzing data. This plan isn't only the specifics of what we plan to do and how we'll do it; it's also how we're defining our research question itself and the aspects of what we're studying. It's through the planning process that we clarify *what* we will study, *how* we will study it, and *why* it's important. This is the foundation of good, professional research. So let's get started as beginning researchers!

Ways of Knowing

People come to know things in many different ways. We learn in various kinds of environments—some more formal than others (e.g., in a classroom vs. from your grandmother)—and we also produce knowledge using different means. If you think about it, you can probably find examples of things you know that you learned or produced in different ways. You might know about a religious holiday—what happens during a service, what families do before and after, and so on—because you've participated in it year after year. You could know that you should buckle up when you're in the car because you were told this by your parents, you learned formally about seatbelt laws and traffic safety statistics in Driver Education classes, and you are reminded about safety through anecdotes you hear about car accidents and what happened to the passengers. Qualitative research is a way of *formally* establishing knowledge but allowing you to capture *folk or vernacular* cultural understandings and agreements. That is, as a researcher, you will draft a formal design to collect data, analyze the data, and

Chapter Learning Objectives

Students will be able to do the following:

1.1 Identify underlying assumptions and connect them to research methods

1.2 Identify how inductive and deductive research work together

1.3 Identify and justify dependent and independent variables

1.4 Understand operational definitions

1.5 Explain how to optimize levels of measurement and units of analysis in research

1.6 Explain the relationship of research projects, methods, and theories

1.7 Recognize common mistakes in ethnographic research

1.8 Explain the factors that lead researchers to select a particular research topic

report about the data. However, the data you will look at will include and encompass your participants' knowledge and ways of knowing. You are producing knowledge about others' knowledge!

The important thing that sets your research apart from journalism or a travelogue or an anecdote is that you start with a formal plan that integrates specific *theories* from your field or discipline, *methods* that collect and analyze data, and *plans for reporting* that present your data to an identified audience. So what do we mean by *methods*? You're probably sitting in a methods class right now (or trying to learn on your own about them). We actually mean three different things when we talk about **methods**:

1. **Epistemology**, or the study of how we know stuff. This involves the question "What do I think are valid ways of knowing?" This bridges theory with method, and it helps you select analytical frameworks (and in some cases, ways of collecting data).

2. **Strategic methods** (what most people initially think of when they hear the word *methods*). That is, specifically how will you collect or analyze data. This answers questions such as "Should I conduct a survey or do participant observation?" Strategic methods are selected in part based on your epistemology and in part for other reasons that we'll discuss in detail later, such as the amount of time you have.

3. **Techniques**, or the nitty-gritty details of how you choose to do what you choose to do. For example, if you choose to do interviews, you might ask, "How will I choose my informants?" Again, as with choosing strategic methods, sometimes you select techniques for reasons of design, and other times you select them based on expediency.

Methods The researcher's approach to collecting and analyzing data; this includes epistemology, strategic methods, and techniques.

Epistemology The study of how we know things.

Strategic methods How data are collected and/or analyzed.

Techniques The details of how a researcher chooses to do what they choose to do.

Everyone—and we mean *everyone*—has underlying assumptions that affect all three of these choices you'll make in methods. Underlying assumptions are working hypotheses and biases you have about the world that affect the way you perceive your surroundings and yourself, the way you would usually gather information and assess it, and the way you view your role as a researcher. Because we're social animals, we're hardwired to develop these assumptions, and they're usually related to our broader culture (our learned and shared behaviors and ideas). They allow us to function with relative ease and calm in the many social interactions we have every day, but they also can hamper our freedom of thought and open-mindedness as researchers. There is no way to entirely escape underlying assumptions, so they are built into even the *grand theories* (the famous, really big ideas about human life) in the social sciences.

Underlying assumptions that influence each of us and the grand theories include things such as these:

- *Constructivist view:* the idea that reality is constructed uniquely by each person (a more humanistic orientation)

- *Positivist view:* the idea that an external reality (outside of us) is waiting for us to discover it through our approximations of this real truth (the scientific method)

- *Rationalist view:* the idea that we know things because we can reason about them

- *Empiricist view:* the idea that we know things because we have experiences of them (through our senses), and we are also always skeptical because we can never be sure of the truth (because our experience changes over time)

If you're in a field like anthropology, which has a lively and long-standing discussion about appropriate underlying assumptions, you might find a sometimes passionate (even argumentative) debate about whether the discipline is a science or part of the humanities. These two broad-based positions treat "truth" as different concepts—and therefore with different ways of studying and understanding it. Science is inherently empiricist and often positivist: science strives for objectivity (replicable studies that don't depend on the researcher's identity) and chases truths that are thought to be external to the individual researcher. Science, therefore, is very explicit in its methods and measurements, with the ideal that another researcher could replicate (do again, the same way, with the same results) a person's research design and that the findings are generalizable (the findings are broadly applicable across the population the researcher defines). Data are acquired through direct observation (whether in experimental design, such as chemistry, or observation alone, such as astronomy). Even though science isn't always experimental, it's always striving for objectivity (even if, arguably, it can't entirely reach this goal).

The humanities have a totally different way of understanding truth—and therefore a different way of trying to capture it. The truth is not an absolute but instead is decided by individual human judgments. Instead of trying to find generalizable truths, humanities scholars attempt to understand and articulate the web of meanings that humans create and live in. They argue that humans are unique in this way, so they have to be studied differently. Many social science disciplines, such as anthropology, live in an in-between space—part science, part humanities. In part, this has to do with the sorts of research questions that people have in such fields. An anthropologist might ask, "How did this particular group affect plant biodiversity through their plant collection methods over the last fifty years?" This question would lend itself more to a science-oriented epistemological framework. Another anthropologist might ask, "What is the meaning of this ritual that this particular group does before it goes to gather this particular plant?" That question is entirely different in its nature and lends itself more to a humanities-oriented epistemological framework. At the same time, both anthropologists may employ the same *strategic methods* and even *techniques:* In this case, both might decide to select a number of key informants (particularly knowledgeable people in a group) to interview and observe.

Beginning students often mistake *qualitative* for *quantitative* methods and data for the science versus humanities debate: They mix up letters (as opposed to numbers) to be about epistemology. But this is not what the science versus humanities debate is about at all. Science can use qualitative methods and data (such as an astronomer's description of an event), and humanities can use quantitative methods and data (such as a historian looking at census records to describe the populations of different ethnic groups in a nation over time). It is helpful if students can try to differentiate by asking these questions:

1. What is the research question? Is the research question better addressed through looking for an objective truth (that is replicable and generalizable) or looking for a variety of meanings people are making—or both?

2. What is the researcher's theoretical orientation? Is it more about finding out one answer or articulating a variety of viewpoints?

3. Does the research question need text-based information and assessments or numbers-based measurements (or both) to be answered?

Deduction A way of conducting research that begins with selecting a theory, then creates hypotheses to test theory, and finally conducts research that generates observations to support or refute the hypotheses.

Induction A way of conducting research that begins with collecting data on a topic, then generates hypotheses based on the data, and finally uses hypotheses to build or discuss relevant theory.

Hypothetico-deductive model A two-stage process that combines inductive research (as the first exploratory stage) and deductive research (as the second confirmatory stage).

Exploratory research The stage of research that explores a research topic through collecting data and using those observations to (1) refine the research question and (2) select and build on relevant theory.

Discussion

Think for a moment (and then jot down) what your underlying assumptions are in how you see the world. Do you find that you trust statistics and measurements more? Or stories and relationships? Do you tend to think there is one truth or answer, or do you think that the truth is always contested and arguable? Are you more apt to collect many different experiences and stories and think all of them are right for different reasons, or do you assess which ones are more reliable and in agreement (and see the rest as outliers)? Can you give one or more examples of how your underlying assumptions have been put to use in your life? (Bonus: Can you think of a time when your assumptions served you well and a time when they didn't?)

Research Stages

There are two basic ways in which research is conducted: deductive research and inductive research. **Deduction** happens when a researcher starts with a theory, creates hypotheses that test the theory, and then conducts research that generates observations that either support or refute the hypotheses (and therefore, by extension, the theory to a certain extent). **Induction** happens when a researcher starts with making observations (that is, collecting data), then generates ideas about what the data are saying (hypotheses), and from there, builds or discusses relevant theory. Many research projects, over the long term, use both of these approaches in the **hypothetico-deductive model**, which combines the two (see Figure 1.1).

How this works is by using a two-stage process:

1. Stage 1 is **exploratory research**: It explores a research question through collecting data and then figuring out from those observations what further refinements to the research question should occur in the future, as well as what theories the data speak to.

2. Stage 2 is **confirmatory research**: It takes what was learned in the exploratory stage and develops a research design that combines these findings with relevant theory to develop hypotheses that can be tested with further observation.

For example, let's use the example of one of the author's (Jan Mills's) doctoral dissertations. She was working on a doctorate in education while also professionally teaching

Figure 1.1 The Hypothetico-Deductive Model

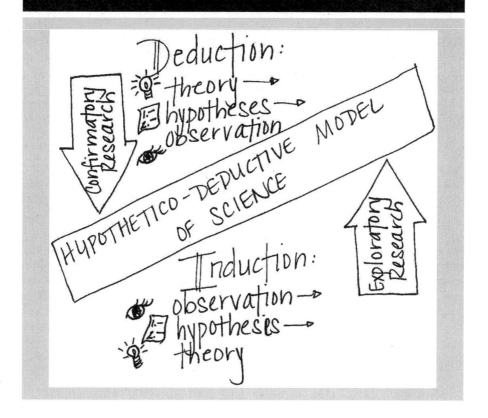

first grade. She was interested in how, in her role as teacher, she could co-create a more functional learning environment for the whole group by helping develop students' individual capacities to self-regulate their behavioral choices. Further, she explored how these interactions between students and teacher linked back to later interactions and student outcomes. She conducted her doctoral dissertation using an exploratory approach, particularly using autoethnography as a method (observing and writing about one's own life experiences ethnographically). Through this, she developed hypotheses about an effective approach to classroom management with a large group of students demonstrating challenging behaviors, based on patterns in student–teacher interactions over time and behavioral outcomes in students. If she wanted, she could have followed up with a confirmatory study, perhaps combining interviews and classroom observations of other teachers with a widely distributed survey to understand their own senses of classroom management under similar conditions and how they reflect on their interactions with students.

Many research projects are carried out this way in the social sciences, and most thesis and dissertation projects that graduate students complete are exploratory research. Then, if students go on to academic careers, they often refine and expand on their initial

Confirmatory research The stage of research that develops a research design to further refine initial findings through developing hypotheses and ways to test them with further data collection and analysis.

work through confirmatory research. When you think about research topics you might like to explore, keep in mind that you are likely to develop a design that follows an exploratory, inductive approach. This way, you won't feel too overwhelmed by the process. You should take the process of finding a topic seriously, because many students find that this can be developed into a suitable master's or undergraduate capstone thesis project—which often later informs a dissertation and even sets the stage for a person's later academic career. But at the same time, remember that you need to start with only a small piece of your larger interest and that researchers also can later change their focus to a certain extent. Don't feel locked in to a topic you pick at this early stage, but also take seriously the process of developing a project—it could lead to your future as a researcher!

Variables

There is a lot of jargon—or specialized language—social scientists use to talk about research. We'll cover some of the basics here. You'll want to begin trying to use these terms in your discussions with classmates, so that you become comfortable and familiar with them. **Variables** are aspects of a research question that can take on more than one value. Researchers define variables, look for relationships between them, and try to understand what causes them. Variables can be **unidimensional**, which means they have a single value for every case and are easy to measure, such as age, birth order, or height, or they can be multidimensional. **Multidimensional** variables have more than one aspect to them and multiple factors that lead to them—and can therefore have multiple values for every case, such as political orientation or household income. These are harder to define and measure. Is political orientation what someone self-identifies as? Or their voting record? Or how their beliefs and values about various topics stack up against official political stances of political parties? Is income considered only salary, or is it also inclusive of occasional side jobs, yard sales, and gifts? Some variables are very challenging to measure and also under debate as to how to define them, particularly because they are charged with emotion and political import: These include variables such as race and ethnicity, gender, sexual orientation, and relationship (formerly marital) status.

Variables can be all sorts of things, including both things we can observe and things we can only ask other people about. They can include the following:

- Internal states (such as people's thoughts, feelings, worldviews, and meanings)

- Demographic characteristics (such as people's age, gender, and race/ethnicity)

- Behaviors (what we observe people doing)

- Artifacts (things that people use or make)

- Environments (both physical and social)

Many studies in the social sciences seek to understand the relationships between many of these variables at once. For example, one of the author's (Kimberly Kirner's) studies investigated the potential relationships between Pagans' beliefs, demographic

Variables Aspects of a research question that can take on more than one value.

Unidimensional A term describing a variable that has only a single value for each case.

Multidimensional A term describing a variable that has multiple aspects to it and factors that lead to it—and can therefore have multiple values for each case.

characteristics, spiritual practices, and household-level sustainable behaviors. In part, what we are often trying to figure out is which of these variables cause the others. That is, which are **independent variables** (those that exist on their own, unaffected by the others), and which are **dependent variables** (those that are affected by the independent variables)? What is the nature of their relationship? In the case of Pagans and their household-level sustainability, we can surmise that household-level sustainability is dependent on other factors, but which ones? Does it depend on how rural a person is? Their age? Their income? Does household-level sustainable behavior happen because a person believes in common Pagan values, such as the sacredness of nature, or are Pagan belief and household-level sustainable behavior unrelated variables (or do people who were already practicing sustainability become Pagans)?

Sometimes, it is relatively easy to figure out the relationship: For example, it is easy to figure out that longevity (lifespan) depends on socioeconomic class in the United States (more money in a capitalist health care system yields better care). Other times, it is hard to figure out which variables drive which. For example, in many parts of the world, poorer families have more children. Is this because they are attempting to generate economic security when they are old? Or is poverty leading to less access to contraception? Or both? Finally, establishing which variables are independent and dependent does not necessarily mean that one causes the other. We know, for example, that in the United States, women earn less than men in the same profession, but we also know that gender doesn't *cause* income. Rather, mediating factors around sexism (such as the expectation that women will do more household tasks, even if they are working, and prejudices against promoting women who are of childbearing age or who are mothers) are what drive gender-based income inequality. We have to take one step at a time and remember that establishing which variables are independent does not mean they are the cause of our dependent variables, and that even **correlation** (a statistically significant relationship between two variables) does not establish **causality** (which variables cause which, and how they do this).

Establishing causality can be really important, not only conceptually but also in practice. Many social programs assume, for example, that action is the dependent variable of thought. That is, if we change how people think, we can change how they act. However, the thought-causes-action model rarely works in practice. Usually, the independent variable causing both thought and action is infrastructural: It's economic or organizational. If we want to change people's behaviors, then, we have to change the systems around them that support the behavior we want. If we try to change only their minds but don't give them the support to change their actions, nothing will change. For example, teaching poor women how contraception can limit family size is generally insufficient for yielding the behavioral change of lower fertility rates. Instead, the broader social system that causes poor women to have high fertility—including norms that do not give bodily autonomy to women and a lack of economic opportunities for women—must change in order to support behavioral changes that lower fertility, such as abstaining from sex or using contraception.

Indicators are ways you plan to measure the variable. They are the general aspects of the variable you think are important. Indicators of household income, for example, are salaries, external support (such as alimony or child support), revenue from investments, side and cash jobs, and sales of household items (such as at yard or garage sales). Indicators are defined by **values**, which are the options that a participant can choose for

Independent variables Variables that exist on their own, unaffected by the others.

Dependent variables Variables that are affected by independent variables.

Correlation A statistically significant relationship between two variables, such that when one changes, the other is affected.

Causality A statistically significant relationship between two variables, in which one variable is the cause of another variable changing.

Indicators One or more measurements for a variable.

Values The specific options an indicator can take.

answering a question about an indicator. For salary, this could include salary ranges (a set of options that the researcher defines, such as $0–20,000 per year), or the researcher could instead ask about the participant's salary in an open-ended fashion, allowing them to provide any numeric value. Variables, indicators, and values do not have to be quantitative in nature, nor do they have to conform to an exclusionary list. For example, a researcher studying cultural norms around first marriage might be curious about how the variable of maturity is tied into the social acceptability of the couple's marriage. In this case, indicators might include the couple's self-described internal states (such as self-control and perceived emotional stability), conflict resolution patterns (skills in resolving arguments and disagreements productively), and socially defined responsibility (such as caring for younger siblings, working at a full-time job, or building wealth). The values may emerge from the interview responses of participants from that culture, which would define the indicators in ways that are meaningful to the culture in question rather than to the researcher's own culture.

The process to define variables, indicators, and values can be deceptively simple: It is often more challenging than it first appears to set up the research design for success. Let's take, for example, gender (or sex) as the variable. Before you simply define it as male/female for your survey (the values you offer the participant as choices for self-identification), let's look closer at how you are setting up your design in measuring this variable. If you set up participants' options as male/female, you are already defining gender as a dichotomous (two-option) variable, rather than a spectrum of maleness to femaleness. You also haven't clearly established whether your indicators are genetics (XX vs. XY), physiology (the spectrum of physical characteristics that we think of as defining maleness or femaleness, such as breasts and facial hair), or culture (the spectrum of characteristics that we associate with masculinity or femininity, such as nurturance or assertiveness). Providing participants with only two options for gender ignores the variance that is present in a population, which might be expressed as intersex, transgender, androgynous, nonbinary, or gender-fluid, among other identities. Is capturing that variance of minority gender expression important? This may depend on your participant population and your research question. You always need to ask yourself, "How am I defining my variable and its potential values by the way I set up my indicators? Am I limiting what my participants can express? Is it a good idea to do that?"

Discussion

Let's say you're going to do a research project on campus that seeks to understand the unique challenges that students who are also parents face and the strategies that they use to be successful. What kinds of variables would you consider important to study? What indicators would you use to measure these variables? What values would define the indicators? After you've mapped out a few variables (and their indicators and values), find a small group of fellow students and discuss. What did you all agree on? What did others contribute that you hadn't considered?

Operational Definitions

In research, we often talk about *defining* variables and their measurements. How is this sort of defining different from using the *Merriam-Webster's* dictionary? Our usual way of talking about definitions—that is, how something is defined in the dictionary—is what we call **conceptual definitions**. Conceptual definitions are abstractions that facilitate understanding. They're generally agreed-on meanings of words. In research, we mostly talk about **operational definitions**. Sometimes, we say this as a verb: that we must *operationalize* something. What do we mean by this? Unlike a conceptual definition, which is abstract, an operational definition provides specific instructions about how to measure a variable. The variable usually already has one or more conceptual definitions, but we still have to explain how we will measure the abstractions for the purposes of our research.

Let's get back to the example of gender. We have commonly agreed on conceptual definitions of what *gender* means. We know it has something to do with femaleness and maleness. But when we seek to measure gender in our participants, that abstract conceptual definition doesn't work well enough for us to start. We still have to figure out how we're going to actually measure maleness and femaleness. Even if we based this on self-identification (the participant telling us what gender they identify as), we will shape their response based on how we ask the question and how we offer the responses (if we don't ask the question in an open-ended way). Consider the following ways of operationalizing gender differently and how you might respond (or how the researcher would assess you):

- What is your gender? Check *male* or *female*.

- On a scale of 1 (least) to 10 (most), how much do you feel you belong in the gender category of male? Of female?

- Do you feel that you are only one gender, more than one gender, or no gender at all? Why?

- Following is a list of traits that are traditionally associated with a specific gender. Please check all that apply, which will help us assess how strongly you are identified with masculinity and femininity: (1) aggressive, (2) warm, (3) analytical. . . .

As you can see, you could ask participants about their gender in many different ways, and each of those ways of operationalizing gender would not only shape the data you receive but also speak to certain theories about gender itself: whether or not it is about the body (as opposed to social roles or internal states); whether gender is two categories, more than two categories, or a spectrum; and how much gender is a category assigned by others versus an identity that is claimed by an individual. You can imagine that if it is this difficult to operationalize a variable for which we have strong shared conceptual definitions, it can be much more challenging to operationalize concepts that are less clear: power, for example, or alienation from place.

However difficult it may be, we have to try to create operational definitions as part of our research design. There are rarely objective definitions of anything. Instead, what we are seeking is a definition for a particular study, in a particular context. Keeping this

Conceptual definitions Abstractions that facilitate understanding.

Operational definitions Definitions that provide specific instructions for how to measure variables.

in mind can help us face the daunting task of defining variables in our study—remembering that it is for our purposes and need not work in every case. It also helps to remember that we can break complex variables into simpler variables. Socioeconomic status (SES), for example, is a complex variable that includes many simpler variables, such as income, household size, consumption patterns, occupation, self-assessment, educational achievement, social networks, and job stability.

Operational definitions help us move from question and hypothesis to data collection and analysis. We can think of them as the bridge between our research question and hypotheses and our ability to explore and test them. In a study designed by one of the authors (Kimberly Kirner), one of the hypotheses was this: *The greater the household's access to flexible labor resources, the higher the environmental health of the ranch.* The first step is to break hypothetical statements into their variables, so that each can be defined:

- Household access to flexible labor resources (Variable 1)

- Environmental health (Variable 2)

- Ranch (Variable 3)

If we try operationalizing just one variable—for example, Variable 1 (access to flexible labor resources)—we find a number of different indicators that measure such access to resources (see Figure 1.2).

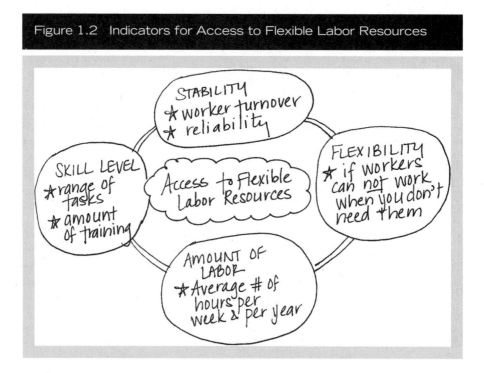

Figure 1.2 Indicators for Access to Flexible Labor Resources

If we are careful in operationalizing each variable, developing the most appropriate indicators that will produce meaningful values, we go a long way toward designing a project that works: one where the data to collect are clearly described and there are clear indicators that measure variables in meaningful and relevant ways, so that we can trust our findings.

Discussion

Consider the term *working student*. Let's say you're doing a survey of your fellow students and you want to establish how many of them are working students and how this affects their study habits. But first, you need to operationalize what a working student is! Write a hypothesis, based on your own experiences or the conversations you've had with other students in the past, about how you think working student status relates to study habits. Then, operationalize *working student*—determining the measurements that would establish, for your participants, whether you consider them to be in this category or not.

Levels of Measurement and Units of Analysis

We can measure variables in various ways, and we can generally categorize these ways into levels of measurement—from more categorical to more numerically exacting. A general rule is that you should *always use the highest level of measurement possible* for a variable. This makes sense, right? The more precise you can be in measuring a variable, the better you will understand it when you analyze the relationships between variables. There are four levels of measurement: nominal, ordinal, interval, and ratio (see Figure 1.3).

It is very common in qualitative research to mostly use nominal and ordinal levels of measurement, because these are best suited to measuring concepts—and that is much of what qualitative research is oriented to do. Interval and ratio data can often augment, though, whenever you can see that a variable could be measured using concrete observations.

Aside from levels of measurement, there are also units of analysis. These describe how big your unit of study is. Most student projects (and most exploratory projects, no matter who the researcher is) are **case studies**: smaller, local projects that have limitations on how generalizable they are (how much they can definitively speak for multiple locations) but that are deep and rich in their description of the people, problem, or place that is studied. They can be contrasted with larger studies that test hypotheses, often by comparing across local, regional, or even global study groups or areas.

Case studies Small projects that have limited generalizability but offer significant preliminary or localized findings.

Units of analysis are not always defined by the number of individual persons: One unit is not always one person. Sometimes, a unit of analysis is a geographically or ecologically defined space, such as a watershed or a city. A unit of analysis might be a social

Figure 1.3 Levels of Measurement

Level of Measurement	Definition	Example
Nominal	An exhaustive list of names; participants select one or more to describe themselves (remember that mutual exclusivity, the ability to pick only one thing, tends to make participants annoyed!)	*Religious affiliation:* Buddhist Christian, Catholic Christian, Protestant Hindu Jewish Muslim None, Atheist None, spiritual but not religious Other (please specify)
Ordinal	Rank-ordered categories, where there is a relationship between the categories	*How much do you agree with the statement?* Strongly disagree Disagree Agree Strongly agree No opinion
Interval	The distance between rank-ordered categories is meaningful—partially quantitative. The distance between the categories is assumed to be equal, which quantifies the spectrum.	*Kinsey scale for sexual orientation:* 0 Exclusively heterosexual 1 Mostly heterosexual, only incidentally homosexual 2 Mostly heterosexual, but more than incidentally homosexual 3 Equally heterosexual and homosexual 4 Mostly homosexual, but more than incidentally heterosexual 5 Mostly homosexual, only incidentally heterosexual 6 Exclusively homosexual
Ratio	Measurements that are intervals with a true zero point that represents the absence of a phenomenon	*Number of times you've moved in your life:* 0, 1, 2, 3, 4 (If you've moved four times, you've literally moved twice as many times as a person who has moved only twice.) *Other examples:* age, income, number of births

organization, such as a household or a corporation. Or it could even be an event, such as a famine or a war. The general rule for selecting a unit of analysis is *always collect data on the lowest level of analysis possible*. It is relatively easy to **aggregate** data (to combine it across multiple units) later, but not the other way around! For example, if I'm curious about gender roles in a particular community, it is best if I keep my unit of analysis at both the individual (for ideas and identities) and household (for interactions and tasks) levels. I can always aggregate across extended families, or neighborhoods, or social networks. But if I start with keeping track of data at the extended family level, for example, I might miss ways key variables such as age or marital status (or household) play into the interactions I am recording.

The Relationship of Projects, Method, and Theory

So let's get back to the question of how method and theory relate to each other. We started talking about this at the beginning of this chapter, and then we entered some of the nitty-gritty details of how researchers talk about the components of their research (and define them at the start of projects). Let's now return to the lofty discussion of how a research project contributes to social science theory—and how that theory informs your research! You'll hear many social scientists talk about paradigms. **Paradigms** are theoretical perspectives, or what we might call *grand theory*. These are broad ways of looking at the world, what anthropologists often call *worldview* or *cosmology* (the nature of the universe and our place in it), but applied specifically to Western science. A paradigm defines the major issues with which a theorist (and researcher) is concerned. Let's take a look at a few examples:

- *Evolutionary theory:* The world is about biology and change in a species over time. How might this be applied to diverse topics? A psychologist might seek to explain certain emotions, such as fear, and their outcomes through a framework that describes how humans evolved this emotion, why it affects us the way it does, its utility, and its disadvantages in contemporary society. A medical anthropologist might conduct a study that investigates human cravings for fat and sugar and relate this to our nutritional needs under the long period when we were hunter-gatherers, describing the social environment as having shifted in ways that are in conflict with our biological drives for nourishment.

- *Idealism/cultural theory:* The world is about what people think (this paradigm underlies structuralism and functionalism). Let's get back to our topics and see how this might influence such studies differently. A psychologist working from an idealist or cultural paradigm might seek to investigate how fear is differently conceptualized by various cultural groups and how this mediates outcomes in behavior from people who feel fear. A medical anthropologist might explain the global trend to eat fatty, sugary foods based on the way people around the world have come to associate them with high status or comfort and convenience.

Aggregate To combine the data from multiple units.

Paradigms Theoretical perspectives that provide broad ways of looking at the world and define the major issues with which the researcher is concerned.

- *Materialist theory:* The world is about people's positioning for resources (this paradigm underlies cultural ecology and Marxism). Let's return once more to our topics to see how such a paradigm might influence our researchers' studies. A psychologist might investigate how fear is related to social environment, especially how the person views themselves in relationship to others' power or capacity for force, leading some people to be chronically fearful due to marginalization. A medical anthropologist might choose to study the phenomenon of food deserts, areas within urban and suburban regions that lack healthy food options (grocery stores, farmers markets)—usually because the residents are low-income.

Hopefully, you can see that there is rarely a "right" paradigm to study a particular topic or research question. Questions such as "Why are people afraid, and what can we do to ameliorate negative outcomes, such as violence when people feel fear?" or "Why are people all over the world increasingly eating fatty and sugary foods and suffering poor health effects from it?" have multiple answers, because they are complex. Researchers operating from different paradigms can each contribute a piece of the puzzle.

While there are sometimes "best" paradigms for a research question (and, more frequently, poorly fitted paradigms), it is also frequently the case that we can learn a lot from a variety of paradigmatic orientations. There is room for all sorts of researchers, aligned with a variety of grand theories, to contribute meaningful findings to our quest to answer compelling questions about human life. As a beginning student, it is best if you identify only one or, at most, two paradigms that you feel speak to your research question and your own interest and theoretical orientation. Keeping your design simpler doesn't mean you won't contribute meaningful findings, but it means that you'll give yourself a stepping stone toward more complex projects and set yourself up for success. You don't want to overwhelm yourself right at the start. If you haven't had a course in social science theory, or you haven't had one in a long time, you might want to learn some basics to select a paradigm that is meaningful to you. At the end of the chapter, there is a list of books that cover social science or anthropological theory at a beginning level.

Discussion

Think about paradigms you've learned about in your social science classes. Which ones speak to you most, and why? Do you think those paradigms are more aligned with your identity or values? More useful for the kinds of applications you care about? More interesting as an area of study? Then, find a small group of fellow students and discuss. Listen to the variety of paradigmatic orientations in a nonjudgmental way, and then think about what each of you can learn from the paradigms that you would not select yourself.

Paradigms are related to what we like to call the *BIG questions*, the questions that social scientists (and philosophers, theologians, and so on) have been trying to answer for hundreds of years (and that may never be fully answered). We can think of these as questions that are broadly interesting and grand (BIG). We can consider these BIG questions and paradigms as the very highest, broadest level of doing social science—where we contemplate some of the driving questions of human life while considering all the studies we've read about (plus our own that we've conducted). These questions tend to be held in common across the social sciences (broadly interesting), and they're extremely ambitious as questions for researchers to tackle (grand). Popular BIG questions include the following:

- Nature versus nurture (what makes you *you*)

- Evolution (how species, organizations, and societies change over time)

- Internal versus external (the way behavior is influenced by values and environment; real vs. ideal culture—or the gap between what people do and what they say they [should] do)

- Social facts (the emergent properties problem—how social forces both emerge from and transcend individual interactions)

At the other end of the research process is your specific question or hypothesis driving your research project. This is likely to be a small, focused question (so that you don't go crazy trying to sort out the biggest questions of all time in a limited time frame, with a small group of people!). In between is what researchers call *middle-range theory*, which integrates theory and empirical research (see Figure 1.4). These BIG questions and paradigms are integrated with those pesky underlying assumptions we discussed at the beginning of the chapter, which then also affect middle-range theory. (Remember, all theory is affected by underlying assumptions!)

Middle-range theory is where the proverbial rubber meets the road, because it guides how grand theory (or paradigms) are actualized in empirical research (where you, the researcher, will go out into the world and collect some data). Middle-range theory is more easily applied to contemporary problems for the purposes of explanation or prediction, and it usually shapes the methods you will use (and is, in turn, shaped by those methods). For example:

- *Optimal foraging theory (evolutionary anthropology):* articulates methods and ideas around why people select resources the way they do from an evolutionary perspective of efficiency

- *Cultural model theory (idealism; ethnoscience + functionalism):* articulates methods and ideas around how people come to have shared but variant idea structures that shape their interpretations of others' actions and aid their decisions about their own actions

- *Political ecology (materialism; Marxism + cultural ecology):* articulates methods and ideas around how differences in power and class affect the ways in which people interact with their physical environments

Figure 1.4 The Relationship of Paradigms to Research Questions

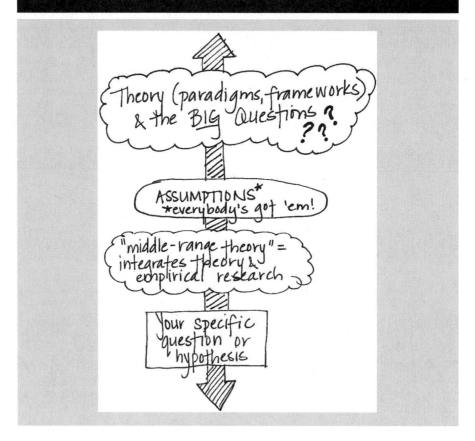

Even though we (especially as students) might primarily work with middle-range theory, which might look like it is focused and logically tied to specific methods, we always have to remember that the assumptions and the goals of grand theory (paradigms) are at work behind the scenes.

Why does theory ultimately matter when we're doing social science research? It matters because it informs the policies and programs societies create to try to get people to change behavior in positive ways. If we want people to do any number of behaviors that might benefit society, such as recycle, wash their hands, or educate their children of all genders, we have to use ideas (theories) about why people do (or do not) select these actions to begin with. Theory informs our basic assumptions that we use to conceptualize social problems, methods to understand them, and potential solutions.

What you'll notice is that the scale of research changes as you move from specific question to paradigm. Almost all student work, and most professional researchers' work (in both academic and applied fields), resides in the smallest scale of research: in specific, focused research questions answered with data from specific, focused places and populations. Most of what social scientists produce are *case studies* (in cultural anthropology, **ethnography**). Fewer social scientists, usually later in their careers, generalize across cases (drawn from their own studies and those of other social scientists), producing what anthropologists call **ethnology**—general theoretical discussions that seek to account for human behavior across many cultural groups and geographic locations. From these, grand theory or paradigms are influenced over time.

Most of the time, researchers don't realize the BIG questions we are chasing until we are mid- or late-career professionals. But thinking about this early, from the time you begin trying out your identity as a researcher, can help you focus on what is meaningful to you. This means you'll have a more integrated career, starting with your earliest research experiences—building research projects that fit together into one or more research programs (longer-term, broader foci of your research career) that link to BIG questions that make you intellectually satisfied.

Discussion

Contemplate the four BIG questions offered earlier (or you might generate one of your own from past classes). Remember, to be a BIG question, it should be broadly interesting and grand. Which of these questions appeals to you? Is there one that you think you'd be curious about for a decade—or two or three—as a professional researcher? Why?

Making Mistakes

All researchers make mistakes, because we're human. It's OK to make mistakes. You'll make lots of them as you practice research design, data collection, and analysis. The main thing is to be mindful of the way you're working through each step of the research process, noting successes and failures, and using these observations to strengthen your capacity as a researcher. The other big concern is to address ethical issues that arise throughout the project, which is the subject of the next chapter.

There are three major sorts of mistakes (aside from ethical ones) that researchers make during the research process: study design, data collection, and data analysis (see Figure 1.5). Of these, mistakes in the study design are most problematic to recover from. This is because mistakes of this nature are embedded in every stage of research that comes after, which causes fundamental problems in the way you collect and analyze data. In such cases, there is really only one solution: to start over. This is why research design and planning are so important and are at the foundation of both this textbook and your research project. Good design is imperative; it ripples throughout your entire project.

Ethnography Writing about a specific culture at a specific place and time.

Ethnology General theoretical discussions that seek to account for human behavior across many cultural groups and geographic locations.

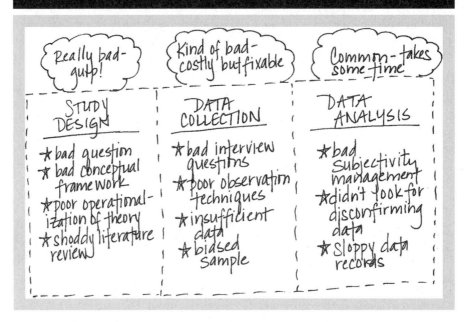

Figure 1.5 Three Sorts of Mistakes

Really bad—gulp!

STUDY DESIGN
* bad question
* bad conceptual framework
* poor operational-ization of theory
* shoddy literature review

Kind of bad—costly but fixable

DATA COLLECTION
* bad interview questions
* poor observation techniques
* insufficient data
* biased sample

Common—takes some time

DATA ANALYSIS
* bad subjectivity management
* didn't look for disconfirming data
* sloppy data records

Mistakes in data collection are problematic, in that you may have to substantially change your methods (techniques) and extend your time and cost to complete data collection. However, if your original design (the relationship between your research question, theory, and method) is solid and intact, problems in technique are not catastrophic—just costly. Mistakes in data analysis, on the other hand, are very common. It is not unusual to find that you've analyzed your data less thoroughly than is ideal. Sometimes you realize this as you begin to work on your conclusions, and sometimes a colleague, supervisor, or reviewer will point out flaws in your analysis and conclusions that prompt you to reconsider. It is normal to take a bit of extra time, either before submitting your findings to a supervisor or reviewer or after they note some weaknesses, to refine your data analysis and conclusions.

As you review your findings and conclusions, you should keep in mind two concepts that describe the extent to which research is accurate. The first of these is **validity**, which determines whether research measures what it is claiming to measure and whether research truly examines what it claims to examine. For example, if your interpretation of your data claims to accurately describe the culture associated with an occupation, such as construction workers, but you didn't investigate whether those cultural trends are related more to socioeconomic class or blue-collar (trades and manual labor) versus white-collar (office and administrative labor) patterns, then your interpretation may not be valid. Validity is threatened by a number of specific problems that you should watch for in your research:

- Premature conclusions (drawing your conclusions too soon, without sufficient data or analysis)

Validity The determination of whether research measures what it is claiming to measure.

- Omission of disconfirming data (ignoring data contrary to what you expect or want to find)

- Not analyzing everything (ignoring certain data or avoiding clearly related topics)

- Not having data to support your interpretations (using very few data to support your conclusions)

The other concept, **reliability**, means that the study results are consistent over time and reasonably complete representations of the population at hand. Reliability generally means that the research study is **replicable**: that similar results should appear in similar settings when the study is repeated. There are some caveats to the concept of replicability in qualitative research. Most notable of these is that (1) studies of specific events (such as wars or famines) may not be replicable, as these are time-limited and often rather localized (i.e., they do not necessarily have a similar setting), and (2) in qualitative research, the individual researcher's attributes may substantially affect the results. That is, a female researcher may be treated differently by the study participants than a male researcher would be, or an older researcher may be treated differently than a younger one would be. You'll learn more about these effects in later chapters, but it is good to be aware of their impact on ethnographic research, which differs in this regard from experimental or statistical/quantitative research models. Reliability is threatened by other specific problems that you should watch for:

- Inattention to detail (you fail to pay close attention through observation or to pay close attention to nuances in the data, which means your representation of the population has substantial missing pieces)

- Poor recording of the process (you take incomplete notes and/or do not adequately track your analysis strategies)

- Fuzzy procedures (your methods were poorly defined and planned, so you inconsistently collect and/or analyze data)

- Failure to be clear (your written documentation of your methods, data, population, and analysis were not clear, so other researchers—or you in the future—can't adequately do the same thing)

In quantitative (statistical) and experimental studies, the ideal is often a combination of replicability and **generalizability**—how applicable a study's findings are to predicting human behavior or interpreting it in meaningful ways elsewhere. A study might be replicable, generalizable, both, or neither. Like replicability, generalizability is tricky for ethnographic studies. It is important to be attentive to whether or not you think your participants and study site represent the broader culture or population you are studying as a whole. However, even if your study site and participants produce findings that are not broadly generalizable, this does not mean your study is without merit. Culture varies a great deal from place to place, and even from person to person. Many smaller-scale, localized studies are still important for understanding humans.

There are three ways you can boost your validity and reliability: reciprocal ethnography, an audit trail, and triangulation. **Reciprocal ethnography** is a methodological process in which you ask your participants to check your validity. You can provide your

Reliability The determination of whether study results are consistent over time and reasonably complete representations of the population at hand.

Replicable The condition that similar results should appear in similar settings when the study is repeated.

Generalizability How broadly applicable a study's findings are to interpreting or predicting human behavior elsewhere (aside from the study site and participants).

Reciprocal ethnography A methodological process in which the researcher collaborates with research participants to review the findings and address conflicts between the researcher's interpretations and those of their participants.

participants with your preliminary findings and ask them to help you identify anywhere you have misinterpreted them. This doesn't mean that you negate your own analyses if the participants disagree, but rather that you use this uncomfortable critical review to work on dealing with the conflicts between their perspectives and your perspective and carefully assess whether your analysis is meaningful and why it is so. This means you can discuss social theory and your ideas with the participants, opening anthropology up as a collaborative endeavor! This process not only helps you refine your findings and clarify the assumptions that went into them but also forges more egalitarian and collaborative relationships with your participants. It's tricky, and not always comfortable, but it can have meaningful effects on your conclusions and your field relationships.

An **audit trail**, unlike reciprocal ethnography, is a methodological strategy that every researcher should use. That is, it isn't tied to any theoretical or ethical orientation but is rather a standard practice for all researchers. An audit trail is a record of your procedures and thoughts. It helps you figure out, especially if you run into mistakes, how you got from point A (the data) to point Z (your interpretation and conclusions). This allows you to carefully backtrack if you find that your conclusions are not valid or reliable. The audit trail should include two types of information: *where* you got your ideas from (data, notes, and peer-reviewed research literature) and *why* you made the decisions you did (your personal notes, journaled in analytical memos alongside data, drafts of your paper, and annotations, which are your thoughts on how you'll use peer-reviewed literature). Finally, researchers can improve validity and reliability by using **triangulation**, which is a search for agreement among multiple, different sources of information. Triangulation will be discussed at length in a later chapter when we cover combining qualitative and quantitative methods. For now, it is enough to know that triangulation is one strategy to improve validity and reliability, and it can happen through using multiple methods, researchers, or disciplinary perspectives and/or checking one's data and interpretations against similar studies.

Discussion

Try to critically assess your personality and the ways you usually approach assignments and tasks. Where are your weaknesses? How do they overlap with the problems related to validity and reliability? How could you improve these weak areas to become a better researcher?

Audit trail A record of the researcher's procedures and thoughts while conducting research.

Triangulation The search for agreement among multiple, different sources of information.

Finding a Topic

The starting point to building yourself as a researcher is to identify a topic (and later one or more research questions) that piques your interest. Also of concern, especially as a student, is that you select a topic that you can actually study—that isn't too far away, expensive, or challenging to do. The way research begins is through planning—through drafting a design. There is an ideal way to design and execute research:

1. Think of a theoretical problem

2. Select an appropriate site and method(s)

3. Collect and analyze data

4. Challenge or support the theoretical proposition that informed your problem

However, there are lots of reasons why this general process gets derailed or altered. A researcher may notice that there is substantial funding and interest available for a research problem that wasn't originally on their radar but is tangential to (and partially answers) questions that they had. The researcher might select a site that is optimal to answer her question but find it problematic logistically: It might be too difficult to get to in the time she has, or be in political upheaval and therefore not allowed by her institution's risk management, or be too financially expensive as a field site. It is very common that researchers select a particular method, only to find during data collection that they can't get enough participants for using that method—necessitating that they get creative about which methods might be easier for drawing in participants. Similarly, it's common for a researcher to end up collecting data on a topic that he didn't really want to explore, because that's what his informants want to talk about. Finally, researchers frequently find that when they analyze their data, there are interesting results in areas of study that they did not anticipate or plan to discuss. All these challenges are part of the way real research is conducted.

As students, it is easy to at first feel frustrated and disappointed in your ability to stick to your design. Try to remember that you'll get better at both design and execution of research over time—more realistic about what will probably happen (and what you can accomplish) and also better at accomplishing it! Yet you'll always find challenges as you begin research projects, because social scientists work with people, so we'll always have an element of the unknown (and the chaotic) to our research. This is OK. You'll adjust over time to this challenge and become more comfortable with adjusting your research to meet the demands of the field. For now, take heart when you feel lost, annoyed, or unhappy with your process and results. We all go through this, multiple times, and it's part of the learning curve in conducting social science research. Stick with it!

So how to select a topic? Start with your interests (both intellectually and personally—more on this in a moment), but also try not to be too much of an optimist about your resources. Acknowledge that, as a student, your resources are pretty slim. This means you need to think in a very realistic (even pessimistic) manner about your available time, money, and contacts (social network). The goal of an undergraduate or master's-level thesis (even a dissertation) is to finish. Always remember that. Yes, you want it to be meaningful and interesting. But most of all, you want to finish your degree, and you want to finish it efficiently—as quickly (and cheaply) as you can. If you select a topic that is too challenging—that requires too long a period of fieldwork, too much data, or a location that is too difficult for you to reliably get to—you'll get stuck in your project, and it will impede your ability to finish your degree. So you want to start with not only ideas of what interests you but also a list of your limitations.

While you might plan to pursue fellowships or small grants to help with your thesis research, these are never guaranteed to arrive—and, indeed, they are rather competitive. You'll want a list of your limitations for what you think you could do without any major influx of resources from somewhere else. Make a brief list of the following: how much money you think you could afford to put toward your research (out of your own pocket or from your family, if they will pitch in), how much time you think you'll have to do your project (most undergraduate and master's theses are based on about three to six months of fieldwork), and contacts you have or think you can make in communities of interest to you.

Now, you need to think about two things: topics that interest you and topics that have a purpose. While you should feel interested in your research topic, it is equally important (if not more so) that your topic has a clearly defined purpose and is meaningful to others—other academics, the public, or both. Remember, people don't exist for you to study them. You exist to serve people through your studies of them. Both participants in your research and organizations that fund research care that your research will contribute to the advancement of method and/or theory and that somehow it will have broader impacts (as the National Science Foundation puts it) for the public at large. Even if you self-fund your research, this is not like taking a trip for pleasure. You're expecting other people—your participants—to donate considerable amounts of time and even discomfort to your research project. Honor their time and assistance by making sure your research has a purpose: that it has clearly defined research questions and is articulated meaningfully with theory and application or advancing the voices of those you are studying. Keep in mind how you'd feel if a stranger knocked on your door and asked if they could hang out with you for a few months, ask you nosy questions, and generally be in the way of your life. This is what you're asking your participants to do, so it is important to have clearly defined descriptions of why they should do it!

While you need to find a topic that speaks to more than your personal interests, your interests are also your own. One of the joys of qualitative research is that it often allows the researcher to work by themselves on topics that are of intense interest to them. While qualitative researchers often make up part of a larger research team on large-scale research projects, they're also able to relatively easily (and cheaply) conduct small-scale research projects that speak to their personal interests. You don't have to justify your interests (so long as your research also serves a purpose, as we discussed previously), but you do need self-awareness. You might not know, right at the start, what your research interests would be. You should conduct a self-inventory to help you think about topics, field sites, and populations or groups that would make you happy in your work as a researcher.

Discussion

Take a self-inventory to help you think about and assess potential research topics. What are you passionate about? What fascinates you? What do you like doing (in terms of tasks)? Where do you like to be (indoors, outdoors, a particular type of environment)? What kinds of people are enjoyable or interesting to hang out with?

Pairing the Textbook and Workbook

As you begin to shape your research topic and question(s) using the culminating activity in the workbook for Chapter 1 (Activity 1.7), remember that your research can be a humanistic form of the social sciences, but it shouldn't be your quest to connect to all of humanity, the divine, or the cosmos; aesthetic assessments; sermons; travel journalism; or a boring diary. What makes your project research is that you connect it to a purpose—theoretically and/or in application—and that you put in the hard work to plug your small project into the bigger questions and paradigms of social science. As you think about your research design throughout this introductory process, keep asking yourself these questions:

- Am I really interested in this topic? Site? Method(s)?

- Is this problem something I can study? Or is it a question that is philosophical, artistic, or spiritual in nature? (These areas are outside the boundaries of social science.)

- Do I have the resources to do this project?

- Will this question, site, or method cause me angst ethically or in advancing my career? (It is best not to rock the boat too much when you are just beginning.)

- Will my results be interesting? Will anyone else care about my project? Who?

Now, leap in to the research design project with the workbook activities! What are your interests? Who will you be and what will you do as a researcher?

Reflective Prompts

1. Reflecting on my learning in this chapter, did I highlight or underline main points?

2. Do I understand the relationships between variables, indicators, and values?

3. Can I describe the various points a researcher must consider in terms of designing a research project?

Case Study

Vélez-Ibáñez, Carlos. 1929–1997. *Carlos G. Vélez-Ibáñez Sterilization Research Collection, 20*. Chicano Studies Research Center, UCLA (University of California, Los Angeles).

Vélez-Ibáñez, Carlos. 1980. "*Se Me Acabó la Canción*: An Ethnography of Non-consenting Sterilizations among Mexican Women in Los Angeles, California." In *Mexican Women in the United States: Struggles Past and Present*, edited by Magdalena Mora and Adelaida R. Del Castillo, occasional paper, University of California, Los Angeles.

See also Carlos Vélez-Ibáñez's interview in Bishop, Katelynn. 2018. "Film Review: No Más Bebés." *Teaching Sociology* 46 (3): 288–90.

The Project

I was asked by two young lawyers in 1978, as a brand-new professor at UCLA, the following question: "What is the impact of non-consenting sterilization on the cultural systems of the Mexican women who are part of a lawsuit against a Los Angeles County hospital?" I thought to myself, "How am I going to answer this? How am I going to find out what the impact is and be able to translate it into a narrative understood by lawyers rather than academics? How am I also going to substantiate my findings?" It's not good enough to just do this stuff; you have to substantiate it so that it supports your original thesis. My original thesis was that depending on where the women are from and how old they were, that this would influence the probable impact of the sterilization not only to them but also to their household. I set out a series of questions to get to that.

What I found out was that among the fourteen women, nine of them were from rural areas. And the average age was around thirty-four, so they were relatively young women. They all came from very large families. Because of this, part of the question I would ask was "What were your social networks like before you were sterilized?" but not that directly.

Based on past research I'd done for another project among Mexican households, I knew that the women were likely to have been impacted in their social networks, especially if they were rural and from large families. I reconstructed their social networks individually, including all the social networks of exchange: children's events, recreation, work, all the social domains they participated in. I figured out the density of those relationships pre- and post-sterilization. What I found was that for all the domains they participated in originally, many no longer participated in them as strongly or frequently. Additionally, a good proportion of the households had drawn all their curtains and made it dark in the house. This gave me a pretty good idea that many of these women were disconnected from their social networks. They said they felt embarrassed at these social events and stopped going because they were asked all the time why they didn't have more children. This was associated with a lot of shame and sadness because they had loved having lots of children. I then proceeded to correlate their responses to a series of depression scales that a psychiatrist on the case conducted, and the correlation was at .05 level of significance when I compared the level of network disengagement to the levels of depression.

The federal case came along, I testified, and among the questions the judge asked me was "How long did you spend in doing your fieldwork?" My answer was six months. He asked if I'd do it any other way, and I said no, or the study wouldn't have been worth anything. It took me six months to decipher and make conclusions about the alleged damage of these sterilizations. The judge ruled that the doctors couldn't have known the impact of their actions, so they won. I never touched another legal case again that wasn't a sure thing. All these years later, that case still haunts me.

How was your research question refined over time?

I paid more attention over time to each woman's relationship to her husband and her children and how this changed over time.

What personal interests led you to this research focus?

You have to know yourself and why you're doing what you're doing. Everything about me led me to this project. You have to really know yourself and your limitations and be really modest about what you think you know. You want to avoid the ego trip you can get under and remember you're not there for yourself.

What do you consider your research's contribution to anthropology to be?

I've always published everything I've worked on. A bunch of books and articles, many based on applied research. That's part of what's expected of us, and I enjoy writing some of the stuff. In a way, the writing is psychotherapy for me. It gets rid of some of the devils I carry around with me as an applied anthropologist.

What do you consider your research's contribution to the public or society to be?

While losing this case for these women still makes me upset, new federal rules were put in place as a result of the case that said doctors couldn't get consent from women undergoing anesthesia and that consent had to be direct and not implied.

What advice do you have about research design, based on your research career, for beginning researchers?

You have this original plan you've built, but the process can move you to a different end than you thought you'd study. You have to be open to the way that your questions will respond to a different process than you thought you'd face. You have to be open to information you never expected, and you move from there to the next decision about changes to your research design. Ethnographic research gives you opportunities to respond to the people you're studying through changes to your design. Rather than a linear design, where you build this original plan and then complete it, anthropology's strength is a processual design, where we change the design based on feedback we get through the ethnographic process.

Case Study Reflections

1. Carlos Vélez-Ibáñez explains the process by which a research project can be initiated by a need in a community, population, or group of individuals. What was the value of doing such work? What was the danger?

2. Why is knowing yourself really important for conducting anthropological research? How
   (Continued)

(Continued)

is critically reflecting on your ego, motives, and biases helpful for the process of research design?

3. How did Carlos Vélez-Ibáñez use his past research experiences to inform his current project? What does that tell you about the way anthropological researchers build their skills and knowledge over time?

4. What does it mean to have a processual research design? How is this arguably better and more suitable for ethnographic research than a linear research design?

STUDY GUIDE

Note: Students should study each concept with attentiveness to defining, explaining with examples, and describing or demonstrating process. This is not a list of terms to define; it's a list of concepts and processes to master.

Methods: epistemology, strategic methods, and techniques

Underlying assumptions and how they affect research

Science versus humanities orientation

Qualitative versus quantitative data

Deduction versus induction

Hypothetico-deductive model

Exploratory versus confirmatory research

Variable

Unidimensional versus multidimensional variable

Independent versus dependent variable

Correlation

Causality

Indicators

Values

Conceptual versus operational definition

Levels of measurement

Units of analysis

Case studies

Aggregate

Paradigm

Theory, BIG questions, and middle-range theory

Ethnography

Ethnology

Types of mistakes

Validity

Reliability

Reciprocal ethnography

Audit trail

Triangulation

Process to select a topic (things to consider)

FOR FURTHER STUDY

Bernard, H. Russell. 2018. "The Foundations of Social Research" and "Preparing for Research." In *Research Methods in Anthropology*, by H. Russell Bernard, 23–82. Lanham, MD: Rowman and Littlefield.

Galman, Sally. 2007. *Shane, the Lone Ethnographer: A Beginner's Guide to Ethnography*. Plymouth, UK: AltaMira Press.

Mayan, Maria J. 2009. "Introduction to Qualitative Inquiry" and "Theory and Method." In *Essentials of Qualitative Inquiry*, by Maria J. Mayan, 9–33. Walnut Creek, CA: Left Coast Press.

Pelto, Pertti J. 2013. "Introduction to Ethnographic Research." In *Applied Ethnography: Guidelines for Field Research*, by Pertti J. Pelto, 21–42. Walnut Creek, CA: Left Coast Press.

Visit **study.sagepub.com/kirner** to help you accomplish your coursework goals in an easy-to-use learning environment.

CHAPTER 2

The Ethics of Working with Human Participants

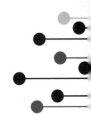

Orientation

In this chapter, we'll dive into the considerations social science researchers must make when working with human subjects, the folks we variously call our respondents, participants, informants, and collaborators. These considerations arise from a long history of developing ethical codes for our disciplines, some of which were the result of debates in cases where researchers may have conducted unethical research—research that harmed the people whom it was studying. As a result, there are standards and processes to better ensure that we do not harm the people we are studying. Our ethical decisions may be the single most important choices we make as researchers and should be carefully considered.

Ethics in Conducting Research with Human Subjects

What do we mean by *ethics*, and why are ethical codes so important when conducting research with human subjects? **Ethics** are standards of what we ought to do in terms of right and wrong: our subjects' (participants') rights, our responsibilities to various others (including our participants), the way our research ought to benefit the people whom we study and society as a whole, and issues of fairness and virtue while conducting research. *Ethics* also means the study and development of ethical standards—that is, the field of research on how to do research ethically. Generally speaking, the purpose of ethics is to provide broad guidelines on how to think through the effects our research has on our participants, and more broadly on the world, and to minimize harm while maximizing positive effects.

Chapter Learning Objectives

Students will be able to do the following:

2.1 Explain what ethics are and why they are important, as well as provide examples of ethical codes

2.2 Describe the responsibilities a researcher has to the people we study

2.3 Describe the responsibilities a researcher has to scholarship and science and to the public at large

2.4 Explain how ethical dilemmas occur despite ethical codes and think through complex ethical dilemmas

2.5 Understand how to identify and problem solve for potential problems concerning population

2.6 Understand how to identify and problem solve for potential problems concerning positionality

2.7 Describe the institutional review board (IRB) process and explain how to work with an IRB to assess and manage risk

Disciplinary associations write **ethical codes**, or documents that are meant to clarify the issues that have been carefully considered by professionals in the field and guidelines for researchers and practitioners. These codes outline the reason why they were written as well as *professional standards* for conducting research or practice—that is, standards that are broadly agreed on by professionals in a field as good practices and considerations to ensure that participants and society at large receive maximum positive effects and minimal negative effects from the research that is conducted. The American Association of Physical Anthropologists (AAPA) *Code of Ethics* (2003), for example, reads:

> No code or set of guidelines can anticipate unique circumstances or direct actions in specific situations. The individual physical anthropologist must be willing to make carefully considered ethical choices and be prepared to make clear the assumptions, facts and issues on which those choices are based. These guidelines therefore address *general* contexts, priorities and relationships which should be considered in ethical decision making in physical anthropological work.

Most professional codes of ethics work this way, in that they cannot anticipate all specific circumstances in which researchers will work, but rather seek to guide a process by which professionals can think about their research and encourage professionals to hold themselves accountable to their professional associations and their participants (and communities or populations they study).

Because of this, professional standards tend to be broadly applicable to a wide range of contexts, highlighting significant considerations across many different places, peoples, and situations. For example, the American Anthropological Association (AAA) *Statement on Ethics* states:

Ethics Standards of what we ought to do in terms of right and wrong actions.

Ethical codes Documents that provide agreed-on guidelines and standards for a profession in order to consistently minimize harm and maximize benefits during the course of the professional's work.

> Anthropologists should be clear and open regarding the purpose, methods, outcomes, and sponsors of their work. Anthropologists must also be prepared to acknowledge and disclose to participants and collaborators all tangible and intangible interests that have, or may be perceived to have, an impact on their work. . . . Anthropologists have an ethical obligation to consider the potential impact of both their research and the communication or dissemination of the results of their research.

In its code of ethics, the AAA outlines a number of considerations for researchers, particularly those of openness and honesty with a number of entities and the importance of using findings in appropriate and timely ways. These professional standards arose both from broadly agreed-on practices that encourage positive and lasting relationships with all groups involved in research (participants, colleagues, and funding organizations) and from responding to ethical problems that have occurred in the past. For example, during some of the wars in the twentieth century, anthropologists were employed or funded by the US military or Department of Defense to conduct research that was not forthright in its purposes with its informants. This was later considered problematic and unethical by other professionals, because it violates the rights of participants to understand what they have agreed to participate in and how the results of their participation will be used. The importance of appropriate and timely dissemination of findings is also important, because when doing research with human subjects, we ask a lot of time from our participants—often without pay. If we don't draft appropriate and timely presentations, manuscripts, films, or other media to share our findings, we have essentially co-opted research and our participants' time and effort for our own enjoyment and amusement—and that isn't social science research.

Discussion

When you consider the professional standards outlined in the AAA code of ethics, you'll note that they don't define certain terms, such as what is *appropriate* or *timely*. Why do you think this is the case, and how might this be both helpful and problematic? Can you think of two or three different dissemination outcomes of a research project that could be appropriate but have entirely different purposes and/or audiences? What factors might affect the timeline to dissemination and make timeliness challenging? How might you communicate or collaborate with participants to ensure that their ideas of what is appropriate and timely are taken into consideration in your plans for dissemination and that their expectations are realistic given factors over which you lack control (such as review timelines for publication)?

The Researcher's Responsibilities to the People We Study

Arguably, the most important responsibilities we must consider in research are those to the people we study—to our participants. **Human subjects** is the term most frequently employed by institutions such as universities and funding agencies when they refer to the people whom we study, who provide us with data through interviews, surveys, or other methods. However, the term *subjects* is framed by a colonialist background, when research often occurred on behalf of (and/or funded by) a colonial government on isolated, "primitive" peoples. As a consequence, it often is unfortunately a put-off to contemporary groups of people, who don't want to be viewed as subjects of the researcher's gaze. While we often have to use the term *human subjects* on forms for universities or funding agencies, it can be helpful to consider other ways to describe the people who are the focus of our study. Some of the popular ways to refer to these folks are aligned with particular methods: Researchers often say they have *informants* for interviews and

Human subjects
A common formal term that means the people whom you study (your participants).

respondents for surveys (though *informant* can also sound a bit like a spy or a snitch in some contexts!).

A neutral term that implies greater equality between the researcher and those who are studied is *participants*. Some researchers who are dedicated to **participatory research** or *collaborative research*—research in which the researcher and the community or population being studied work more intensely and equally together to define the purpose, methods, and outcomes of the research—prefer the term *collaborators*. This is also a particularly good way to refer to key participants who are more heavily involved in one's research and devote a lot of time and effort to it. Unlike in the early days of ethnography, such collaborators are increasingly given not only more power over defining the research project and its outcomes but also more credit, including becoming coauthors with researchers to acknowledge the significant contributions of their intellectual property to the project. In this textbook, we'll use *participant* to refer to people whom we study and who are participating in our project, *key informant* only in cases where we are narrowly referring to specific individuals who are heavily utilized for interview research, and *collaborator* to mean persons who (whether academics or not) are involved in research design and/or dissemination of results.

The responsibilities we have to our participants, and more broadly to the community or population we study, are the most important ones we have as social science researchers. Why? There are ethical and practical reasons for this. Ethically, we arguably have a social (and some would even say moral) obligation to reciprocate in kind the gifts of trust, time and effort, and openness our participants give us (and, more broadly, the information they provide arising from their cultural knowledge). In a practical sense, if we behave badly and break down trust in a community or population, people are likely to paint all of us—all the researchers in your discipline (and sometimes even in other disciplines)—as untrustworthy, rude, or careless people. This makes it much more difficult for future researchers to effectively work with those communities or populations. The ways you interact with your participants now have a ripple effect far beyond yourself and even your lifetime. Remember that you're working on behalf of not only your own project but also your institution, your discipline, and researchers everywhere.

There are a number of responsibilities that, when met, help ensure we are adequately reciprocating our participants' generous gifts of trust, time and effort, and openness (see Figure 2.1). We reciprocate trust by *avoiding harm*, *respecting well-being*, and *giving back*.

In order to return the trust our participants give us, we keep their needs and safety first in our minds. This is why research design begins with assessing risk to our participants and going through an institutional review board (IRB) process (which we'll cover later in this chapter), which allows fellow researchers to review our purposes, methods, and projected outcomes to double-check our minimization of harm.

Beyond avoiding harm, we need to respect our participants' well-being. This means that we not only minimize risk but try to maximize the positive effects of our research on our participants and their communities. For example, we try to anticipate how compensating participants may be perceived as unfair by the broader community and limit any negative social effects that may occur from participation. We treat our participants as we'd treat colleagues or friends—we make sure that we are sensitive to overstaying our welcome, being too intrusive, and showing our participants that we value their time.

Participatory research Research in which the researcher and the community or population being studied work more intensely and equally together to define the purpose, methods, and outcomes of the research.

Figure 2.1   Reciprocity with Participants

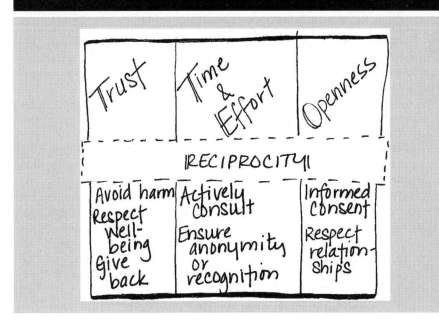

Finally, we try to avoid exploiting our participants by finding culturally appropriate ways of giving back. This can take many different forms, from gift cards or raffles for iPads in research conducted across a US county to volunteering to teach English at a rural school for a community in Guatemala. Sometimes giving back involves direct payment or compensation to participants who devote many hours (even years!) to our research as key informants (informants who usually have specialized knowledge and whom we rely on heavily)—this is especially the case if those informants are considered experts in their communities and are sharing uncommon knowledge with us. Other times, giving back—especially in cases where we are studying commonly held cultural beliefs, knowledge, or behaviors—may take the form of broadly useful or welcomed community-based assistance, such as providing supplies or human resources at schools, medical clinics, or community centers. It can be helpful to take a collaborative approach to the question of how to give back in these cases and incorporate culturally appropriate activities that allow the community to decide what it would like in return (but within a range of services or activities you can actually provide!).

A special consideration, especially if you are collecting specialized knowledge or information about cultural heritage, is to consider the issues around intellectual property. **Intellectual property** consists of creations of the mind, such as art, literature, inventions, and uses of things (such as cures derived from plants). Legally and ethically, people have a right to their intellectual property and fair compensation when it is used. We should engage in protecting our participants' intellectual property rights and give back to them in reciprocity for sharing it with us, but how? We have to consider the questions of

Intellectual property Creations of the mind, which may be held individually or collectively.

whom we choose as key informants and fieldworkers and how these jobs given to certain members of a community—especially if they are individually compensated—will affect how the person is perceived by others in their community. We also have to ask ourselves how widely such intellectual property is shared. Expert knowledge, such as what we might receive from a *curandero* (folk healer) on herbal remedies, may be appropriately compensated at the individual level in some cases. Broader aspects of culture, such as an annual performance that is part of a group's cultural heritage, may necessitate creative ways of giving back to entire communities or cultural groups.

We reciprocate time and effort by *actively consulting with participants* and *ensuring anonymity or recognition* (as participants wish). Aside from the question of giving back, we have to consider how we can return the time and effort participants give us in more intangible ways. We can honor their knowledge and willingness to participate by being more inclusive in our project design and implementation and in publicly giving them acknowledgment (or not, as they desire).

Active consultation with participants can, at its most inclusive and collaborative level, take a form of advocacy on behalf of communities in which the researcher designs their research project around purposes or goals that the community itself has established. In these cases, the researcher is more like a consultant to the community, and the ultimate goal is often to train community-based researchers so that they are eventually independent and self-sufficient in conducting their own research and advocating for themselves. Even in more standard, ordinary academic research (which is generated from the interests of the researcher, as we discussed in Chapter 1), there are ways in which we can consult with our participants throughout our research project. These can include honoring established community-based decision-making frameworks, such as going before the Tribal Council of a Native American tribe to request permission to conduct research in their community and to ask how you might ensure that your findings are returned to them in a meaningful way. It can also include (in bigger projects) hiring **fieldworkers** (paid workers who help collect data) from the community itself rather than from outside institutions or locations. We can also implement consultation on a micro scale in our research, such as periodically checking in with a participant during a long interview to ensure the person is comfortable and doesn't need a break. If we remember to consistently humanize our participants and treat them as we'd like to be treated, we'll find that we remember at all turns to consult them for their feelings, thoughts, and reflections on the research process.

Finally, in research in which people provide substantial time and effort, such as providing long interviews or sessions of participant observation, we should discuss with them their preferences on anonymity or acknowledgment in our manuscripts and other final products. In some cases, our research topic may be tied to conflict, or a participant may not wish to be identified by name for some other reason, and it is best to provide acknowledgment in anonymous, general ways, such as by thanking "all the participants who made this research possible." In other cases, participants may wish to be acknowledged by name, such as when an expert on healing is repeatedly consulted over the course of a year as a key informant.

Finally, we reciprocate openness by securing *advance informed consent* and *respecting close and enduring relationships*. We ask our participants to open up about their lives, often rather deeply and sometimes even painfully or intrusively. Imagine if a researcher

Fieldworkers Paid workers who help collect data.

showed up on your doorstep, asking if they could hang out with you for five hours a day and observe your life! Would you let them in? Letting people into our lives and being open and honest with them is challenging and often socially uncomfortable. Surprisingly, participants all over the world agree to donate significant time, effort, and discomfort to qualitative studies. We need to show gratitude by reciprocating with our own openness and by respecting the relationships we forge with our closest participants.

We primarily model openness from the beginning of our researcher–participant relationship through obtaining advance **informed consent**. We'll talk about this in detail later in this chapter, but this is a process that informs potential participants *before they begin participating* about our project's purpose, what it entails, and what risks they might face. It's our way of building trust, and while most new researchers find it awkward at first to obtain advance informed consent, it's a key part of being open and forthright with our participants.

Once we build those relationships, we need to remember that if we work with our participants deeply and repeatedly over time, as is often the case in ethnographic research (where we often return to a location many times over the course of several years or even our entire research career), these relationships often become more than professional. These close and enduring relationships become friendships as our participants share in our joys of discovery, our frustrations, and sometimes (for both parties) our tragedies and challenges. In conventional ethnographic research in smaller-scale communities, this means that over time, there is often little privacy between the researcher and the participant—and we may be asked to interweave ourselves ever deeper into the lives of our participants and their community. Ethnographers have become godparents of participants' children, loaned participants money for medical bills, and even sponsored participants to become US citizens. It isn't unknown for ethnographers who return to communities for many years to be treated as both insiders and outsiders at once, or even to have romantic relationships with members of the community. It's important to critically reflect on your role as a researcher throughout your time spent in a community and with particular participants, establishing boundaries that honor your needs and concerns for meeting your research goals while also finding ways to respect your participants' close relationships with you.

Discussion

Reflect on the research topic you selected in Chapter 1 of the workbook. What do you anticipate using as your field site, and whom do you anticipate having as participants? How close do you think you'd get to your participants over the course of your research? Would you rather have a short-term project only or eventually return to the community or site again and again? What are some initial ways you think you could give back to your participants (and, more broadly, the community or population you're studying)? How could you consult with your participants? How could you find ways to respect relationships you build with them?

Informed consent
A process that informs potential participants about the project's purpose, what it entails, and any risks they might face before they begin participating in the project.

The Researcher's Responsibilities to Scholarship and the Public

While researchers' most significant responsibilities are to the people they study—and those responsibilities should be first and foremost—our responsibilities don't stop there! We're also responsible to scholarship and science and to the public as a whole. Our responsibilities to scholarship are sometimes framed as how we give back "to our field" or "to our discipline." Basically, such responsibilities ensure that we facilitate rather than impede the advancement of social science as a whole, our discipline, and the work of our colleagues. Responsibilities to scholarship cover three focus areas: planning, sharing, and reputation.

Responsible scholarship in *planning* includes considering potential ethical dilemmas that may arise and planning for how to handle them, as well as including ethics in research proposals—both in terms of considerations of how to ensure that funding mechanisms support ethical standards and in terms of having proposals reviewed by an IRB whenever possible.

Responsible scholarship in *sharing* refers to the "appropriate and timely" dissemination of findings that the AAA code of ethics referred to earlier. Basically, researchers should use their results in meaningful ways, disseminate their findings so that other researchers (as well as policy makers and others) are informed by them, and share data after they're done using the information for new publications and presentations. By sharing data and findings with other researchers, we contribute to the advancement of entire fields and we capitalize on the time and effort our participants have already provided to research.

Finally, responsible scholarship is attentive to maintaining the *reputation* of the discipline (and science) as a whole. As we discussed in the section on our responsibilities to those whom we study, if we behave ethically, we preserve fieldwork opportunities for other researchers who come after us. By being honest and transparent, we provide positive interactions between researchers and participants, which encourages people to be willing to participate in the future. The logical bookend to our own transparency and ethical conduct is a willingness to report misconduct we observe by other researchers. If we come to find that a colleague is not operating with informed consent, is causing harm or unnecessary risk to participants, or is otherwise behaving badly in the field, we are responsible to report this for review by our professional associations or universities. While difficult and uncomfortable, peer-review accountability structures—from research design to fieldwork to dissemination of results—challenge our colleagues and ourselves to do research as ethically as we all can and to produce the best findings possible.

What about our responsibility to the public? Do we have responsibilities to society as a whole? We do. Arguably, the single most important responsibility we have to the public at large is to understand the potential harm that may come from the products we disseminate and to make our results available but in ways that minimize harm. On the one hand, we need to accurately portray the people whom we study. On the other hand, we have many choices to make about how to tell their stories and how to present our interpretations. We need to critically reflect on how our writings, films, or other products we disseminate—including our interpretations—may affect how the public views this group of people who are our focus. A classic example of the potential harm that can come to people as a result of choices in what and how to disseminate is the way in which the public's perception of the Yanomamo was slanted toward focusing on violence and brutality—even primitiveness—as a result of Napoleon Chagnon's portrayal of them in his ethnography. Even if we are not advocates or activists, we should always keep the risk to those whom we study in mind and remember that the public, to a greater or lesser degree, may be influenced by our work.

We also have a responsibility to conduct our research with integrity—not just in terms of virtue but in terms of maintaining the research design's necessary conditions and requirements to answer the research question. We shouldn't agree to conditions that funding agencies or other entities set that would substantially change the research (in ways that make it impossible to answer the research questions) or that compromise our ethics. In short, we need to be willing to improve our research design in various ways— to address peer reviewer concerns from funding-review or IRB panels, to collaborate with participants and incorporate their feedback, and to respond to emergent limitations and challenges in the field—but we also have to be vigilant about not compromising our ability as researchers to answer our research questions and to act in accord with ethical standards.

Discussion

Consider all the different groups to whom you have responsibility as a researcher— participants, the community or population that you study, fellow researchers and your discipline, and the public at large. In what ways do you think these different responsibilities support each other—what works together? In what ways do you think these different responsibilities may conflict? Can you generate one or two examples of potential conflicts in responsibilities and how you might respond to them?

Ethical Dilemmas

Ethical dilemmas are almost inevitable if someone conducts research for any substantial length of time. This isn't because the researcher has a poor moral compass or is unprofessional. Rather, there are gaps between professional standards and personal ethics (the overarching and very general standards set by professional associations and the specific ways in which you feel you should act within certain contexts). Ethics in codes and on paper, before you are in the field, usually seems easy. But the world is messy, and you're bound to be faced with uncomfortable, awkward, or even dangerous situations where you must make a choice about specific actions you will or won't take. Some of these dilemmas happen so frequently across fieldwork in many different contexts that we can discuss them ahead of time and begin to pose questions to ourselves about whether or not we anticipate encountering them for our own research topic. These dilemmas are built into the nature of social science research itself and have to do with conflicting (or multiple) "goods"—that is, positive goals that conflict with each other by their very nature in certain contexts.

Cause versus Culture

Activist anthropologists, particularly, may find themselves torn between a cause (such as ending human slavery or having equal rights for women) and the culture of the people they are studying. All sorts of practices that are widely decried in Western cultures, such as child labor, child marriage, slavery, and limiting the rights of women—including to their own bodies—exist in many cultures all over the world. Researcher responses to this have ranged from moral relativism on one end of the spectrum to activism on the other. **Moral relativism** posits that no one can judge another culture's practices, because morals are relative to their historical and cultural context. That is, we can be against child labor in our own culture and nation, but we can't tell a group from somewhere else that they can't (or shouldn't) have children work. **Activism**, on the other hand, positions the researcher in service to a cause—for example, the cause of ensuring global human rights for children, including the right to education and to not be put into working environments at the expense of education. Somewhere in the middle is **cultural relativism**, where the researcher seeks first to understand a practice or belief within its own historical and cultural context (and without judgment) and may later take a stand, but with this outsider position acknowledged and kept in mind.

Human Rights versus Cultural Continuity

Moral relativism The idea that no one can judge another culture's practices, because morals are relative to their historical and cultural context.

Activism The idea that the researcher is in service to a cause.

Cultural relativism The idea that the researcher first seeks to understand a practice or belief within its own historical and cultural context, without judgment, but may later take a stand.

In a similar but broader vein, researchers often must face questions about whether they attempt to align with the concept of universal human rights or whether they uphold the right of cultures to continue as they are (if they wish to do so). As the world has become more globalized, international political structures and nongovernmental organizations have increasingly pushed for certain inalienable universal human rights. These rights include access to meeting basic needs (e.g., food, water) and having basic securities and freedoms (e.g., not being physically harmed for one's religious beliefs). On the positive side, a movement toward universal human rights often protects groups within any society that are most marginalized and vulnerable—those who have the least amount of power to advocate for themselves. Outside bodies, such as the United Nations or human rights watch organizations, provide external checks on societies to attempt to avoid horrible abuses of power that can result in genocide, widespread sexual assault and violence against women, and other acts that widely—in many cultures—are thought to be tragedies. Yet at the same time, human rights declarations and reviews by outsiders also carry on a legacy from colonialism that posited Western values, beliefs, and practices as superior to non-Western peoples' cultures. Just as the Christian ideas of manifest destiny (the idea that Western Christian people had not only the right but the god-given destiny to convert and change "primitive" people) led to a great deal of suffering and cultural erasure for indigenous peoples all over the world, arguably human rights rhetoric carries the same implications—that Western or outsider values should trump the rights of a culture to continue its practices and beliefs.

Conflict within Cultures

One of the most difficult dilemmas arises from the variance within cultural groups themselves. Let's return to the first two dilemmas. It's one thing to consider how you'd respond if an entire cultural group wanted to maintain a practice that you disagreed with. But how would you respond if only *some* of the people in the group wanted to maintain the practice, and others wanted to get rid of it? What about if you noticed differences in power between these disagreeing groups—that one group was more powerful and perhaps benefited more from the practice, while the other was more vulnerable and paid the price of the practice? Disagreements within communities or cultural groups we study are common and are usually uncomfortable for the researcher to respond to. If we conduct participant observation and live in a location for months or years, it often becomes even harder to navigate these complex differences among our participants and maintain openness and trust while also potentially trying to work with disagreeing people. We may also develop our own opinions or experiences that cause us to feel as if we'd rather take on an activist or advocate role for one group, which comes at the expense of the other. There are no easy answers to this dilemma, but it's important to consider whether we may face it in our research. Some topics are specifically oriented to studying conflict and may make us more prone to encountering this dilemma than others; if we anticipate such "warring factions" within our participant group (or, more broadly, the community or population we study), it behooves us to think about how we'll handle this ahead of time.

Place versus People

Finally, there is a problem that is a bit like a subset of the cause-versus-culture dilemma combined with the conflict-within-cultures dilemma—and this is particularly challenging for environmental researchers, such as environmental anthropologists or political ecologists. This is the dilemma of place versus people. Environmentally oriented researchers frequently address research questions that attempt to understand why people manage resources in a certain way, what the environmental outcomes of that management system are, and whether they are negative—how to persuade people to change so that we become more sustainable on local-to-global scales. In this way, environmental researchers face a particularly interesting and unique cause-versus-culture dilemma—particularly because in some cultures (whether the researcher's or those they study), places, plants, animals, and other natural nonhuman beings are considered persons—complete with their own rights. Geographically bound places or specific resources frequently have competing stakeholder groups who are at odds as to how the places or resources should be used, distributed, and managed—and power differences, just as they play out for other cultural practices, usually matter for whose knowledge counts, whose voices are considered, and which groups are given rights to manage and use resources. Environmental researchers may feel torn at times, not only between these different conflicting stakeholder groups but also between their work toward sustainability overall for a place or resource and their commitments to not harming participants. The question of harm to participants is particularly problematic with regard to environmental research because such topics may have short-term versus long-term consequences that are at odds with each other. For example, research that exposes poor management practices in a fishery may cause immediate economic harm to fishermen in the study area when new regulations are put in place, but those regulations might ultimately preserve the fishery for future generations in the community. The complexity of environmental issues, often with many unknowns about how certain actions will eventually affect people in the study area, make it particularly difficult to assess risk over time.

Discussion

Think about your research topic or one that you've read about for any class. Identify one or more ethical dilemmas that were present in the topic or fieldwork scenario and how you would respond to them. Now, consider the four problems of multiple goods as a whole. Where do you stand on these issues? How would you define yourself as a researcher—more activist or advocate? More neutral observer? Try to imagine one or two scenarios that would test your sense of identity and baseline stance on these matters—how would you respond?

Vulnerable Populations

Aside from multiple goods, a rather specific issue that arises when conducting social science research, especially in the United States, is the issue of vulnerable populations. **Vulnerable populations** are already at greater risk in their lives than the rest of the population of a cultural or social group. Generally, vulnerable populations include certain age groups (minor children and the elderly), institutionalized populations (in prison or inpatient mental hospitals), minority groups (based on ethnicity, religion, gender and sexual orientation, etc.), and disadvantaged people (such as immigrants, those who do not speak the national language, and low-income people; see Figure 2.2).

Vulnerable populations are less likely to be able to advocate for themselves and are often more easily taken advantage of, and they are at particularly high risk for negative effects (including being negatively perceived by the public). As a consequence, researchers have to be especially careful when assessing risks and benefits for vulnerable populations involved in their studies. They need to weigh the immediate risks to participants in a vulnerable population against the greater good that may come to the population as a whole. For example, if we study sexual assault on college campuses, there is considerable emotional risk to victims who participate in interviews about their experiences and decisions about reporting. At the same time, if we design our research well and commit ourselves to disseminating findings in ways that speak to policy, such research could illuminate the barriers to reporting and prosecuting sexual assault cases on university campuses and lead to substantially better experiences for victims in the future (as well as eventually reduce incidences of sexual assault).

Vulnerable populations Groups within a society who face greater risk in their ordinary lives than the rest of the population.

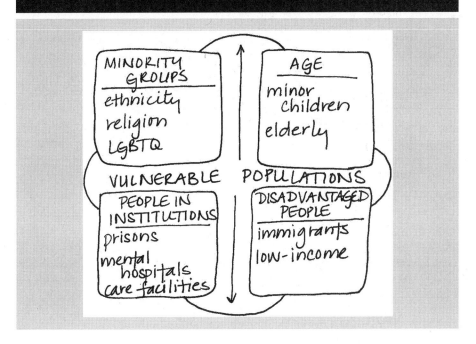

Figure 2.2 Vulnerable Populations

MINORITY GROUPS
ethnicity
religion
LGBTQ

AGE
minor children
elderly

VULNERABLE POPULATIONS

PEOPLE IN INSTITUTIONS
prisons
mental hospitals
care facilities

DISADVANTAGED PEOPLE
immigrants
low-income

In studies of broader research questions that could or could not include vulnerable populations as participants, we need to carefully consider whether the inclusion of vulnerable participants is necessary and whether excluding such participants would further marginalize them. There is no one right answer; it always depends on the research question and context. For example, a student might do a project on how people perceive the benefits of yoga and why they selected yoga as a form of exercise. The student decides to focus on drawing participants from three different yoga studios in their town. While they imagine that yoga might have some particularly unique benefits for people who experience mental illness, is it the best choice for them to specifically ask participants about their mental health and try to recruit participants who have experienced mental illness? Or will that do more harm than good in establishing trust and answering the overarching research questions? On the other hand, another student might do research on how people respond to extreme-heat warning days—when meteorologists warn that the temperature is high enough to cause people physical distress. In that case, the student should consider that if they exclude a vulnerable population such as the homeless, they are further marginalizing a population that is most likely to be the most negatively affected by the topic they are studying. Special efforts to reach out to these vulnerable populations, under those contexts, should be made—including finding ways to give back (or monetarily compensate when appropriate).

Consider the research topic you selected in Chapter 1 of the workbook. What vulnerable populations may be involved as participants? Do you think it is necessary to include them, to make efforts to exclude them, or does it not matter? Why? If you are planning to exclude vulnerable populations, what negative effects could occur as a result? If you are planning to specifically recruit certain vulnerable populations, how will you minimize their additional risk?

Positionality and Privilege

Aside from considering our population and whether some members may be vulnerable, we have to consider our positionality relative to the people we are studying. **Positionality** is how facets of our identity are positioned vis-à-vis our participants, usually based on class, ethnicity, and other attributes that describe how we are alike or different. Are we wealthier or poorer? Of the same ethnic background or different? More or less educated? Positionality matters for two primary reasons. First, in ethnographic research, you interact with your participants. This means that they will respond to their own assumptions and biases about your assumed sociocultural characteristics. It is best if you acknowledge the ways in which you are positioned relative to your participants, as well as whether or not this is likely to cause challenges in developing **rapport** and how it might affect the types of responses you receive and topics you can address. When one of the authors (Kimberly Kirner) studied cattle ranchers and cowboys, her experience was different from what she would've experienced if she'd been a man. In fact, cowboys would tell her how they would take care of her, giving her the best horses and making sure she was out of harm's way, because she was a woman. This afforded her lower physical risk than if she'd been a male researcher, whom some cowboys said they would have hazed with problem horses and harder and more dangerous physical tasks. At the same time, she almost certainly didn't receive access to all the same conversations that a male researcher would have, given the male-dominated nature of the occupation. Whether or not this matters depends on the research questions. Because the focus was on land management, it was unlikely that the participants would have responded substantially differently to a male interviewer. But had the study been on occupational culture, gender, and sexuality, that could have been very different and more problematic.

The second way positionality can affect your research is through your own bias, often due to assumptions based in privilege or because you have insufficiently recognized the ways your worldview differs from your participants. **Privilege** is a way of describing the additional, special benefits and advantages that some groups receive in a diverse society. Most people have some ways in which they have privilege relative to other groups and some ways they do not. For example, the authors have privilege

Positionality How facets of our identity are positioned vis-à-vis our participants, usually based on class, ethnicity, and other attributes that describe how we are alike or different.

Rapport Trust between a researcher and their participants, such that participants feel that they can be open and honest.

Privilege A way of describing the additional, special benefits and advantages that some groups receive in a diverse society.

as white women, compared with people of color. They don't face the same systemic racism as people of color. However, the authors have less privilege than men. Privilege can affect your research in multiple ways. You have to be careful not to assume that your own experience would be like that of your participants, and you also should not assume that your experience as a researcher would be the same as another researcher. You also have to handle the challenges that arise when you have more privilege (and sometimes more power) than your participants. It's important to be aware of the ways you might receive special advantages in the broader society and the ways in which your representations of your participants can help or hinder them, especially if their groups are routinely marginalized by the broader society. It is important to always remember the first rule in ethics in anthropology: *Your responsibility is first to the well-being of your participants.*

Ultimately, as researchers' careers progress and the support they receive is from diverse entities, they may face increasingly complex ethical dilemmas that arise from attempting to meet the directives of many different entities: their own research interests and personal ethics, their family's needs (especially if they take their family with them to the field), the people they study (in all their diverse, potentially conflicting subgroups), funding agencies providing financial resources to do the work, agencies from which permits or permission was necessary to do the work (national governments, local community leaders, etc.), the researcher's university or research institution, the researcher's colleagues and research team members, and the myriad laws and procedures that are required for both the researcher's nation and the host nation. Practicing anthropologists, who operate in applied settings outside of universities to solve social and environmental problems, may face even more challenges. In many social science fields, the majority of practitioners operate in nonacademic contexts (whether clinical or applied research). In anthropology, for example, more than 50 percent of all anthropologists work outside of academia, including 22 percent of PhDs. Employers, often nonprofit organizations or government agencies, bring their own agendas, biases, and standards to applied research—and practicing anthropologists frequently must orient their research agenda and practices to their employer's goals and procedures. While this sounds complicated and challenging—and sometimes is—practice-based or applied research has the capacity to do what academic research rarely can: to effect meaningful change for people in the short term. For many practitioners in the social sciences who desire to make a difference in the world through their work, this is worth the additional effort it takes to navigate the complexity of applied research.

Discussion

Consider your sociocultural attributes: your gender, sexual orientation, class, ethnicity, and so on. When you reflect on the research population you selected in Chapter 1 of the workbook, how are you positioned relative to your participants? What challenges might arise as a result of your positionality? How will you handle these challenges?

The Institutional Review Board Process

We've been mentioning the institutional review board (IRB) throughout this chapter, which is one of many layers of peer review (or review of one's research by colleagues) involved in academic research. **Institutional review boards** (or **IRBs**, which refer to both the board and the process) review and approve all research involving human and animal subjects. They are usually made up of administrators and faculty and are internal entities to all universities (there are also independent IRBs paid to provide oversight to non-university entities). All universities have specific IRB procedures and documents that researchers must file, and sometimes there are additional documents that the researcher must file with funding agencies, such as the National Institutes of Health. Every research project has to be approved by the IRB first, before the researcher can get started with data collection. IRBs provide review of our research to ensure that all participants are protected from physical, emotional, and financial harm and that they are warned of project activities and potential risk and impact in advance of a decision to participate. The IRB will designate research *exempt* from further review (usually, because the project carries no risk and collects no **identifying information**— no names, addresses, or other ways to track participants) or *non-exempt*, which means that further review is necessary before approval. Non-exempt research usually has one or more of the following features: It collects identifying information, it carries risk of some kind, and/or it requires informed consent. The more risk and lack of anonymity a research project demands, the more scrutiny the IRB will generally give the project. This means that participant observation and survey projects, which are often low- or no-risk and anonymous, are often considered exempt, while intensive interview projects—especially on emotionally difficult subjects, such as war or immigration— would be non-exempt.

You might recall from earlier in this chapter that informed consent is a form and process that ensures respect for participants' autonomy by giving them all the information up front about the project, answering their questions and concerns, and asking them to sign off that they understand their rights. Informed consent is a process, often entailing revisiting questions and concerns as they later arise, and the informed consent form is not a legal contract so much as the start to a conversation. This conversation details what participants can expect to experience in the project, how much time and which tasks will be asked of them, what (if any) risks they will face, and what the proposed products for dissemination and impact will be of the project. The form is a guide for that conversation, ensuring they understand their rights to anonymity and confidentiality, to withdraw their participation (and when it is too late to do so), and where and how their information will be stored and used. The informed consent form should, as much as possible, be in language understandable to the public (free from jargon and at a basic reading level) and should be discussed with potential participants, encouraging them to ask questions about what they don't understand or what concerns them.

Generally speaking, IRB documentation includes a **protocol** (a detailed plan that presents the significance of the research and plans for dissemination, the sampling and

Institutional review board (IRB) A board or process that reviews and approves all research involving human and animal subjects.

Identifying information Information that identifies participants and allows them to be tracked in the real world.

Protocol A detailed plan that presents the significance of the research and plans for dissemination, the sampling and methods, an assessment of risk to participants, and how the researcher will minimize risk.

methods, an assessment of risk to participants, and how the researcher will minimize risk) and auxiliary forms, such as informed consent forms, method instruments (such as surveys or lists of interview questions), and evidence that the researcher is qualified to conduct the research (a curriculum vitae or résumé). Collectively, the documentation demonstrates that the researcher has carefully considered the potential positive and negative effects of their research and adequately planned to minimize risk and harm. The documents also ensure there is a clear plan that outlines the proposed methods, tools and instruments, and dissemination outcomes. Because of this, IRB protocols can serve as useful frameworks not only to plan for participant risk but also more generally to plan for the implementation of the proposed research project. A researcher's protocol details the what, why, where, when, who, and how of the research project, providing clarity for both the researcher and others. While such details often change once the researcher is in the field (and these changes are communicated back to the IRB and approved as needed), having a plan to begin with provides the maximum chance for the researcher's success and a baseline from which to modify as conditions demand.

Pairing the Textbook and Workbook

As you think carefully about your own ethics and how you'd integrate them with field research, and as you work toward your culminating activity for this chapter in the workbook (Activity 2.7), it is important to remember that ethics is grounded in a combination of your interpretation of your discipline's professional standards, the unique risks and circumstances your field situation involves, and the ways in which you are positioned relative to your participants. Keep asking yourself these questions:

- How can I best protect my participants? How can I best demonstrate reciprocity with them?

- What is my position relative to my participants, and what challenges may happen as a result? How can I plan to meet these challenges?

- How do I interpret the standards written by my professional association(s)? What do these mean to me?

- What potential kinds of risk are involved in my research, and how do I plan to minimize these risks?

Reflective Prompts

1. How do I take notes or call out important terms or concepts while reading?

2. Can I explain how ethical dilemmas occur despite ethical codes?

3. Do I understand potential problems concerning recruitment, population and positionality, and risk assessment and management?

Case Study

Magliocco, Sabina. 2005. *The Two Madonnas: The Politics of Festival in a Sardinian Community.* 2nd ed. Long Grove, IL: Waveland Press.

Available for free through www.academia.edu.

The Project

I did this project for my dissertation and post-doctoral field research, funded by two Fulbrights. I worked in northwest Sardinia, an island off the coast of Italy, and I looked at religious festivals and the effects of globalization. At that time, I talked about globalization as social and economic transformation. There were changes that had introduced a market and tourist economy. In the 1960s to 1970s, government-subsidized sheep pastoralism occurred, and prior to WWII, this had happened with wheat production. I looked at how these impacted one particular town and its surroundings.

One theme that emerged was the change in gender roles. There were huge changes for women in the period of the 1930s through the beginning of the twentieth century: They gained economic autonomy, they became more highly educated than the men, they participated in wage labor, and they participated way more in the planning of festivals. Some of the other themes were the close relationship between local festivals and local politics. Festivals served as a way for people on the upper end of the social scale to offer hospitality to others in the community and gain social recognition. But because of how the festivals were financed by the end of the twentieth century, it also allowed them to demonstrate their ability to navigate bureaucracy. So people who were more experienced in organizing festivals were more

likely to run for political office and win, since they demonstrated that skill.

There were merged inside and outside versions of identity; the harvest festivals in summer became tourist attractions. But there were other festivals revived for generating *communitas* among community members. Tourist festivals became expensive and included non-participatory events to demonstrate regional identity. Smaller, ancillary festivals were about local identity; people put on these events for themselves. They included local musicians, local food provided by individual donations leading to communal meals, and participatory dance. These were temporary returns to communal identity at a time when global economic and social forces were pushing people to a more individualized identity and pushing the town's identity more toward one oriented toward tourists—outward-looking rather than inward-looking.

What ethical issues arose during your research?
Let's start with my relationship to the community. My relationship to the community came from a personal connection to a woman who had worked as a domestic helper for my grandmother for many years and retired back to her village. So she was both a mother figure for me, and there was also this class difference. Domestic labor can be exploitative. She was not a social equal to my grandmother. Italian society was quite hierarchical. Many of my ethical difficulties in the community stemmed from that. As a daughter-like figure in her home, I was expected to adhere to all the social norms and rules as if I were in that relationship in

the family. This included not forming political relationships with opposing families and not borrowing things from others outside the family.

But my responsibilities as an ethnographer were very different. I needed to not limit my contacts to only one particular subgroup of society. So that created unease. I truly tried to talk to people all over the village: every social class, every political persuasion, every gender. Sometimes that created tension inside my living situation with the woman who hosted me and her family. I might talk to a family they didn't have good relationships with, for example. I became close to some people, one of whom was vice-mayor, and she belonged to a political party that my host and her family didn't belong to. So the situation was complex. It got more complex, because during my fieldwork, one of the festivals was taken over by the Christian Democrats. They took control of the festival from my friend on the left, who was in name running it, but who let them take control because she wasn't that invested in the festival. As a result, the Christian Democrats were elected to city council immediately following my fieldwork. This was interesting for me in terms of studying festivals, but it created a lot of tension between my host, my friends, and me.

I wanted to work with a local ethnographer who offered me the opportunity to publish my book in Italian in a series he was doing on Sardinian ethnography. I was thrilled by this, because I had the idea of giving back to the community that had hosted me. So I worked on the translation, and I asked for feedback from the community on the book so it would be their book as well. Then I got it from both sides. Both sides felt I got it wrong and felt I listened too much to people from "the wrong side." This was the result of interfamily politics in families that for generations had been on different political sides. I ended up with hard feelings on both sides of the political spectrum, and it was really a tough time for me. When that went down, the publisher decided he didn't want to publish the book anymore because it was too politically controversial, and he himself lived in a town dominated by Christian Democrats and he didn't want to be on their bad side. So I had to publish with a different publisher. When the book was eventually published, with help from friends on the left, the right-wing city council took this out on my host by taking away a piece of her property. I felt awful. For a long time, I felt I couldn't go back to the town. I felt that by trying to give back to town, I hurt the person I was closest to and to whom I owed the greatest debt.

What are your reflections on these issues now?
Obviously, hindsight is 20/20. I wish I'd understood going in that in Sardinia, politics are family-based and there is no expectation or understanding that anyone could be neutral. My mistake was going in as an outsider and thinking that I could be neutral. This idea did not exist to the people I was studying. If I'd understood that from the beginning, it might have been easier to cope with. But the situation was complicated, and it'd be difficult for anyone to be caught up in these local politics.

What advice do you have on ethics, based on your research career, for beginning researchers?
You have to be honest with people about what you're doing. You have to be honest with yourself, about your own biases and limitations going into the field and how they might color the way that you see things. And I think you have to get over any romantic notions you have about trying to do good or help people in the community. There's
(*Continued*)

(Continued)

a limited amount you can do to help people in the community. I'm taking a group of students to the town in Sardinia where I did fieldwork this summer, but this was initiated by the community, and we're using all local vendors. It is a different kind of process. This will give back to the community economically in a very concrete way, and was their idea. But does our ethnographic work help communities? It's really difficult for that to happen. It's very challenging, because there are many competing forces at work. The best way I have given back to that community is through friendship. It's the relationships we build in our field communities that give back the most. We're giving back emotionally, but on a very small-scale, individual basis.

Case Study Reflections

1. Reflecting on Magliocco's experience in the field and what she wishes she'd known before she started it, what kinds of information should you try to find out before beginning your fieldwork?

2. Micro-level politics (conflicts in power and wealth between families, local groups, or local villages or towns) are relatively common around the world. How can you prepare yourself for handling conflicts between your participants in the field?

3. Why do you think it is difficult for ethnographers to meaningfully give back to the communities where they study? Why is academic research and publication often insufficient for meaningfully giving back?

4. What do you think Magliocco means when she says that our relationships in the field (our friendships) give back the most? If you approach your participants in this way (as friends), how does this change the way you would conduct your research and approach relationships in the field?

STUDY GUIDE ●━━━━━━━━━━━━━━━━━━━━━━

Note: Students should study each concept with attentiveness to defining, explaining with examples, and describing or demonstrating process. This is not a list of terms to define; it's a list of concepts and processes to master.

Ethics

Ethical codes

Responsibilities to people we study

Human subjects

Participatory research

Key informants

Intellectual property

Fieldworker

Informed consent

Responsibilities to scholarship

Responsibilities to the public

Moral relativism

Activism	Privilege
Cultural relativism	Institutional review board (IRB)
Common types of ethical dilemmas	Peer review
Vulnerable populations	Identifying information
Positionality	Exempt and non-exempt research
Rapport	Protocol

FOR FURTHER STUDY

American Anthropological Association Committee on Ethics. n.d.-a. *AAA Ethics Forum.* Accessed July 22, 2018. http://ethics.americananthro.org.

American Anthropological Association Committee on Ethics. n.d.-b. *Briefing Papers on Common Dilemmas Faced by Anthropologists Conducting Research in Field Situations.* Accessed July 22, 2018. http://www.americananthro.org/ParticipateAnd Advocate/Content.aspx?ItemNumber=1835.

American Anthropological Association Committee on Ethics. n.d.-c. *Handbook on Ethical Issues in Anthropology.* Accessed July 22, 2018. http://www.americananthro.org/LearnAndTeach/Content.aspx?ItemNumber=1942.

Mayan, Maria J. 2009. "Ethics Boards, Risk, and Qualitative Research." In *Essentials of Qualitative Inquiry,* by Maria J. Mayan, 125–31. Walnut Creek, CA: Left Coast Press.

REFERENCES

American Anthropological Association. 2012. *AAA Statement on Ethics: Principles of Professional Responsibility.* Accessed June 26, 2019. https://www.americananthro.org/LearnAndTeach/Content.aspx?ItemNumber=22869&navItem Number=652.

American Association of Physical Anthropologists. 2003. *Code of Ethics.* Accessed June 26, 2019. http://ethics.iit.edu/codes/AAPA%202003.

Visit **study.sagepub.com/kirner** to help you accomplish your coursework goals in an easy-to-use learning environment.

CHAPTER 3 Sampling

Orientation

In the previous chapter, we discussed the ethics related to working with human participants. But how do we choose participants to begin with? In this chapter, we'll return to some Chapter 1 concepts, such as generalizability and reliability, and explore how the size and type of our sample—our group of participants—affect the ways we can answer our research question. Sampling tends to be a challenging topic for students, so hang in there as you read about the different types of sampling and how they are related to research topics. Review frequently if you need to, and if it helps you, remember that you can create graphic organizers to help you differentiate between the sampling types and organize your thoughts about them.

What Is a Sample?

A **sample** is a way of representing the wider world through a small population that you study. Most researchers use samples, because unless you are working in a very small community or population, it is almost impossible for you to include everyone as participants (what we call a **total sample**). Researchers have to decide what kind of sample to employ, and the most basic of these decisions is to determine whether they should use a probability or nonprobability sample. **Probability samples** are best for research that focuses on how individual attributes (such as gender, ethnicity and race, or age) affect certain characteristics of interest across a diverse population. They're often used for survey (questionnaire) research in complex, large populations or societies. Most qualitative research is conducted using **nonprobability samples**. These are samples that collect cultural data—behaviors, beliefs, and knowledge that are widely held

Chapter Learning Objectives

Students will be able to do the following:

3.1 Define the term *sample* and explain how it relates to a study population

3.2 Define *nonprobability sample* and describe the types of studies for which it is appropriate

3.3 Understand what to consider when selecting an appropriate type of nonprobability sampling plan and justify why it is appropriate in a specific research context

3.4 Identify the main problems in selecting key and "expert" informants that must be addressed in research planning

3.5 Define *probability sample* and describe the types of studies for which it is appropriate

3.6 Understand what to consider when selecting an appropriate type of probability sampling plan and justify why it is appropriate in a specific research context

3.7 Compare and contrast nonprobability and probability sampling plans and relate them to the hypothetico-deductive method

in specific groups. The assumption when using this type of sample is that the information or phenomenon you're studying is shared across many members of a group, so using a smaller and more directed selection of participants will not cause you to lose a great deal of the variance and detail you would find with a larger sample. See Figure 3.1 for a summary of the differences between probability and nonprobability samples.

Some qualitative researchers, such as anthropologists, did not always use sampling. In fact, for many years, anthropologists frequently went to small, relatively bounded groups (such as rural villages), so they were able to have a total sample—working with all willing participants in the field site. Because sociologists and psychologists more frequently worked in large, complex nations, they used sampling much more frequently, because samples are the only way to address

Sample A smaller population of participants in your research study that represents the larger population you are studying.

Total sample A sample that includes all willing people from the larger population you are studying as your participants.

Probability samples Samples in which every unit (whether individual, household, or another unit of analysis) should have an equal chance of being drawn into the study sample.

Nonprobability samples Samples that collect cultural data, so they can use a small number of participants who represent the whole population of study.

Figure 3.1   Nonprobability versus Probability Samples

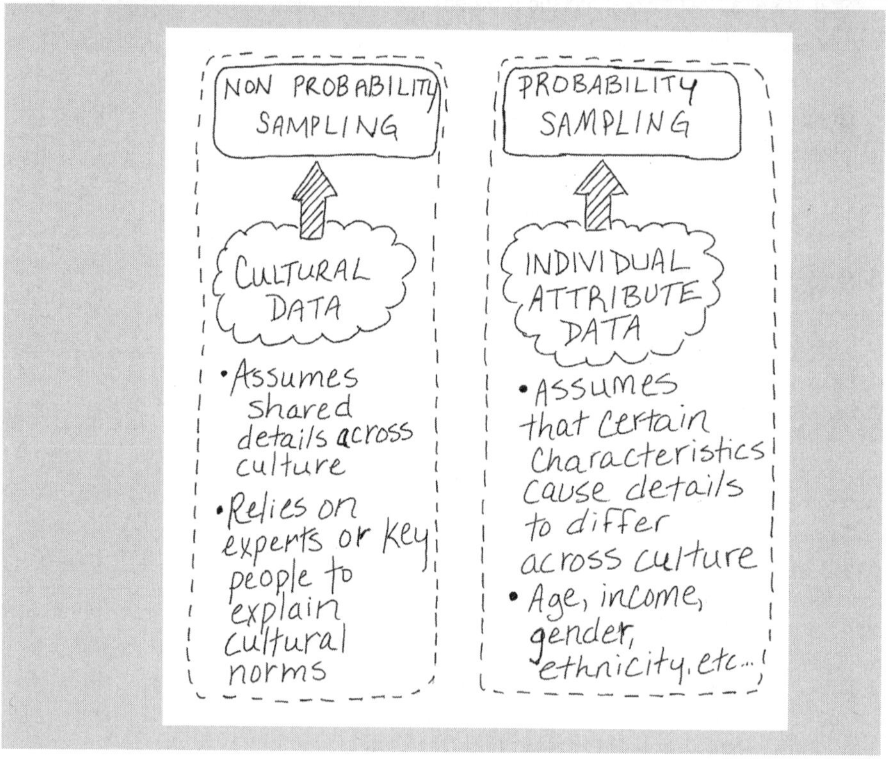

NON PROBABILITY SAMPLING

CULTURAL DATA

- Assumes shared details across culture
- Relies on experts or key people to explain cultural norms

PROBABILITY SAMPLING

INDIVIDUAL ATTRIBUTE DATA

- Assumes that certain characteristics cause details to differ across culture
- Age, income, gender, ethnicity. etc...

research topics in an impossibly large population. If the community or population you're studying is much more than about one hundred people, or if you plan to conduct intensive research, such as in-depth interviews, oral histories, or participant observation, you'll need to consider which participants you'll select and which people you won't—or you'll never get past the data collection stage! In addition, sampling ensures that if major changes (social, environmental, or otherwise) happen midstream in your project and disrupt your data collection, you can move forward with your project's integrity still intact. Starting with a defined sample and moving iteratively through phases (for example, an introductory interview, followed by a period of participant observation, followed by an in-depth interview), rather than working intensively with only a handful of people (intending to work with others later), ensures that if your research is disrupted—let's say, by a flood—you are able to return later to the same sample of people to compare before- and after-event responses or to work with a different sample that has similar characteristics to finish your study. It protects the integrity of your research design by minimizing the negative impact that emergent disruptions can have. When you start with a defined sample, it also tends to boost your chances of successfully finishing your research project, because you'll be less scattered in your approach—more focus generally equals more productivity and timeliness.

Discussion

Reflect on your research topic that you've been working with. Do you think it's best for probability or nonprobability research, and why?

Nonprobability Samples

As we've discussed, researchers often choose to use nonprobability sampling when their research question covers cultural data—broadly held, widely distributed beliefs, knowledge, or behaviors. This doesn't mean we should assume there aren't variances across the study group—there always are—but it does mean that if we're most interested in the overall pattern in the group (the culture), we can be less concerned about the variance (the outliers). Nonprobability sampling, therefore, is particularly useful for some kinds of research questions. Aside from broadly held cultural data, nonprobability sampling is also useful for capturing what is considered expert knowledge. For example, if an ethnobotanist (someone who studies the knowledge about and uses of plants in cultural groups) wishes to develop comprehensive lists of plant-based cures from a cultural group, they're best served by intensively working with a handful of expert healers, rather than anyone and everyone in the cultural group.

Selecting nonprobability sampling is also tied to practical, logistical limitations of certain qualitative research methods. If a researcher proposes to deeply explore a subject using labor-intensive methods, such as in-depth interviews or oral histories (especially for sensitive topics for which it takes a lot of time to build trust first through participant observation and simply hanging out), it is unlikely that they'll be able to manage a huge number of participants. In fact, narrative-based studies, where complex, lengthy narratives are collected from participants, rarely exceed fifty participants—and that is still a ton of data! Nonprobability sampling is also commonly used in exploratory, or pilot, stages of research projects wherein the researcher may not have sufficient time or money to conduct a larger-scale project with a bigger sample size. However, in all cases of nonprobability sampling, each of the participants counts for a lot, so researchers need to pick their participants wisely and document biases that arise from the sample.

How big should your sample size be? This depends on the type of study you intend to conduct (see Figure 3.2). In grounded theory studies (where the data drive the development of theory—more on this in later chapters) and ethnographic studies, a sample size of thirty to fifty interviews is optimal. Some participants may be more deeply engaged than others—for example, when you work with a smaller number of participants intensively through participant observation and combine this with a wider number of interviews. In cultural domain studies, where your focus is narrower (and therefore, frequently, there are fewer "experts" or optimal participants to engage) but you work with participants more intensively, ten to twenty knowledgeable persons is a sufficient number. For example, if you're interested in how a community manages its water, and there are specific people in charge of this process, working intensively with these people will allow you to gather all the data you need. Finally, in phenomenological studies, which focus on the participants' perceptions, perspectives, and understandings of lived experiences in particular situations, a very small number of participants is used, usually because these studies go into great detail for each participant and are very narrowly defined in their scope.

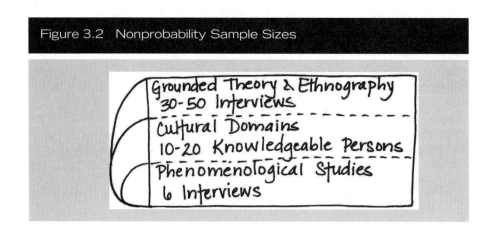

Figure 3.2   Nonprobability Sample Sizes

Grounded Theory & Ethnography
30-50 Interviews

Cultural Domains
10-20 Knowledgeable Persons

Phenomenological Studies
6 Interviews

Discussion

For now, focus on aspects of your research question that could be addressed through nonprobability sampling—whether you envision this as an exploratory phase or as the optimal form of sample to address your questions. What kind of research are you proposing? Is it likely to be an ethnographic study? A cultural domain study? A phenomenological study? How do you know? How many people, optimally, would you engage as participants?

Types of Nonprobability Samples

Once you've determined how many participants you will attempt to recruit, it's time to figure out how you will recruit them. To do this, you'll select a type of nonprobability sample to generate (see Figure 3.3).

Again, the choice depends on both your research question and logistical concerns, such as finding enough participants. **Quota sampling** is a stratified sample, which means that you determine certain categories of participants—often capturing key variables for

Figure 3.3 Types of Nonprobability Samples

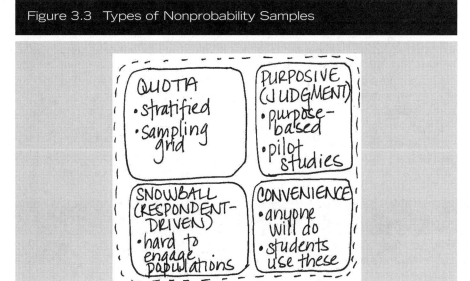

Quota sampling
A stratified sample based on certain categories of participants, in which the categories are assumed to matter for answering the research question.

the study—and then recruit a certain number of participants into each combination of categories. Unlike a probability sample, participants aren't chosen at random; rather, the quota framework provides a way for the researcher to ensure they have enough participants from different groups to answer the research question. Quota sampling is widely used for qualitative studies, especially interviews. It's based on a **sampling grid** of the variables you want to compare. For example, a study seeking to describe the experiences of young women in a period of "discernment" for becoming Catholic nuns (a period in which they strongly consider this choice, often while living in a convent) may consider a number of variables that might affect their experience: whether they are in an enclosed or open convent (an enclosed convent means the nuns do not leave, and they do not have frequent visitors), whether they came from a Catholic or non-Catholic family, and whether they came from a high or low socioeconomic status (SES; see Figure 3.4). In this case, eight groups would capture the variety set by these categories along these variables. While quota samples are biased toward people who are easy to engage as participants, when quota sampling is done well, it approximates probability sampling at a fraction of the cost, all while producing more data because of the depth with each participant.

Purposive (judgment) sampling is based on first defining the purpose you want participants to serve and then including all participants who are willing. There is no overall sampling design, but rather simply a direction of whom you are looking to engage. This form of sampling is frequently done for **pilot studies** (studies conducted before larger studies on the same question or topic), for intensive and critical case studies, and for hidden, stigmatized, and hard-to-find populations. Because purposive sampling is opportunistic, it is frequently deployed for pilot studies because researchers are exploring a new question or topic, and this is an easy way to engage participants for the study without investing a great deal of time or resources. Purposive sampling is also helpful for case studies, especially when a small number of participants are intensively engaged in identifying and describing a cultural phenomenon or providing life histories. Finally, this type of sampling can be useful for populations who are difficult to engage. If a study seeks to understand the lives of undocumented students, for example, it may be quite challenging for a researcher to recruit participants, because they may feel vulnerable. A purposive sample allows the researcher to focus on engaging as many willing participants as possible, without excluding some of them due to specific sampling frameworks (as might happen with quota sampling).

Is a purposive sample the same as a convenience sample? They're very much alike, but, no, they're not the same. A **convenience sample**, which many students employ in methods classes when they are first trying out various methods on participants, is

Sampling grid A table that outlines the variables you want to compare and how many participants you need in each of the resulting categories.

Purposive (judgment) sampling Sampling that includes all willing participants, so long as they meet the purpose of your sample.

Pilot studies Studies conducted before larger studies on the same question or topic.

Convenience sample: A sample that engages anyone willing to participate, usually starting with people the researcher knows.

Figure 3.4 Quota Sampling Grid

Young Women in Discernment Period for Becoming a Nun							
Enclosed Convent				Open Convent			
From Catholic Family		From Non-Catholic Family		From Catholic Family		From Non-Catholic Family	
Low SES	High SES	Low SES	High SES	Low SES	High SES	Low SES	High SES

Note: SES = socioeconomic status.

basically engaging anyone who will participate. When students are just starting out, they often find that the easiest way to get participants is to ask friends, family, roommates, and classmates. (If you're in a methods class, you might find all your friends running in the opposite direction by the time you're halfway through the course, to avoid the method of the week!) Convenience sampling is completely acceptable for the beginning student who is trying out topics and methods for a class. However, by the time you reach the master's thesis level, your sample should be more carefully planned. What shifts a convenience sample to a purposive sample is making sure your participants represent the topic or research question you have. Rather than grabbing any person who is around you, you're looking for people who have direct links to the research question. Convenience samples are helpful for trying out methods or getting a sense of how people—anyone, not specific groups—think about a certain domain or topic. However, because the sample is not carefully chosen, it usually isn't sufficient to make findings or conclusions that can be shared with others. It's more for exploring a topic in order to create a research design than it is for implementing a research design.

What does a researcher do if the population they're trying to study is particularly difficult to engage? This can happen for many reasons. The group may be hidden or hard to find—that is, not apparent or clustered in a location in any way. Pagans in the United States, for example, are challenging to locate because they are distributed across the entire nation and often don't meet in public or identify themselves publicly as Pagan. Some groups may be stigmatized (repeatedly treated by the public as problematic, bad, or inferior), which generally reduces their visibility and their willingness to engage with a researcher. Undocumented workers, for example, may be very reluctant to identify as such and join a research study. Finally, some groups are simply hard to study—they're not stigmatized or particularly hard to find, but they're also unlikely to agree to participate. For example, CEOs of companies or very wealthy people may not be reachable by a researcher. In all these kinds of cases, a **snowball (respondent-driven) sample** is probably best. This allows the researcher to start with just one or two people with whom the researcher has an "in" and prior rapport, then ask these people for referrals to others who are in the group (see Figure 3.5 for an example). Alternatively, the researcher may advertise for the first few participants and offer payment, then hope that they can refer to other participants from that point. While the sample can often be skewed along social networks, it allows the researcher a way to engage sufficient participants from populations that are otherwise inaccessible. This makes it very popular as a sampling method for research on groups that would otherwise be too challenging to engage at all.

Discussion

Reflect once again on your research question you've been working on. What kind of nonprobability sample do you think is optimal for answering your question, and why? Do you anticipate it being easy or challenging to acquire that sample? What are one or two contacts or places you could start with for recruiting participants?

Snowball (respondent-driven) sample A sample drawn from the social (referral) networks of only a few people whom the researcher knows, who fit the category of participant needed.

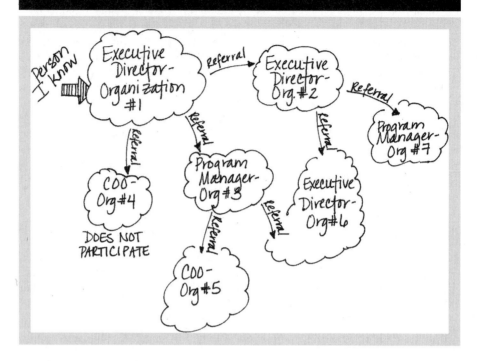

Figure 3.5 Snowball Sample

Choosing Key Informants

Key informants
People who know
a lot about their
culture and are
willing to participate
in your study.

**Specialized
informants** Key
informants with
expert, specialized
knowledge in a
specific domain of
the culture you are
studying.

In qualitative research projects that have few participants, where each participant will count for quite a lot in the analysis, another consideration researchers have to make is how to select individual informants for interviews. That is, if you will spend a great deal of time interviewing participants, how will you select who is best to interview? Rather than the question of sampling (how to engage a sufficient number and type of participants), this is a question of individual judgment: Will this particular participant be a good informant? **Key informants** are people who know a lot about their culture and, for their own reasons, are willing to share this information with you. Most qualitative researchers have key informants in their field site, and these people are often the most engaged in their research over the years—frequently providing not only interviews but also referrals to other participants and conversations that mull over data. Usually, these folks have their own reasons for wishing to participate so deeply in your work: They may have a vested interest in the outcome, have above-average interest in scholarship or your discipline, or might just be very friendly and gregarious and enjoy the company. **Specialized informants** have a special competence in a particular topic—for example, healing, agricultural knowledge, or religious practice. They're like key informants but with expert knowledge not shared by most of the other people in the group you are studying.

Good informants are invaluable to researchers, and usually you'll find you have only a few really good informants in a study with many more participants. Good informants will talk easily with you, will understand the information you need, and are glad to work with you to get the information. Usually, their personalities and interests align with your research project, and they find personal satisfaction in providing time and effort toward the project. With really good informants, you can teach them how to be ethnographers on their own, and they become co-investigators (and sometimes coauthors) over time. As you engage participants, remember to approach people with skeptical friendliness. Your first informants aren't necessarily the best informants. Informants may have their own agendas, they might lie, and they might assume things about what you want to know that are inaccurate. Approaching people with both a friendly demeanor and gratitude for their time, while also holding off on assessing their accuracy of information until you've collected quite a bit of data, is a good balance for the researcher to maintain to ensure that you're open-minded and engaging but don't rush to conclusions based on a handful of participants' initial information.

Probability Samples

If you remember from the beginning of this chapter, probability samples are used when the individual attributes of members of a population may matter, given your research question. If you suspect that the type of research question you're asking would result in different kinds of answers, trends, or experiences depending on your participants' age, income level, religion, ethnicity, or other key individual attributes, then it might be best to structure your research study around probability sampling. Probability sampling is also most commonly used in complex, large, diverse social groups in which subgroup members' lifeways, experiences, behaviors, and ideas are likely to substantially differ. For example, you might ask: How do extended family members contribute to childhood socialization in the United States? This is likely to be structured differently based on US families' ethnicities, household structures, income levels, and perhaps even geography (such as whether a family lives in an urban, suburban, or rural area). Because there are more than three hundred million people in the United States, and they differ in many ways from one another, any question that is likely to be different across those demographic groups would require probability sampling.

Remember that in probability sampling, every unit (whether individual, household, or another unit of analysis) should have an equal chance of being drawn into the study sample. Because there are likely to be so many differences in the data across various demographic groups, it is not sufficient to rely on key or expert informants; instead, it's necessary to get a lot of different people who will represent the broader population you're studying. This means that you'll usually have a very large sample size compared with nonprobability sampling. This large sample size makes it almost impossible to use in-depth interviews and other time-consuming methods for data collection. Imagine trying to conduct 1,500 one-hour interviews for your master's research! You'd be in graduate school forever! But what about the depth of data collected, and how do you weave in participant observation or participants' voices? There are several ways you can approach such challenges as a student researcher focused on such questions:

1. You could select a nonprobability sample but consider your project a pilot study;

2. you could narrow down the population of study while retaining the core research question and consider your project a case study (such as by maintaining a focus on childhood socialization, as described earlier, but changing from the United States in general to Korean American families in Seattle); or

3. you could make your primary research method something like questionnaires (surveys), which allow you to collect more shallow data over a much larger population.

We'll cover questionnaires as a data collection method in Chapter 8, as well as how you might integrate this method with more qualitative ones that provide depth. But for now, let's further explore how probability sampling works.

Sample accuracy in a probability sample depends on making sure that every unit in the population has the same chance of being selected for participation: that is, that the sample is not biased. Maintaining our same research question on childhood socialization by extended family in the United States, let's imagine that you recruit all the families in your neighborhood. This might be an easy way to reach participants, but your sample is biased. Whatever your neighborhood's dominant income level, age structure (some neighborhoods tend to be younger adults vs. older adults), and ethnicity will bias your sample so that it really isn't about the entire United States anymore. Instead, it's about only a much smaller, more specific subset of the population. In this case, your sample would be an inaccurate portrayal of the US population.

Sample precision can be increased by increasing the size of unbiased samples. This is why you want a relatively large sample. Let's return to our example about childhood socialization. Let's say you recruit two families from every state, and you're careful to do quota sampling (remember that type of nonprobability sample from earlier in the chapter?). You have one hundred families in your study, and there are representatives from every income level, ethnicity, and state. But when you think about it, even if you're very careful to recruit representatives of all these different groups of people, with only one hundred participants, there won't be very many representatives of *each* of those groups. You might have only a couple of Native American families, for example. Are those two Native American families really representative of all the Native American families in the United States? This is why to have more precise data, you need a relatively large sample size. A larger sample size decreases the margin of error (also known as the *confidence interval*) and increases how representative your participants truly are of the broader population they represent (also known as the *confidence level*). You can calculate optimal sample sizes for probability samples using online calculators once you've found an estimate of your research study's total population size. For example, for our childhood socialization study, we'd need about 1,100 participants if we wanted a reasonably accurate and precise sample, and closer to 2,000 participants if we wanted it to be highly accurate and precise!

Sample accuracy
The condition that the sample isn't biased; every unit in the population has the same chance of being selected for participation.

Sample precision
The condition that the sample really represents the population being studied, and your results really would be how people in your study population would respond.

Types of Probability Samples

As was the case with nonprobability samples, once you've determined how many participants you'll need, it's time to recruit them. In the case of probability samples, recruitment can be a lot more difficult and complicated. You'll have to start with a **sampling frame**, a list of units of analysis from which you'll take the sample and to which you'll generalize. Popular sampling frames include telephone directories (though this has become more difficult in the era of smartphones), tax rolls, or even a community census you produce yourself (which is especially helpful in areas in which the total population is not too large but lacks a readily available sampling frame). There are various problems inherent in the use of sampling frames, and it's important to consider how they'll affect your data collection, given your research question. These include poverty (Who doesn't have a phone? Who doesn't have a home?), undocumented immigration (Who is hiding? Are they on any government lists?), and age (young adults may not have landlines or pay taxes yet; older people may not use the internet). If you think that these problems will affect your research question, you may have to be very careful to select a type of probability sample that corrects the issue or to take special care to make extra efforts in recruiting people who are hard to find with the sampling frame you select.

Discussion

Thinking about your research question you've been working on, what would your optimal sampling frame be, and why? Would you miss any significant participants in specific groups? How would you avoid this?

As is the case with nonprobability samples, there are different types of probability samples; we'll discuss the three most commonly used in anthropology. The one that you've probably heard of in the past is the **simple random sample**. In this type of sample, every person (or unit) theoretically has an equal chance of being selected. For example, let's say you're working in a village with 500 household dwellings. You would number them on a map and then pick 250 of them with a random number generator. The simple random sample is easy to understand and can be done systematically in any sampling frame with a random starting number and specific interval, such as starting with the ninth person in the telephone book and selecting every twenty-first person after that. However, simple random samples often don't work very well in real life. Why? Well, several types of groups are rather difficult to recruit with such methods. These include groups that are hard to find, such as people who practice a marginalized minority religion. This method also is challenging to use if you need participants from groups who don't want to respond to inquiries, such as CEOs of companies, or participants from groups who aren't readily available using a sampling frame, such as homeless people. In all those cases, you have to make special efforts through recruitment to locate and engage

Sampling frame
A list of units of analysis from which you'll take the sample and to which you'll generalize.

Simple random sample A sample in which the sampling frame is queried based on randomly drawing participants on a numbered interval; every person (or unit) theoretically has an equal chance of being selected.

your participants. Additionally, in cases in which representation from diverse groups is necessary (such as our example on childhood socialization), you'll need to ensure that key subpopulations are included in sufficient numbers in your sample.

In all those cases, it might make more sense to use a **stratified random sample**, which divides the sampling frame into subpopulations based on key variables and then takes a random sample. Common key variables for subdividing your sample in complex societies include age, gender, socioeconomic class, and ethnicity/race. You may also have specific harder-to-recruit categories of participants you make a special effort to recruit. If a subpopulation is likely to be underrepresented in the whole (such as Native Americans, who make up only 1.3 percent of the US population), you'll use **disproportionate sampling**, which actively recruits more members from that subgroup so that your sample really represents the subpopulation as well as the population as a whole.

Finally, there are cases in which your research question or recruitment needs dictate that the optimal probability sample type is **cluster sampling**. Cluster sampling is based on the way humans live their lives in groups. In cluster sampling, you begin with a location as your sampling frame for recruiting participants, and you rely on this location as a means to create stratified random samples (see Figure 3.6 for an example). Cluster sampling is especially useful when you need to sample populations for which there is no convenient sampling frame, such as schoolchildren, community members, practitioners of a specific religion, hidden or stigmatized populations, or people in a public health district.

For example, let's say you're interested in how people in Chicago are using health clinics during extreme weather events of abnormal heat or cold. The city of Chicago is a large, heterogeneous group, but like all cities, it consists of neighborhoods that tend to draw people who are more similar to one another. By carving up the city into smaller, more homogenous areas that represent meaningfully diverse groups, you have generated

Stratified random sample A sample in which the sampling frame is divided into subpopulations based on key variables, prior to randomly drawing participants on a numbered interval.

Disproportionate sampling Actively over-recruiting and accepting more participants from a particular subpopulation due to the subpopulation being underrepresented otherwise.

Cluster sampling Using geographic space as a way of dividing people into subpopulations and then using geographically defined spaces and places as a sampling frame.

Figure 3.6 Cluster Sampling

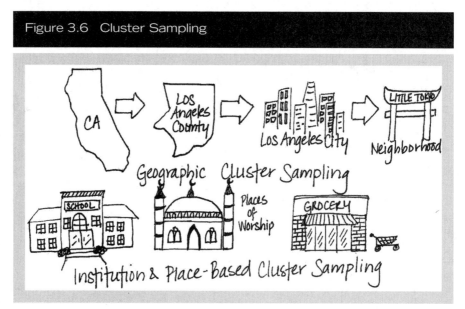

a geographically based stratified sample. Then you might select certain types of locations as your sampling frame to recruit participants through the randomness of who shows up. It is important to recognize that this means you have to be careful to select locations that would draw all the different types of people within each neighborhood. A school, for example, will draw only people who are involved with youth. A church will draw only people in organized religions. However, places such as convenience and grocery stores draw many different types of people. Alternatively, you might consider a number of different locations, each of which may draw specific subgroups in a neighborhood. Using place-based sampling can often help you locate those participants who would otherwise be very hard to engage, such as homeless people or recent immigrants.

Discussion

Reflect once again on your research question. What kind of probability sample do you think is optimal for answering your question, and why? Do you anticipate it being easy or challenging to acquire that sample? What strategies might you use to recruit participants?

Sampling in the Hypothetico-Deductive Method

We'll cover **mixed methods**, or the combination of qualitative and quantitative approaches, when we get to the chapter on questionnaires. But for now, you might want to reflect on how nonprobability and probability sampling might both be utilized in the hypothetico-deductive method. Remember how you learned that research may start off as being exploratory, with a small group of participants, and later become the springboard for confirmatory research that uses a much larger group? Or how research may start off with a large group of participants to shallowly explore a topic and later recruit a smaller group to explore the topic in depth? In these cases, a researcher may develop their research in phases, using one type of sampling to explore their research topic and a different type of sampling when they are seeking to confirm hypotheses or more deeply explore their topic. For example, a researcher working on the impact of women's hospital versus home birthing experiences on their early sense of identity as a mother might begin with a quota sample (hospital vs. home birth) in which they conduct in-depth interviews, then develop some hypotheses, and later use a stratified random sample (including age, income level, education level, and hospital vs. home birth) to collect questionnaire data to confirm or negate their hypotheses. Conversely, a different researcher might choose to collect questionnaire data using a simple random sample of new mothers across the entire United States and find results that demand more explanation for why women choose home birthing and whether it is strongly related to their identity as mothers, choosing to follow up on their survey with a series of snowball samples based on midwifery services.

Mixed methods
The combination of qualitative and quantitative approaches.

There is no one right way to select a sample and recruit participants, though there are ways that are a poor fit for your particular research question and circumstances. Always remember that your selection of your sample type and size, as well as the strategies you use for recruiting participants, will affect your research study's generalizability and reliability. However, as a student researcher, some data are better than no data! Recognize your limitations (of expertise, time, and money) and do the best that you can! Your research can contribute to the broader conversation about your research topic. Just be sure you are honest with yourself about your optimal sample, what you modified your sample to be and why, and how that affected your results.

Pairing the Textbook and Workbook

Many students struggle with sampling, because they are not used to thinking about how the parameters of a selected group of participants affects the conclusions researchers make. If you're feeling a bit lost as you work toward your culminating activity for this chapter in the workbook (Activity 3.7), don't worry—you're not alone. Review the concepts in this chapter as many times as needed. It's a frequent "muddy point" for students, so work with your peers and your professor until you feel more confident about your understanding of the different kinds of sampling and when you might use them. Keep asking yourself these questions:

- Am I mostly studying a topic for which individual attribute data are important, or is my topic focused on cultural data?

- Who do I need to find for my research study?

- How many people would be optimal for my research study, and why?

- How can I find those people?

Reflective Prompts

1. What strategies did I use to deepen my understanding?

2. Can I describe the difference between nonprobability and probability sampling plans?

3. Can I determine why it would be appropriate to select a probability sampling plan in relation to a research context?

Case Study

Kronenfeld, David B. 1973, "Fanti Kinship: The Structure of Terminology and Behavior 1." *American Anthropologist* 75, no. 5: 1577–95.

Kronenfeld, David. 1980. "A Formal Analysis of Fanti Kinship Terminology (Ghana)." *Anthropos* 75, no. 3/4: 586–608.

Kronenfeld, David B. 1991. "Fanti Kinship: Language, Inheritance, and Kin Groups." *Anthropos* 86, no. 1/3: 19–31.

Kronenfeld, David. 2009. *Fanti Kinship and the Analysis of Kinship Terminologies*. Champaign: University of Illinois Press.

The Project

My research question for the project with the Fanti was "Did behavior co-vary with kin term category?" That is, if you knew someone was your uncle, did it impact your behavior choices toward him? The traditional discussion about kin terms was treating them as role terms: Each term meant that there were behaviors attached to the role. A father or mother does this or that. Entering my research, I had doubts about this, so I investigated the question. My field site was a small enough town (three hundred people) that I could include in my sample most of the men in town and a nontrivial number of the women. I knew enough about this small town to avoid being unduly affected by clear outliers. If anything, my sample was biased toward the central. There were two kinds of sampling in my cognitive research: first, the sample of participants, and second, the sample of the concept being inquired about—here, the frames and terms I was using. First, I generated a list of kin terms in Fanti, and I talked to lots of informants regarding questions such as "What does a father do? An uncle?" I came up with a list of behaviors from these interviews and from my observations of behavior. Then I constructed a sample of abstract people—that is, relational descriptions (such as "mother's brother's son" and "friend," where I knew which kin term each relational description belonged to). For

the first survey phase, I asked each respondent, "Do Fanti people do X behavior to Y person?" for each combination of behavior (X) and each relational description (Y).

This first survey phase of research was on abstract behavior, which allowed me to quantify everything. For comparison, in a second survey phase, I asked similar questions but based on real relationships to gather information on real behavior. Here, I selected a smaller sample of respondents, and I based the questions specifically on their social network—on specific people they knew and with whom they were in particular relationships. This participant sample had to fulfill a number of requirements: They had to represent the diversity of real people and social networks in the community; I had to know them well enough to construct a meaningfully contrasting set of relationships to interview them about; and they had to have the patience and attention span to do the interview, because it was tedious. I was trying to maximize in- versus out-lineage, kin term categories, and generational differences—this was similar to a quota sample but not quite so formal. I had to make sure that each participant was different from the others. I was basically getting a controlled diversity in the sample. Each person was asked questions about their behavior related to ten to twelve specific people in the community. I went through the question "In your relationship with *[person's name]*, have you ever done X behavior?" What I found really structured behavior was not kin term category but a combination of relative age, generation, social status and seniority combined, and closeness. Lineage was very important to people, too, but for identity, not behavior (except for inheritance).

(Continued)

(Continued)

What's the difference you've found in your research between sampling the way they do it in, say, political science or sociology, and the way that we do sampling in anthropology?

In anthropology, you're asking questions that aren't generic, like what you get in political science. You're asking culturally meaningful questions. When you begin with ethnographic data, you're set up nicely to do different kinds of surveys that are easy and cheap. This produces a traditional sampling problem: Do you try to include everyone in the target population or settle for just a sample of them? In the conventional rural village setting, you can include everyone who is willing to participate. In a larger, more urban setting, you still want a representative sample, so you have to construct a random sample. There are several ways to do this, including randomizing a selection of blocks, and then houses on those blocks. What you don't want is to do something that feels random to you (but isn't carefully constructed to be random—called a "haphazard sample"), because then all your biases come through (plus biases inherent in the place). You're going to end up avoiding challenging, strange, or uncomfortable situations. So randomizing it helps you avoid the biases that ruin your results.

What are things researchers should be aware of when they're trying to align their sampling plan and their research questions?

You have to be aware of the ways inaccuracy can creep in, which can be through your sampling plan, your methods, or your techniques for asking questions. Having done a census in the small village I lived in when I was in Ghana, I knew all the houses and the people who lived there—and based on that experience, I sometimes made

guesses about questions, such as "How many people live in a typical house?" When I finally got around to adding up the actual numbers, I discovered that my guesses were pretty bad! This is why it's important to sample and to do the real counting work, and to formalize the questions and format of them, because otherwise our salience bias (what we notice) creeps in.

If you're only doing surveys, you do have to worry about accuracy based on participants lying or not knowing, and that not being apparent in the responses. Sometimes this depends on the way you ask the question. In one study, when I asked, "What was this house lot before you got here?" (because it was apparent the houses and lots had changed), people said, "It was always like this." But when I did residence histories, mapped these out, and then asked people about particular plots and houses based on carefully elicited ownership and residence histories, it was clear that the place had changed, and even relatively recently (former farming and grazing fields had become residential lots). That detailed history is additionally a way to get enough quantitative data to do statistics that are meaningful. Because sometimes the group is really too small for results to be statistically significant, unless the trends are overwhelming. The method of doing these histories gives you a much bigger sample, not based on people but based on events. For example, for eating history, a group of ten people times five days of meals yields far more meals (data points) than if you just got a group of ten people to take a survey about their most recent meal.

And also, there are issues of accuracy of what the data represent as a whole. On a typical survey, you'll get the typical lunch on a workday if you ask someone about their most recent meal. If you do a history, you get a much better picture because you not only have more data, but you have more of a chance to see the not-default cases: the fancy dinners and snacks and such. This is also the case if you have a population where there are really important minority groups, but you aren't likely to pick them up through a typical random sample because their numbers are too small, yet they really matter for your research question—implying a stratified random sample. So you have to think carefully about the relationship between how you sample, your sample size, and the questions you're asking.

What advice do you have about sampling and recruitment, based on your research career, for beginning researchers?

With sampling, it's not that there's a universal right answer. You have to ask: What am I sampling, and why? You don't want to get just any kind of sample. You want a sample that represents the universe relevant to the question you're asking. The distribution of people in categories is important to think about. If you want to look at social linkages, snowball samples are great. For initial exploration, these work great, but later you'd want to understand how you're positioned in that broader group because of the snowball. Conversely, let's say you're random sampling. You might have really good sampling for some questions but not about social networks, which is where the snowball sample comes in.

Too much of social science is built like cookbooks, with recipes based on random samples. But you really have to ask yourself, "What am I randomizing?" and "Why?" and "Is the random sample process necessary, and does it really answer the question?" You have to figure out what entity you want to talk about: Individuals? Families? Communities? Generations? And what kinds of things do you not want to have bias in? Many of these end up being stratified random samples, but not always. For a lot of anthropological questions, you can get away with very few people because you are interested in broadly shared collective patterns of behaviors and ideas.

Case Study Reflections

1. In Kronenfeld's study of Fanti kinship, how are different kinds of sampling used to generate the results? What is another example you can think of where multiple types of sampling might work together for the most valid and comprehensive collection of data?

2. Kronenfeld gives an example of how his participant observation (being there) was not sufficient to accurately answer a question about the average number of people per household. Why might this be the case? Why is it important to do actual counting and statistics for certain types of information, based on this example?

3. If you are struggling to find enough people to take a survey about times in their lives they've felt stressed, what might be a better way to approach the sampling and the question to increase your number of data points?

4. What are some circumstances under which a stratified random sample might not be the best type of sample? What are the underlying questions that Kronenfeld encourages researchers to think about when selecting a sampling plan?

STUDY GUIDE

Note: Students should study each concept with attentiveness to defining, explaining with examples, and describing or demonstrating process. This is not a list of terms to define; it's a list of concepts and processes to master.

Sample

Total sample

Probability versus nonprobability sample

Nonprobability sampling (why/when?)

Quota sampling

Sampling grid

Purposive sampling

Pilot study

Convenience sampling

Snowball sampling

Key informant

Specialized informant

Probability sampling (why/when?)

Sample accuracy

Sample precision

Sampling frame

Simple random sampling

Stratified random sampling

Disproportionate sampling

Cluster sampling

Mixed methods

FOR FURTHER STUDY

Bernard, H. Russell. 2018. "Sampling I: The Basics," "Sampling II: Theory," and "Sampling III: Nonprobability Samples and Choosing Informants." In *Research Methods in Anthropology*, by H. Russell Bernard, 114–62. Lanham, MD: Rowman and Littlefield.

Davis, Anthony, and John Wagner. 2003. "Who Knows? On the Importance of Identifying 'Experts' When Researching Local Ecological Knowledge." *Human Ecology* 31, no. 3: 463–89.

Pelto, Pertti J. 2013. "Sampling and Counting in Ethnographic Research." In *Applied Ethnography: Guidelines for Field Research*, by Pertti J. Pelto, 141–56. Walnut Creek, CA: Left Coast Press.

Visit **study.sagepub.com/kirner** to help you accomplish your coursework goals in an easy-to-use learning environment.

Participant Observation

Orientation

Having discussed how to design a research project, how to address ethical issues within it, and how to select participants, we will turn to participant observation as the first of the data collection methods we'll cover. Participant observation is the cornerstone of ethnography, or "writings about culture," and is deceptively simple to students. As Geertz put it, **participant observation** is "deep hanging out," or hanging around people with a purpose. This sounds easy enough, but as most students find out with their very first experience of it, it isn't. Participant observation is likely to initially bring up many feelings of awkwardness and discomfort, followed by the realization that we haven't usually trained our minds to be fully present and mindful, much less to remember details about places, people, and events. However, practice makes improvement in anything, especially in participant observation, and this foundational method of ethnographic research is well worth a student's dedicated effort.

The Advantages of Participant Observation

Participant observation puts you on the ground alongside the people you are studying, which gives you greater access to data. By experiencing the lives of those you study and reflecting critically on this experience, you'll build not only a better dataset but a better capacity to analyze the data you collect. Participant observation has great value for boosting the validity of findings—that is, how accurate and reliable the findings are. This method offers this because it makes it possible to

Chapter Learning Objectives

Students will be able to do the following:

4.1 Describe the advantages of using participant observation in research studies

4.2 Describe the different roles a researcher can take in fieldwork and the advantages of each

4.3 Describe the core skills field researchers need and how to build those skills in everyday life

4.4 Understand the first steps in entering the field

4.5 Understand the common characteristics of the fieldwork cycle

4.6 Understand how to write jottings that show raw material (data), not interpretations or assumptions

gather data that would otherwise be inaccessible. In fact, some research problems, such as those concerning how interactions or decisions work in practice, are incredibly difficult (or nearly impossible) to answer in any other way but with participant observation data. Participant observation also reduces the problem of **reactivity** (people changing their behavior because they know they are being studied). When a researcher is at a field site for a long time, such as a year, people eventually tire of formalized, polite patterns that are prompted by the arrival of an outsider. The guard eventually comes down, and people revert back to ordinary, everyday patterns of living. The researcher is then able to gain insight into the **real culture** of a group of people (rather than the **ideal culture**, or what people think they ought to be doing). Further, participant observation provides the basis for refining research questions and the language in which you'd ask your questions to get the optimally rich, detailed responses from participants in interviews or questionnaires. Most researchers are initially awkward in their field sites (and their nonnative languages); participant observation allows them to improve both their linguistic and cultural skills in their participant community or population. When it comes to analyzing data, participant observation provides the researcher with a more intuitive understanding of the interactions they observe and a greater confidence in interpreting their data.

It is participant observation that, when paired with writing, generates ethnography. Ethnography is where the researcher's personal, direct experience of a social setting and the lives of their participants meet the tasks of critically thinking and writing about this experience. The critical reflection and liminal space of the researcher—caught between their own life and the lives of their participants—leads to an interpretation of the social worlds of the participants and concern for the processes, sequences of interactions, and interpretations that emerge from the data. "Doing" participation observation and "writing" about the experiences is a dialectical practice—a dialogue that constructs each activity vis-à-vis the other.

Fieldwork Roles

Participant observation involves three processes that are key to producing, in an interactive fashion, valuable data: immersion, resocialization, and reactivity. **Immersion** is the process of living within our participants' communities and hanging out for the everyday tasks and interactions of their lives. Immersion enables us to see from the inside of a different lifeway how people live their lives, experience their everyday practices, and understand what they themselves find meaningful. In immersing ourselves in their lives, we undergo a process of **resocialization**. Resocialization occurs as we enter their social system and approximate (though never replicate) their experiences. We are trained into a new culture, in many ways as a small child is initially trained—learning how to properly perform a variety of tasks, processes, and interactions. Throughout both immersion and resocialization, we experience *reactivity*. Reactivity occurs when our participants react to our presence by performing their lives differently for a while, and this gives us valuable clues about how people form social ties, what is important to people, and how they construct meaning (if we keep detailed notes throughout our time there).

Participant observation Collecting data through spending many hours with the people you are studying, participating in their activities and observing them in their ordinary lives.

Reactivity People changing their behavior because they know they are being studied or in response to characteristics of the researcher.

Real culture The behavioral patterns that people demonstrate under usual conditions.

Ideal culture The behavioral patterns that people view as ideal or optimal.

Immersion The process of living in our study participants' communities and participating and observing in their everyday lives.

Resocialization Training the researcher in a new culture and social structure during immersion.

We can be involved in these processes from a variety of **fieldwork roles**, or ways in which we are positioned vis-à-vis our participants. If we are a complete participant, our participants do not know we're an observer. This involves deception—we don't reveal who we are or what our purpose is. We rarely do this as anthropologists because it violates the American Anthropological Association's code of ethics and usual standards of transparency. At the other end of the spectrum is being a complete observer. In this role, you simply watch and reflect on others' behaviors. You don't personally engage in activities with your participants. The most usual role for an anthropologist is either an observing participant or a participating observer. The **observing participant** is a researcher who studies a group to which they belong already. You begin by being an insider and then add critical reflection. This can take the form of participant observation (in which you add protocols to your usual interactions as an insider) or autoethnography (which is when you add critical reflection on events from your own life that have already occurred—we'll cover this more in the next chapter). The **participating observer**, on the other hand, begins by being an outsider to the group they study and has to enter the group specifically to participate as a researcher.

The authors of this book have done both. In the role of observing participant, Jan Mills conducted research on classroom management covering an entire school year, seeking to identify the most effective behavioral interventions for a large group of highly disruptive primary students with high needs. Also as an observing participant, Kimberly Kirner studied how Pagan belief and practice intersected with conversations about and actions for environmental sustainability by triangulating a questionnaire and a year of participant observation at regional ritual gatherings, interpreted through the lens of her own understandings of Paganisms as a practitioner of Druidry. In contrast, as a participating observer, Kirner lived in a rural ranching community for a total of a year, across three different years (for a longitudinal, or "over time," study), in order to study ranchers' decisions about range management and their emotional connection to the landscape. In this study, she entered their world from the outside and attempting to learn enough to interpret their decisions and, more generally, their cultural lives.

Both roles have their advantages and disadvantages (see Figure 4.1). Observing participants, as insiders, often have more contacts and can get started immediately on the substance of their research question. Participating observers, as outsiders, usually have to take some time in the field to orient themselves to the community, to build rapport and locate key informants, and to master enough basic tasks, dialogues, and interactions to be able to tackle more substantive research questions.

On the other hand, the participating observer is unlikely to be as biased in their analysis and interpretation of their data. Having no prior basis for a complex understanding of their participants, they are less likely to make assumptions. The observing participant has to be extra cautious in misinterpreting data based on their assumptions, because the lure of the insider's knowledge is always present. In all cases, full engagement in the lives of participants builds empathy for local ways of feeling and acting. Whether we begin as an insider or outsider, it is the writing process (taking notes, refining them, and interpreting them) that reminds us that researchers are in a liminal space and have the power to determine what is remembered and recorded. Writing is, therefore, as critical to participant observation as participating and observing.

Fieldwork roles Ways in which we are positioned relative to our participants (whether in-group or as an outsider).

Observing participant A researcher studying a group to which they already belong.

Participating observer A researcher who begins as an outsider to the group they study and enters the group in order to conduct the study.

Figure 4.1   Advantages and Disadvantages in Fieldwork Roles

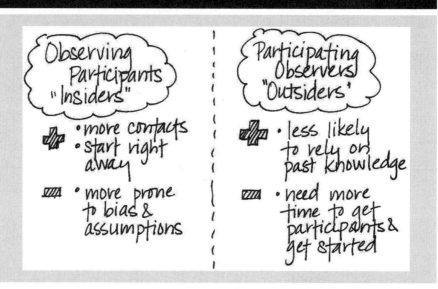

Discussion

Consider your research question you've been developing since Chapter 1. Are you positioned as a participating observer or an observing participant? Why? How do you feel about your role? What might be easy about the role you've assumed? What might be difficult?

Skills for Participant Observation

Most students will recognize, as they try out participant observation for the first time, that some of the skills they use in everyday life are foundational to quality participant observation (see Figure 4.2). These skills are often simply underutilized, insufficiently developed, or not brought to conscious awareness prior to methodological training and practice. However, they are skills that most people have to some degree in order to navigate the complex social world that they live in. These skills can be practiced well ahead of your time in the field, so that you hone them before you will rely on them.

Explicit awareness Mindfulness about what you are doing and experiencing.

One of the most basic of these skills is to build **explicit awareness**—that is, mindfulness about what you are doing and experiencing. Participant observation demands that we are consciously aware of what is going on around us, our responses to it (both

Figure 4.2   Skills for Participant Observation

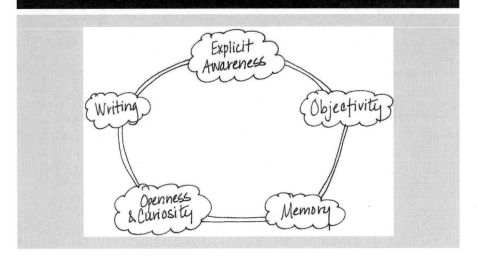

internally and in our behaviors toward others), and others' responsiveness to us. If we aren't aware of it, we can't write about it. This is much more challenging than it appears, and it is one of the hardest skills for most students to refine. For most of us, our Western culture has enculturated us to expect new sensory input constantly and to "tune out" much of what is around us (the noise of our world) so that we can avoid being overwhelmed. We often distract ourselves from what is going on through our smartphones, tablets, music, and television. We construct inner worlds and dialogues and daydream our way out of what our minds consider boring or uncomfortable. All these tendencies remove us from mindfulness and full presence in the place and time we are in, and this means that we miss valuable information in it. It can be very helpful for social science students to begin a mindfulness practice that becomes part of their everyday lives: quiet, undistracted time for reflection and trying to limit distractions and focus on present interactions, settings, and one's own internal and external states. Ask yourself throughout your day: "What am I doing right now? What are the details of what I am seeing and hearing? How do I feel about this? What are my body and my facial expression conveying?" Begin to develop a consistent awareness of yourself and what is around you.

Another critical skill is to develop an *openness and curiosity*, while finding ways to ask questions of others without appearing unduly naïve or intrusive. Most of us think that it is easy to be friendly and curious with others, until we try to get to know complete strangers. Building the rapport (trust) with strangers that is necessary to get them to agree to be interviewed or let you hang out with them can be challenging, and many students find that they feel socially awkward when they first try to do so. The best way to hone this skill well before you must rely on it is to try it out, consistently, in your everyday life. Try to get to know the person next to you on the bus, in line at the coffee shop, or at the flea market.

While you are at it, try to develop your *memory*, or your ability to remember these interactions. We interact dozens, even hundreds, of times per day. Our ability to write down these interactions as they happen is usually incredibly limited—this is true of participant observation as well. As a consequence, we have to be able to remember our interactions, circumstances, and responses for hours until we are somewhere we can write about them. The only way to expand your ability to remember these events is to practice the skill, so begin treating everyday life as your laboratory for doing so!

How can you assess your memory? Through *writing*, of course. Though most students will feel that they practice writing enough through coursework, the academic writing you do in classes is not like the field notes you have to write as a professional researcher. Field notes are more like a journal of the day's events, in great detail, and are inclusive of your reflections on the day. As such, they are quite different from the more ponderous, far less descriptive writing you practice for research papers—and they rely on and demonstrate the memory for these social interactions. It is through trying to write what happened that most students find their memory has significant gaps, and they then can work to strengthen their memory by noting what they do not include (senses, parts of scenery, etc. they routinely do not remember). Daily writing in a journal will help you build not only your memory but also your ability to write for hours each day, an eventual requisite of being a professional social scientist. The participant observer often closes each day in the field by writing thousands of words on the details they observed—after all, this is their dataset for later analysis (and the entire process of participant observation works only if data are recorded as close to the time they happened as possible). So write, write, write, until you feel comfortable with it and your memory appreciably improves.

When you first begin a writing practice, simply let yourself get into a rhythm of sitting down at a notepad or computer each day and forcing yourself to write. Some people find it useful, if they are resistant, to set a minimum length (one page, three pages) or a minimum amount of time (thirty minutes, one hour). At first, don't worry about the content or sequencing of your observations. Just write. You can reflect on your writing after you've done it. After you have sufficient field notes for the day, reflect on your writing. First, note your gaps in memory so that you can improve this through mindful awareness in your interactions in the future. Second, reflect on your demonstrated capacity for **objectivity**, which is a way of turning mindfulness inward. Objectivity isn't about distance from what you study but rather is mindfulness of your own biases, experiences, responses, and engagement. Objectivity, therefore, isn't **value neutrality** (without passion or a value-engaged agenda). Suspending judgment of interactions in order to understand them does not mean that you eliminate your bias or your values. It means that you practice "showing, not telling." That is, you should describe in enough detail for the reader to see, hear, and touch what you did, rather than explaining or interpreting what happened—interpretation is based on later analysis. You may write initial impressions or ideas that are analytical in nature, but these should be clearly separate from the details themselves—maintaining a distinction between descriptive and analytical writing in your notes.

Finally, a note on language skills: If you plan to conduct research in a group of people who do not speak your language, it is imperative that you begin to learn their language as early as possible and focus on conversational fluency. It is much more challenging to build rapport with people if you can't personally talk with them, and people usually appreciate the effort of conversing in their language (even if they also

Objectivity Descriptions of human behavior that include reflections on one's own biases, assumptions, and responses so that the researcher is clear about what they are bringing into their observation and interpretation.

Value neutrality A condition where the researcher would have no biases or values of their own and would be entirely neutral as an observer.

speak English or another common world language). A few tips for preparation can be helpful:

- Emphasize vocabulary and pronunciation over grammar. Most people can understand what you're trying to convey if you have enough words and your pronunciation is clear, even if the sequence of your words is odd. If your grammar is excellent but you're missing sufficient words, or if your accent is too thick, people will be lost.

- Even if you're speaking the same language as your participants, make sure you know slang and jargon that are meaningful in their cultural group. Having some foundation in specialized language will help you understand interactions you observe.

- Consider an intensive summer or other field course that emphasizes conversational fluency. The common progression of formalized academic study in a language often sacrifices conversational fluency for grammatical correctness, which is the reverse of what field social scientists need.

With practice ahead of time, you'll no doubt not only feel more comfortable and confident in the field but more readily adjust to the work and gather accurate, detailed data.

Discussion

As you review the skills necessary for participant observation, are there skill areas that you feel more confident in? Why? Are there skill areas that you think would be a struggle for you? Why? What kinds of commitments to practice could you make now, as a student, in order to build those skill areas that you struggle with?

Getting Started

So you've practiced and improved, and you're getting ready to head to the field to do some research. What should you know about to get started? First of all, selecting a field location is a crucial part of this process. Your field site should be a good one (you think it will answer your research question) and easy to enter (you can get the appropriate permissions and get in touch with people there). Students particularly should try to avoid selecting field sites that are politically fractious, challenging to access, or otherwise projected to make your data collection very difficult. You'll have enough to worry about without adding layers of difficulty to simply getting there and finding participants. Use existing personal contacts to help you, and try to make it as easy as you can for yourself.

Before you head to the field, you need to do some practical and research-related preparation. First of all, you need to assess gear and health-related needs you may have. If you're going to a climate you're unused to or engaging in activities that require specialized gear, you should plan for this ahead of time. You should also remember that if you're going to be in extreme environments—high elevation, very hot or very cold climates, and so on—you'll want to plan for time to physically adjust to the environment. This is also the case in environments that will be a shock in terms of drinking water, food, and sanitation. You're likely to get ill at first, so plan for it. Make sure that you ask questions of other researchers who have gone to similar places, so that you know what to expect and what they wished they had brought. Talk to your doctor about your expected travel early, so that you can get any necessary immunizations and medications they'll want you to take with you.

Second, you need to prepare research-related materials and the "elevator pitch" you'll use to describe who you are and why you're there with locals. You need to enter the field with a lot of documentation about yourself and your project: informed consent forms, approved flyers that describe the project, and endorsements from your university that you are a student there and you've been cleared to do this research. You'll also want to have prepared an elevator pitch, or a two-minute informal chat about yourself. You'll want to consider how you'll answer (in accessible, informal ways) the many questions people will have: Who are you, and what are you doing here? Who is funding you, and why? What good is this research going to do? What do you want to learn? Why did you pick this place/us?

Finally, once you arrive, spend time getting to know the place. Figure out how to navigate the physical and social world there. Walk around a lot, sort of aimlessly, to get to know where things are and to become known to people there without leaping into formal introductions. Pay attention to how you are feeling and take care of yourself. Give your body and mind time to adjust to the place before you try to tackle the observation process and recruit participants.

What to Expect When You're Doing Fieldwork

You've prepped, you've packed, and you've arrived! Now what? What can you expect in your fieldwork experience? H. Russell Bernard (2018, 301–05) wrote an excellent discussion of the fieldwork cycle and the common feelings and experiences that ethnographic researchers have during this cycle, which we summarize here. Well, initially, you usually experience one emotional extreme or another (or both in a cycle): euphoria (*I'm finally here! Yay!*) or misery (*OMG, what did I get myself into?*). This is entirely OK, and it's likely to happen whether or not you go far from home. It's a natural consequence of the stress of starting a new big project and adjusting to a new environment. Try not to panic, and just be present in your feelings. Both extremes will pass and fade to more temperate emotions (days you're really quite excited to be doing the work, and days that you wish you were back home).

Culture shock Depression or other emotional discomfort that people experience when they enter a culture that is unfamiliar to them.

Culture shock is likely to set in after these initial extreme emotions. **Culture shock** is a kind of depression and discomfort that sets in after contact, usually within a few weeks, and it often hangs around for quite some time. As the novelty of being in the field wears off, you'll realize you have a lot of work to do, and you'll likely feel overwhelmed by it. After all, for most of your student experience, you were guided step by step, week by week. Now all you have is some research questions, some paperwork, and a long period of time to figure out how to make it happen. It's disconcerting to students—and even to seasoned researchers when they first enter a new project at a new field site. As you become increasingly aware of the work you have to do, it's also common to have **imposter syndrome**, where you feel like you're really not at all qualified to do what you're supposed to do. You're likely anxious about your skills and abilities to get the work done. This is also common, even for seasoned researchers. While you're physically alone, you're not alone in your feelings. It can help to simply acknowledge the discomfort and name it, and then keep going.

Paired with these feelings of inadequacy and performance anxiety, you're likely to start to feel really lonely. This is even more the case if you are an extrovert and are used to spending all your spare time with other people. But even those of us who are introverted (like both of your authors) miss home: We miss our family, pets, and familiar places. This loneliness is heightened because you don't know anyone yet, and even if you've introduced yourself, you're likely seen as an outsider and no one wants to hang out with you yet. Coupled with loneliness, you'll likely feel homesickness. The more different your field site is from your home, the more likely it is you'll feel an acute sense of disorientation. Even basic things, such as toilets, parenting habits, food, and privacy (or the lack thereof), may be very different in this new place. This makes many people frustrated and even angry. In order to cope with all these feelings, you'll want to bring some items (even small items) from home that help you feel connected to your life before fieldwork. This might be a novel, a magazine, or a photo album. You might start your field notes daily practice by simply journaling your feelings so that you can express them to an audience. And while you feel this sense of discomfort, start working. Trust the process that thousands of social scientists have trod before you, and start in on basic task-oriented work: mapping the space, introducing yourself to contacts, and attending public events. Try to begin to learn how to do the basics—whether this is shopping at the local market, cooking with local foods, hauling water, lighting your cook-fire, or navigating the new city streets—and be open to meeting one or two informants who are extra friendly and will not only participate in your research but generate hospitality and friendship.

After this initial wave of discomfort, you'll start getting more comfortable at going out and doing participant observation. As you do, you'll start systematically collecting data each day and writing up field notes. At this stage, you usually have people beginning to let you into their lives, either hanging out with you or agreeing to be interviewed. Often, especially if it's your first time doing fieldwork, you'll experience a new wave of euphoria at *discovering all the things*. You'll feel like you're discovering new things every day, because you are. The only caveat is that you're usually discovering what is obvious to everyone else. Later, you'll find this very humorous, but enjoy the feeling—you're finally out of the depression of your initial culture shock, and you haven't yet felt that you're not really getting anywhere with answering your research questions. Enjoy the feeling of belonging in your new role, with "your field site" and "your people."

Right about at the point you begin to feel pressure to attend every event and talk to every person, and to never take any days off, if your fieldwork period is long (such as six months or a year), you should take a short break. While you might be tempted to avoid this in order to maintain the momentum, there are good reasons to do the opposite. Usually, though you feel like you're in the full swing of things, your participants are getting tired of hosting you. They need a break from you. In addition, in leaving for a short while, you will relax and restore yourself, and you'll get some much-needed distance from "doing" fieldwork in order to think about it. The best thing to do at this point is to

Imposter syndrome A state when you feel that you aren't qualified to do what you are supposed to do, even though you actually are qualified.

go to a university and share your preliminary work with colleagues (even informally). This can generate much-needed perspective-taking that allows you to reassess what you know in your research and what you have yet to find out. When you return to the field, this also strengths the rapport you've built with your participants. They now know that you will return to them, even if you are gone for a while.

Generally, the short break will leave you refreshed and focused. You'll have a much better sense of what you still do not know and what to do with the remainder of your time in the field. You'll make modifications to your research design as necessary and implement these. (Don't forget to check in with your institutional review board to get approval for all modifications involving changes to human subjects protocols!) Making these changes may give you some anxiety again, but they're worthwhile. Most researchers make some changes to their plans midstream in order to accommodate what they've learned from their time in the field.

At some point, if your fieldwork period is long (like a year), you'll start getting tired. Really tired. You'll feel like you have asked every question there is to ask and seen everything there is to see. But you haven't. Your exhaustion is likely causing you to miss the last gaps between what you wish to find out and what you already know. It's time for another short break. Distance and perspective-taking, again, will restore and relax you and will also allow you to now have a very narrow focus on what you still have yet to discover. Following this short break, most researchers return to the field rather frantic to try to collect the last bits of data they realized they didn't have while on break. The perspective-taking usually shows you that you could actually spend years at this field site and never really know all there is to know. But you have only a couple more months, so make wise use of them.

Finally, while it was almost impossible to imagine leaving the field during the initial depression of culture shock and homesickness, it will be time to depart. This is a critical stage. It is very important that you don't simply leave one day. You need to **debrief** your participants, or wrap up the process with everyone before disappearing. Researchers often use this last bit of time to give gifts to key informants or the community as a whole and to express their appreciation in culturally appropriate ways. Many of the final days are spent in social engagements rather than research, in saying goodbye the way you would with friends or colleagues at home. You'll need to assess whether there are expectations for relationships to be long-term or permanent—either if you intend to return again (which should be asked of, not imposed on, participants) or if your participants expect that you'll return to share findings or visit. Even if you want at this point to leave your field site forever, you might consider doing otherwise for the sake of your participants, for other future social scientists wanting to study at your field site, or for keeping your own options open. When you eventually return home, be sure to give yourself some adjustment time yet again. If you were somewhere quite different from home, you may experience **reverse culture shock**. For example, if you've become accustomed to leisurely mornings filled with going to a local farmer's market, tending a cook-fire, and making some food from scratch, you might find it overwhelming to go back to buying groceries for a week at a grocery store. If, like one of your authors (Kirner) was, you became used to physical activity outdoors for ten hours a day, it is a major adjustment to return to a sedentary student life as you write up your findings. Again, give yourself time, acknowledge your feelings, and practice self-care, as you might go through a bit of post-fieldwork blues.

Debrief A period of time in which you communicate to your participants and field site community that you are leaving soon, answer any questions they have, give back in meaningful ways, and make plans for how and when to return to the site in the future with your analysis and conclusions.

Reverse culture shock Feelings of disorientation or depression when you return home and reenter your own culture.

The standard amount of time academic researchers devote to participant observation for ethnography is one year. A full year is optimal because it gives participants plenty of time to warm up to you (it usually takes a couple months), it gives you plenty of time to discover rich details about your participants' lives, and it provides you with an opportunity to see your field site through all seasons (especially important if you're studying agricultural, pastoral, or hunting-and-gathering groups). The time of one year is standard for an ethnographic dissertation to attain your doctorate. However, there are many reasons why researchers conduct research in less time than this. Before the doctoral level, most students have more limited time and resources, so MA-level students often limit themselves to three to six months of fieldwork. Some research is event-specific and therefore is time-limited on its own (for example, a study of a boot camp or a social movement around a particular proposition that will be voted on during an election cycle). Some research is narrow enough to allow rapid research, such as studying how people interact with each other and the built environment in a restaurant. Applied research often has unique limitations on time, as it often must be timely for policy making or executive decision making.

In all these cases, the challenges in doing more rapid research are the same: Gaining rapport is more challenging, and your data are subject to greater error. To reduce the potential level of error in your data, because you don't have the time to let increasing rapport and long-term observation correct inaccuracies, you'll want to consider triangulating your data and asking your participants to review your findings. For example, a researcher doing a study on children's labor in rural communities might combine observations while working on farms, interviews with children and their parents, and work diaries in which children jot down the tasks they do each day. Collecting multiple types of data and looking for the points of agreement reduces the probability that you won't fully understand or observe what is happening in your field site (due to your limited time there) and will misrepresent it. Finally, selecting key informants as collaborators and reviewers for your paper or thesis can greatly enhance not only your accuracy in representing them but also your rapport for future projects.

Discussion

Consider the trajectory of fieldwork and what you might encounter. What do you think you'll adjust to easily? What might be more challenging for you? How can you optimize your response to your challenges?

Jottings

As was discussed in the section of this chapter on skills, half of ethnography is writing. Writing **field notes** at the end of the day usually requires jogging one's memory about what happened throughout the day. Because it's usually impossible to write detailed notes as events unfold (unless you are largely observing an event in which you do not have to participate and at which it is normal to carry a notebook), researchers take

Field notes Narrative descriptions of your observations and reflections that are used as a dataset to analyze.

jottings throughout their day—brief phrases or photos that help them remember what to write about later. Researchers jot these down in a variety of ways: in a small portable notebook, as texts in their phone, or as scrawls on napkins or index cards carried in a pocket. The main thing is that jottings have to be done quickly, and generally they must be easily portable, so that you can do them at key points throughout the day.

Researchers choose a method of making jottings, including when and how to do so, based largely on two factors: their comfort level (what works for them as an individual) and the field situation (what works in a practical sense with whatever else they're doing). Openly showing your note-taking while you're observing has the advantage that you can maximize accuracy about what you're seeing and hearing. However, this limits your participation (it's hard to write and do most other things), and it often disrupts the flow of interactions. People often feel awkward when they're watching someone take notes on them. This technique works optimally in environments where it is natural to take notes and others may do the same.

Kirner (one of your authors) used this technique while attending Pagan gatherings in order to record conversations and interactions pertaining to sustainability and folk ecological knowledge. Because many other participants also carried notebooks to try to remember the workshops they attended, this worked well for all the gathering events except religious ritual, where no jottings could be made for the duration due to behavioral norms. Another technique is to get away from the action for a few minutes here and there throughout your day to rapidly jot down phrases to help you remember. Your other author (Mills) used this technique for her autoethnography on her classroom, periodically going to her desk throughout the day to jot down notes to flesh out later in the evening. This technique also tends to have high accuracy if you do it frequently, and it disrupts the flow less than taking notes in front of people. However, it can look a bit odd to leave periodically, and you might miss interactions while you're gone. Furthermore, in both of these cases, it might be totally impossible to do this.

When it is impossible to jot down thoughts throughout the day, the only options are to write at the end of a day or participant observation session and/or to use other devices for recording. One of the authors (Kirner) found it impossible to write during her participant observation on ranches, because she was usually on horseback or actively working alongside cowboys and ranchers with cattle. Obviously, this was not an environment in which notes could be made—or that she could periodically leave. The downside of waiting until the end of the day to write is that accuracy is lower and the impact of your memory bias is enhanced. However, the advantage is that it maximizes participation. If you must do this, it's best to make jottings about your day the instant you return home or somewhere you can write. Don't try to write field notes right off the bat—just brain-drain your impressions, memories, thoughts, and feelings in short phrases onto the screen or paper. You can then have dinner, take a shower, or otherwise take a short break before returning to your desk to write up your field notes from these jottings. There are sometimes creative methods you can employ to get around the challenge of full participation interrupting jottings. One of the easiest of these is to take photos throughout your day to jog your memory. You can do this even without people in the photos (there are additional protection of human subjects and informed consent issues with having recognizable people in your photos). Kirner found that taking photos was much easier while on horseback or working and could capture key moments and places in the day, helping her write up field notes later.

Jottings Brief phrases or photos that help you remember what happened during participant observation so that you can write longer descriptive narratives (field notes) later.

Think about your research question you've been working on since Chapter 1. When you consider doing participant observation, which of the techniques we just reviewed makes the most sense to try as your method for making jottings? What do you think will be the advantages of that technique in your particular case? The disadvantages?

It's worth noting that making jottings and writing up field notes will be much easier if you develop some basic skills that allow you to write more quickly. Learning shorthand or creating your own abbreviations of commonly used words will help you write jottings more quickly. Learning to type quickly and with high accuracy is a valuable skill—not only for writing field notes in the evening but also for later writing up your academic papers. The advantage to being a quick, accurate typist can't be overstated, because it allows your writing to keep up with the speed of your thoughts. This makes it enormously easier to write up your memories, especially in detail.

So what should you write, exactly, in making jottings? What events and thoughts are worth jotting about? In general, you'll write all sorts of things that help preserve your memories for expanding on later: direct quotes from participants, bits of action to frame up full interaction sequences, sharp details as mnemonic devices (a mental device that helps you remember), interactions, descriptions of people who are present, and your own actions or conversational prompts to put context around your participants' responses. Your jottings should capture details to help jog your memory later, such as sensory impressions (what you see, hear, taste, smell, and touch), emotional expressions and experiences, behaviors and sayings of your participants, and your feelings and thoughts. You should focus on "showing, not telling." That is, your jottings (and later field notes) should be raw material (data), not already digested interpretations. They are meant to jog memory of detail, not characterize or summarize scenes or events. See Figure 4.3 for examples of showing versus telling.

When you first arrive at the field site, be sure to capture your initial impressions of the place and the people. They're often wrong, but the comparison of your initial impressions with later field notes is important for analysis: It speaks to your own biases and assumptions, it may speak to broader cultural trends of how your cultural group or groups perceive the places and people that you study, and it shows your socialization into the cultural group you are studying over time. It is also important to jot frequently about your participants' meanings: what your participants find important and significant, their reactions, and their discourse about events or issues—this will help provide contrast with your initial impressions. You'll want to write as much of this down as you can, because you often won't be able to tell what is important until much later in your fieldwork.

Two other things you should routinely jot about are the opposites of one another: routine actions and unexpected and significant moments. The former should record fine details of interactions, which will help you understand the processes through which your

Figure 4.3 Showing, Not Telling

Showing	Telling
The child sat down in front of the glass portion of the gorilla exhibit. A female gorilla was sitting on the other side of the exhibit with her back to the onlookers, against the glass. The child took a small toy stuffed animal out of her backpack and pressed it up against the glass. "Mama," she inquired, looking up at a woman, "Maybe the gorilla would like a toy?" The child began tapping quietly on the glass. The gorilla refused to look back toward the glass, leaning away from it. "Do not tap the glass," the child's mother warned, "it's likely to annoy the gorillas."	The child sat down in front of the gorilla exhibit and tried to make friends with the female gorilla who was on the other side of the glass. The gorilla seemed annoyed.
The community party was lively, with a live band and about forty people standing around in small groups talking. A few couples were dancing, along with six children of various ages, who were also laughing. I stood at a table heavy laden with food, serving myself some tortillas and carnitas. I could see on the other side of the picnic area that a young man was engaged in a passionate conversation with a young woman. I couldn't hear them over the music, but they were waving their hands about and gesturing with so much liveliness that they were spilling their drinks.	The community party was lively, with a live band and about forty people standing around in small groups talking. A few couples were dancing, along with six children of various ages, who were being silly, worn out from being up past their bedtime. I stood at a table heavy laden with food, serving myself some tortillas and carnitas. I could see on the other side of the picnic area that a young couple were arguing with each other, their elaborate gestures causing their drinks to spill.
The priest, with the help of several teens who were called "altar boys," gave everyone "communion," a small wafer and a sip of wine. This represents the body and blood of Jesus, who the parishioners believe was both human and divine. To receive the wafer and wine, the parishioners lined up, walked to the altar, knelt on the little pillows, and returned to their seats. They sang hymns the whole time.	The priest gave everyone communion as the parishioners lined up, walked to the altar, knelt on the little pillows, and returned to their seats. They sang hymns the whole time.

participants construct, maintain, and change their social worlds. Routine actions also help you find patterns in how interactions occur and to notice the common variations and outliers, which will help lead you to answer questions of why these patterns and variations occur. The opposite of this is recording significant and unexpected moments—either in your own experiences or in your participants' reactions. These often record "aha" moments of insight on your part, where a number of thoughts and feelings crystallize into an understanding, or record key moments of realization or change for your participants.

Your jottings—and later field notes—should capture not only what is happening around you but also what is happening inside you. **Reflexivity** is the idea that a person's thoughts and ideas tend to be biased, so you should turn the critical gaze back on

Reflexivity Turning the critical gaze back on one's own experiences, feelings, and thoughts to investigate one's own biases and assumptions.

yourself. Reflexive writing looks carefully at the two-way street of interactions and impressions: what is happening outside you and what you are doing in return. It looks for cause and effect in the interactions you're a part of. Your jottings should mostly record what is happening around you—your shorthand observations to unpack later. But if an interaction or event brings up strong feelings or thoughts in you, your jottings should also record what is happening inside your own mind. These short notes are key to fully unpacking significant events from the day later in the evening as you sit down to write up field notes.

Pairing the Textbook and Workbook

Having discussed the main elements of the process of "doing" participant observation, from selecting a site to writing up notes, it's time to try it out! As you work toward the culminating assignment for this chapter in the workbook (Activity 4.6), it's particularly important for you to begin to use your daily life to build your observational skills: becoming more present, more aware, more mindful of your own internal responses to what is happening, and used to storing observations in your memory for later. Continue to work on building skills in remembering details from your daily life and journaling them each day. The more you practice these skills, the better (and more comfortable) you'll be at using them.

Reflective Prompts

1. Do I know the skill areas that are challenging for me? To build up those skill areas, what commitments to practice should I make?

2. Can I describe the importance of reflecting on my own memory bias in participant observation?

3. Do I have questions about field challenges related to jottings in regard to my own research project?

Case Study

Cruz-Torres, María Luz. 2004. *Lives of Dust and Water: An Anthropology of Change and Resistance in Northwestern Mexico.* Tucson: University of Arizona Press.

The Project

The main research question I had, entering the field, was to understand how these communities dealt with environmental and economic issues in the region. I started from a historical perspective. It was a region that, for a long time, nothing was changing there. And then the *ejidos* started—communally farmed land owned by the community itself, with all the decisions made by the people in the community. It was very interesting because I didn't initially know about all the struggles for

(Continued)

(Continued)

access to land and for building these communities from scratch, from nothing. I found my particular community by accident. I went to a different part of Mexico, and then I found out this community was a better place for fieldwork. I didn't know anything about Sinaloa at that time. I went for a visit to the community first, and then I went back to the university to write my proposal. Before I got back to the field, Mexico had a new election, and a new president, and everything changed, so I had to start again. I was very interested in following these two communities and seeing all the different changes that took place.

Most of the families were still there, so I could spend a lot of time doing participant observation. I went to see how people fish in the communities, how they grew different things like corn and squash. There was a coconut plantation in the community, and I looked at how they used the coconuts. I talked to the women a lot, because they knew the most. You had to be a part of the *ejido* to participate in the board, and women weren't allowed to participate in these meetings. So here's these meetings at the school house, and all the men are inside, and the women are all outside the building, listening. The women were the ones who organized the signatures to get water in their houses; initially, there was no running water in the community.

When I went there, gender wasn't one of the questions that I was going to address, but it became a huge part of my research. Because women were the ones who were keeping the community running all the time. So in terms of participant observation, I spent lots of time doing activities with the women, working alongside them—doing the work, meeting at their houses, having meals with them, talking about schooling and issues with children. Sometimes going with them to do the laundry at the river. But mostly we were at their houses: eating, talking, laughing, working. Going to the beach and to church. The farmers would take me around to see plots of land and show me what they grew. I got to know the communities—the places important to the people.

Why was participant observation particularly important for data collection, given your research question?

Participant observation was very important for many reasons. I didn't know anything about Mexico or my communities. I had an idea of the topic, of what I wanted to do, but once I got there, everything seemed so different. I had to build rapport, to gain the trust of people. Because in Mexico it can be hard. They wonder how you'll use that information. So I did things like survey at the end, but the participant observation gave me more of an understanding of the dynamics of the community and built rapport with the people so they could know me.

What is something that you learned regarding your field site or community you couldn't have known if you hadn't done participant observation?

People have the different categories; the people who came recently to live in the community were like outcasts, because no one knew them yet. Some of them migrated from the highlands to the coast. I didn't know that until I did participant observation. Also, one of the issues that came up in my fieldwork was domestic violence. When I went to the field, I didn't think of it at all. It came out later in my interviews, but it started being brought up during my participant observation with the women. Also, I had no idea about gender roles in Mexico. When I did participant observation, the men have their own spaces and the women have their own spaces. Even in public spaces, men were on one side and women were on another side. My own gender limited what I could do. I couldn't go fishing with men alone. I had to invite their wives or other women with me. No one told me to expect something like that when I was in school. It's how you're supposed to look, too. A group of women stopped me once and invited me to their house, and then told me that they were worried that I wouldn't find a husband because I never dressed up or wore makeup. I wasn't being very womanly. They always saw me in jeans and no high heels. This told me a lot about what it was like to be a woman in Mexico.

When you first entered the field, what did you find difficult? Did you experience culture shock, and what did it feel like? How did you respond to these feelings?

Everything was culture shock for me. I had to learn about Mexican food. I had no idea what *nopales* or tortillas were. I had to learn everything. I speak Spanish, but the Spanish spoken in Mexico is different from the Spanish spoken in Puerto Rico. The meaning of the words were different. So I made a lot of mistakes. Someone would be laughing, and I'd figure out that I had made a mistake: I'd said a bad word and shouldn't have said that. It took me a while to figure out the language for that particular place and learn new words for the region of Sinaloa. Another challenge was finding a place to live in the community. At first it was hard to find a place to stay, but later people invited to stay with them, and I got to know those household dynamics. That was one of the hardest challenges because I didn't know anyone initially. And you think about it, this woman

who knows no one going into this rural area—it just didn't make sense to them. But people were very nice at the time.

How did you gain rapport with your host community?

Rapport came with time, but it was also strategy, because I had to convince people I wasn't a problematic woman. They had all these hypotheses about who I was, like was I running away from home. No one really came to this community, so they kept questioning what I was doing there. I had to convince people that I was doing research, that I was an anthropologist. I found out later they had all these theories about who I was and why I was there. Because as a woman in rural Mexico, you are supposed to marry and have children by a certain age, so when you don't fit into these stereotypes, they wonder why? What are you doing there?

How long did you stay in the field? How many times have you gone back, and why?

The first time, I stayed for a year. And then I went back two years later, annually, to finish my book, for five more years—during summer and winter on breaks from teaching. The process took me a while.

What advice do you have about participant observation, based on your research career, for beginning researchers?

You have to go in with an open mind, because you don't know how the project will evolve. You need to read a lot before you go to a place—as much as you can. When you get there, relax about it. Researchers want to do interviews and everything right away, but participant observation is there to provide an entry into people's lives. So this is the first thing to do. Get to know the people in a more relaxed way. Accept all kinds of invitations—to people's houses and such. It can be hard, and you

(Continued)

(Continued)

get overbooked, but it helps, and I was glad I could visit everyone in the community. And this told them that I was there for my work and I wasn't taking sides in the community. You get more information in participant observation, in ethnography, than in any other method. You get this really rich, descriptive, thick ethnographic information—this is the distinctive factor of anthropology. And it's fun! You get to go to all these parties, and dinners, and people's homes—playing *Lotería* and eating tamales and all that. It's a great technique to use for you to learn about the community and all their dynamics, even in specific households.

Case Study Reflections

1. What were the various challenges that Cruz-Torres faced in conducting her fieldwork? What did you learn about how to face these challenges?

2. Why are there often significant gaps between the preparation a researcher does (through reading the literature and planning a proposal) and the circumstances they encounter in the field? How should an ethnographer respond to these gaps?

3. What is specifically unique and valuable about participant observation as a method? In the case of Cruz-Torres's study, what did participant observation make possible that another method would not?

4. Cruz-Torres spent many years in the field before finishing her ethnography, which is fairly common (even though many students finish their dissertation after only a year of research). Given her research question, why would it be advantageous for her to not only spend more time in the field but return to the field over the course of many years?

STUDY GUIDE ●

Note: Students should study each concept with attentiveness to defining, explaining with examples, and describing or demonstrating process. This is not a list of terms to define; it's a list of concepts and processes to master.

Ethnography

Participant observation

Reactivity

Ideal versus real culture

Immersion

Resocialization

Fieldwork roles

Observing participant

Participating observer

Skills for participant observation

Explicit awareness

Rapport

Objectivity

Value-neutrality

Selecting a field site (major points)

Preparing for the field (major points)

Fieldwork experience cycle (major points)

Culture shock

Reverse culture shock

Imposter syndrome

Debriefing

Time constraints in fieldwork (major points)

Field notes

Jottings (what, where, how, when)

Showing, not telling

Reflexivity

FOR FURTHER STUDY

Bernard, H. Russell. 2018. "Participant Observation." In *Research Methods in Anthropology*, by H. Russell Bernard, 272–307. Lanham, MD: Rowman and Littlefield.

Emerson, Robert M., Rachel I. Fretz, and Linda L. Shaw. 2011. "In the Field: Participating, Observing, and Jotting Notes." In *Writing Ethnographic Fieldnotes*, by Robert M. Emerson, Rachel I. Fretz, and Linda L. Shaw, 21–44. Chicago: University of Chicago Press.

Galman, Sally. 2007. *Shane, the Lone Ethnographer: A Beginner's Guide to Ethnography*. Plymouth, UK: AltaMira Press.

Pelto, Pertti J. 2013. "Participant Observation." In *Applied Ethnography: Guidelines for Field Research*, by Pertti J. Pelto, 127–140. Walnut Creek, CA: Left Coast Press.

Tierney, Gerry. 2007. "Becoming a Participant Observer." In *Doing Cultural Anthropology: Projects in Ethnographic Data Collection*, edited by Michael V. Angrosino, 9–18. Long Grove, IL: Waveland Press.

REFERENCE

Bernard, H. Russell. 2018. "Participant Observation." In *Research Methods in Anthropology*, by H. Russell Bernard, 301–05. Lanham, MD: Rowman and Littlefield.

Visit **study.sagepub.com/kirner** to help you accomplish your coursework goals in an easy-to-use learning environment.

CHAPTER 5

Writing Field Notes

Orientation

As we discussed in the previous chapter, writing is a critical part of participant observation. Writing is half of ethnographic fieldwork, and it takes up a good deal of the researcher's time. Field researchers will often write at least several hours of notes per day—sometimes you'll spend more time writing up field notes than you spend "doing" participant observation. What exactly do you write down? Well, the truth! That is, you write about the truth as you experience it, contextualized by your perspective and relationships. Emerson, Fretz, and Shaw (2011) say fieldworkers "inscribe reality"—that is, because different descriptions and interpretations of events are possible, the researcher actually creates reality through their writing, determining what the audience will ultimately understand as truth. There is no best description, because the researcher's observations are filtered through their unique characteristics. The writing process, beginning with one's daily field notes, is itself a form of (often subconscious) analysis: the first step in a process of moving from data collection to interpretation.

The Truth as Subjective

As you hopefully realized in the previous chapter, participation observation is a messy, though very useful, means of data collection. "Truth" in an absolute sense doesn't exist in participant observation, because your body, memory, and writing are your instruments to collect data, and these will vary from one researcher to the next. So truth in ethnographic research

Chapter Learning Objectives

Students will be able to do the following:

5.1 Explain how truth is subjective in ethnographic research

5.2 Understand the process of ethnographic writing

5.3 Describe the descriptive components of field notes and how jottings become field notes

5.4 Consider audience, stance, style, and perspective when writing narratives

5.5 Describe the analytical components of field notes

5.6 Identify and correct writing pitfalls

5.7 Define *autoethnography* and explain how it differs from autobiography and ethnography

is subjective to a certain degree. Common differences between researchers include the following:

- Perception (or **orientation**—what the researcher is attentive to)

- Interpretation (including underlying assumptions and theoretical lenses)

- Reactivity (people changing their behavior because they know they are being studied or in response to characteristics of the researcher)

- Context (position, place, timing)

- Chance (every researcher will run into different events, interactions, and people to meet)

- Writing choices (how your choice of words, style, and other mechanisms as a writer affect your representation of observed events)

Some of these differences between researchers are consciously chosen (such as writing style and interpretation), and some are not (such as reactivity and chance). Field notes, by necessity, reduce the chaos of the world into manageable chunks that you can analyze. But in doing this, you necessarily pre-analyze your information before it even becomes data. You have to determine what is important to pay attention to, to remember, and to write about. Even if this is subconsciously done, you're analyzing the world around you even before you sit down to write up your field notes for the day.

Orientation What the researcher is attentive to.

Selection The analytical process through which the writer decides what to write about and what to leave out.

Presentation The analytical process through which the writer chooses how to present information, including writing style and point of view.

Emic Insider (i.e., in the cultural group under study).

Polyvocality Inserting a variety of participants' voices into field notes and the final manuscript.

The process of writing field notes is a process of both selection and presentation. **Selection** is an analytical process in which the researcher decides what to write about and what to leave out. Because it's impossible to write about everything, this selection process automatically limits the data the fieldworker produces, eliminating some interactions, observations, and events at the very beginning. The researcher also frames the events they write about in particular ways, controlling the **presentation** of the data. The writer's presentation of the data influences the way the audience views and understands the culture the writer studied. The audience accesses their understanding, then, through the ethnographer's choices. Selection and presentation are informed by the methodological and theoretical approaches of the researcher and the attendant underlying assumptions. The bottom line is that writing field notes—choosing what to write and how to write it—is a messy process. Researchers should try to be critically reflective about it, but at the same time, you must write notes—and you can't write everything. So forgive yourself for what you don't include.

As you can probably tell, "data" in participant observation are inseparable from the process itself. Part of the data is your own feelings, circumstances, and interactions. "What happened," as you write it in your field notes, is not fact but rather a certain truth with a specific context. In order to collect meaningful data, you should be attentive to **emic** (insider) meanings and concerns, which will balance your discussion of your own perspectives. You can't eliminate your biases, but you can acknowledge and limit them. Remember, however, that **polyvocality** (inserting a variety of participants' voices into your notes and eventual manuscript) is not an easy fix to the problem of bias. Though you may include your participants' voices, you are still the editor of these voices—selecting who is heard, how their voice is framed up, and which parts of their narratives you include in your notes. Your participants' perspectives on and interpretations of their own lives are critical information, as is the detailed context of interactions and events. Your impressions and experiences, your participants' interpretations, and details on the context combine to generate an understanding of not only *what* is happening in a given social group but also *why* and *how* it is happening.

Remember that your writing style, not just your theoretical lens, frames the understanding of the audience. Pay attention to how your favorite authors influence (for better or for worse) your own writing. Do you tend to provide highly descriptive scenes? Do you focus more on dialogue? Field notes, though they are a means of recording data, are also narrative writing. Style and tone affect how your audience will experience the culture you are representing. We'll talk more about writing style and choices later in this chapter. For now, you should start reviewing some of your creative narrative writing and explore how your style and tone may be reflecting favorite authors, including what that might lead you toward in strengths and weaknesses.

Discussion

Our writing is informed not only by our data but also by our style. Is there an author or two whom you particularly admire? This might be an ethnographer but might also be a novelist or nonfiction writer. What is it about their work that you enjoy? How could you incorporate some of their style that you enjoy into your own writing?

The Process of Writing

In order to capture rich detail, it is absolutely critical that you write field notes as soon as you possibly can after the interaction or event is over. Humans rapidly experience loss of fine-grained detail in memory and distort their memories over time. The sooner you write notes on what occurred after the event has passed, the less likely you will be to struggle to remember properly and fill in your gaps of memory from assumptions—which distort your data. Furthermore, not only does timely field notes writing generate higher-quality, more accurate data, such detail is also important for developing ethnographic texts that will interest readers. Hearing participants' voices and having a clear vision of the context in an ethnographic narrative is more exciting, compelling, and convincing than reading interpretations without sufficient data-based detail.

Field notes should be written daily, if at all possible. In the previous chapter, you already started attempting to unpack your jottings into narrative statements. This was preparing you for the longer narratives that are your daily field notes. The complete participant observation research process follows a trajectory from jottings to ethnography (see Figure 5.1).

Figure 5.1 The Ethnographic Writing Cycle

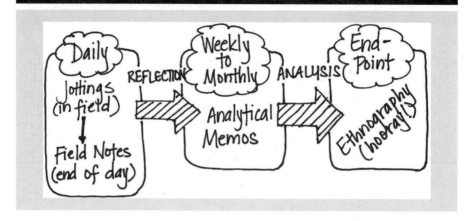

Just as you make jottings (ideally) as you observe behaviors and discussions in the field to ensure as clear a memory as possible, your field notes should be a daily writing activity in order to capture a high level of accuracy (which makes your ethnography valid) and detail (which makes your ethnography interesting and relevant to your discipline). Your field notes should strive to be nuanced, textured (with quotes from your participants), and detailed.

To begin a writing practice, you should develop periods of focused writing time. Just as you've seen with other methodological skills, the more you practice, the better you'll get at it. Start with short periods of participant observation (an hour or two) and then sit down right afterward to write up field notes and work toward being able to have a full day of participant observation. The most common pattern for ethnographers in the field is to have a full day of participant observation during which they make jottings and then to write for several hours in the evening, unpacking those jottings into field notes narratives. A common process through the ethnographic research life cycle (as you read about in the previous chapter) is to initially focus one's jottings and field notes on ordinary routines, tasks, and processes in the everyday lives of your participants. Once field notes feel relatively complete regarding the everyday life details, many researchers will shift their field notes to focus on more extraordinary or significant events. That is, you don't have to repeat yourself over and over throughout your field notes, but at the same time, you do want a relatively complete, detailed set of notes about everyday life before you shift your focus to rarer events.

Because you want to continue to "show, not tell," and this requires a very good memory to capture fine-grained details, it can't be overstated how important it is that you develop a daily field notes writing practice. If for any reason you can't write daily, you need to try to find ways to capture the detail until you can unpack it into a complete narrative form. This might mean taking more extensive handwritten jottings, paired with photos or sketches, or recording narrations (by using a voice recorder). When you sit down to write, the goal is to write as much as you can remember, as fast as you can. Initially, you don't have to worry about editing. You can worry about that later. It will interrupt the flow of your memories to try to edit as you write, so focus first on simply getting the memories into words on the page. Field notes often look like stream-of-consciousness writing: just one memory and thought after another, often without writing transitions and with a lot of grammatical errors. Once you have your field notes written, you can always return to them to tidy them up!

Discussion

How do you feel about writing? Do you experience writer's block or anxiety related to writing? If you have negative feelings about writing, it's time to start developing a positive relationship to the skill, as it's absolutely necessary in qualitative research. Try to develop a journaling practice, recalling things about your day and letting your mind wander into analysis about your own life. Journaling is an excellent daily practice to prepare you for writing field notes as an ethnographer, because it will help you remember what happened during your day and formulate ways to understand it.

Strategies for Field Notes

What does your field notes daily entry consist of? There are two kinds of descriptive components plus preliminary analysis (see Figure 5.2). We'll cover preliminary analysis later in this chapter, but let's discuss the two kinds of descriptive components: sketches and episodes.

Figure 5.2   Field Notes Entry Components

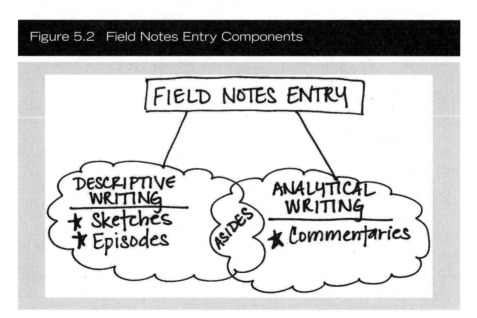

Sketches are highly descriptive narratives that set the stage. They don't focus on sequences of actions so much as they contextualize dialogue or observations of actions. Think of them like a landscape painting or photo: They help the audience understand the social and natural environment of the interactions you will portray. Sketches should help the reader feel like they're at your field site, which not only provides rich detail for interest but also helps the reader understand the social interactions you describe. In this portion of her field notes from working with cattle ranchers, one of your authors (Kimberly Kirner) recounts what the ranches look like as she meets one rancher for an interview:

> I maneuvered my truck up the long drive, bouncing slowly over the rocks and ruts in the dirt toward the corrals and house in the distance. I was heading toward an interview with a millionaire. I parked the truck and gazed around me, unsure of which building was the right one. The corrals lay to my left, the complex maze of chutes and holding corrals and gates empty. In front of me stood a newer manufactured home of modest size. To my right lay several small campers and an old manufactured home with a slightly decrepit look, guarded by several lazy collies. I did not have to hesitate long. The owner of the ranch opened the door and waved me up to the bleached deck, smiling and absent-mindedly patting several dogs, which promptly joined us inside. Perching myself on an old vinyl chair and plopping my notebook on the Formica table, I looked around interestedly. No one would guess that this man, who built a sizeable herd and beautiful ranch over the last several decades, was any different from a ranch hand. The couch was reminiscent of those my college friends acquired for free from neighbors or family and was situated cozily close to a small television. I turned back to my informant. He looked at me benevolently and leaned back in his chair, ready for a long chat.

Providing the context in which the ranchers live and work was necessary to help the reader understand the ways they identified with their land, the economic struggles family ranchers have, and the environmental and economic decisions they made.

Sketches are the context for **episodes**, which are portions of your field notes narrative that are action-oriented. Episodes are more like videos: They provide dialogue or observations of interactions. These actions may be routine or specific extraordinary incidents. Like all action sequences, such narratives have characters who are the actors in the scene. Episodes can stand alone or be linked together through transitions. Your other author's (Jan Mills's) field notes about a day in her classroom record the interactions between students and between students and herself, the teacher:

An example of an episode focused on interactions between students:
> Jeff is at the next table group, being very small of build with a piercing twinkle in his deep blue eyes under long dark lashes. He sits behind Ron and kitty-corner to Bryan. As part of the 3-some, Jeff and Nyles climb under their desks, stand on chairs when I use the overhead projector, and play with water bottles and each other. They delight in shooting the geoboard rubber bands across the room and crashing the pattern blocks. They talk incessantly together as Jeff sits on his feet, folder underneath him in the seat of his chair. Jeff tries to whistle in class, hums a

Sketches Highly descriptive portions of narrative that contextualize your recorded observations.

Episodes Portions of narrative that are dedicated to describing sequences of actions.

drone, shouts aloud about jumping his dirt bike and crashing, and squirms all day long in his seat. As the whole group sings the music teacher's new song, Jeff slams full-body contact into another student, bounding off from the impact as he loudly continues to sing out, "A-chi-chi-cha, a-chi-chi-cha, a-chi-chi-cha-cha!" Though he tries to stop talking when asked, he's quiet for only 1-2 minutes before he's off again. He changes math workplaces before the 15 minutes are up and wanders the room, primarily visiting Jared, who has a new dirt bike that he says Jeff might be able to ride sometime. . . . Today he climbed the ladder hanging on the wall in the hallway outside our room.

An example of an episode focused on dialogue between students and the teacher:
　　Jared sits across from Carl and Bryan but seldom plays or interacts with them. Jared is one of the top 2 readers in our class and will go to second grade for small group instruction. :) He asks to go to the bathroom every 30 minutes or so and most often chooses spelling and reading activities rather than game activities during language arts centers. He says he misses his mom and calls out many questions and comments throughout the day, often mid-sentence during the direct instruction time. "What time is it? When is lunch? (Either mom or dad has made it in every single day so far.) When is recess? When is it time to go home? Can I go see Mr. Cartwright?" (counselor). It's very hard to meet his intense need for emotional support within the current context that is our classroom climate. He seems anxious and nervous—Dad says Jared gets "24/7 individual attention as our only child and the only grandchild on both sides." Jared, too, plays the center of his own universe, demanding immediate attention for every thought that makes it out of his head and onto his tongue, seeming to be impatient with the fact that "others" also have needs to be met.

An example of an episode focused on interactions between teacher and parent with dialogue:
　　Earlier today Jules' mom called me about the behavior letter she received yesterday. She was positive and supportive, saying she was grateful because she's tried to speak with Jules' dad about misbehavior before. According to mom, dad thinks she exaggerates about Jules' misbehavior, telling me that Jules' dad is "kind-of macho." She said it helped to have the teacher letter in writing, causing the dad to take it more seriously and to have a talk with Jules. She said Jules cried himself to sleep, "which means he cares." Mom thanked me and emphatically said I am "doing a GREAT JOB with this class of kids!" (Good to hear!) She said that Jules was even showing more affections towards her! :) So I made it a point to call Jules' mom at work this afternoon to tell her what great choices of behavior Jules is making today. (He chose to finish his work instead of becoming angry over not having earned the privilege of playing with playdoh this week.) I encouraged her to celebrate tonight after school!

Each sketch or episode might be one or more paragraphs, and you can choose to link them together using transitions or have them stand alone. Often, they should be paired so that you are providing a reader with both the details of the context and what happened.

So what should you do in order to move from jottings to sketches and episodes—that is, a day's field notes entry? There are different strategies that people employ, and the first thing to remember is that the primary goal for writing field notes is to drain your memory of everything you can remember that you feel was significant. Another goal is to write interesting, textured, rich narratives to later use in an ethnography—but you can edit your initial field notes into this more polished narrative. The first order of business is getting thoughts down on the page. To do this, many researchers find that it is useful to chronologically unpack their jottings from the day, particularly in the beginning of their time in the field. During that time, if you recall, you will mostly focus on recording observations of everyday, ordinary life. Because of this, it makes sense to simply unpack your jottings one at a time, as they happened throughout the day. Each jotting should be unpacked into a statement, as you learned in the previous chapter. But then these statements should be further unraveled into rich, detailed narratives. Mills's field notes about a portion of her day in the classroom used this chronological strategy (see Figure 5.3).

Another strategy that is popular to employ, particularly once you've been in the field a while, is to focus on extraordinary or unusual incidents (once you've recorded the everyday, routine interactions). And finally, especially in studies in which the researcher is narrowly focused on a particular set of research questions, the researcher might focus

Figure 5.3   Jottings to Field Notes Example 1

Jottings	Field Notes
am - roll call, Maggie out of seat, run; Kyle poured out "brain water" am - rdg, 7 stus tug me, out of seat, yelling in my face -Kyle, Dav, Anna, Jared, Aub, Tye, Shar	Maggie started our morning out of her seat, running laps around the perimeter of our classroom. Kyle poured his "brain water" from the water bottle I'd given each of them all over his desktop, swishing it around for the minute or two he was in his seat, then jumping up and running through the room, later following me around tugging on my shirttail, calling out, "Teacher, look. . . . Teacher, teacher. . ." with pencils or crayons or scissors in hand, while David, Anna, Jared, Aubrey, Tye, and Sharon all do this exact same thing at the same time! I can hardly walk through the room as they cling to me while I'm saying, "I can't hear you. I can't see you. You're not in your seat like this," demonstrating by raising my hand quietly.
pm - math ctrs, Colb bump, push, took crayons, threw pattern blks, polydrons x desks; Carl/Nyles - geobd rbbrbds x rm-crash pattern blocks	Meanwhile, Colburn bumps and pushes people, takes their belongings, and throws the math pattern blocks sailing through the air during exploratory Bridges math learning centers. Later at the polydron math center, Colburn was rolling around on the floor, crying and moaning, complaining that he had to sit on time out after he looked purposefully at the polydron container and then swung his arms and swept the entire container of polydrons over, sending them clattering across the desktops. Carl and Nyles shoot geoboard rubber bands across the room and crash over other people's work in the pattern block center, though they are in a different work group at a different workplace.

their field notes on systematically recounting interactions related to their specific area of interest. In Kirner's research on the ways Pagans (people who practice contemporary/newer nature-based religions) interact at gatherings to learn about, discuss, and make decisions regarding environmental sustainability, she focused her jottings and field notes specifically on her research question. This allowed her to filter out the thousands of interactions she watched each day that didn't relate to her topic of interest (see Figure 5.4).

You might find it most useful to bounce back and forth between strategies in organizing your daily field notes entries. Remember, writing field notes is a creative exercise as much as it is an analytical one. Experiment with yourself as a writer and a researcher, two halves of one whole ethnographer.

Figure 5.4 Jottings to Field Notes Example 2

Jottings	Field Notes
Father to preteen son: "When you say you don't care, it really upsets me. You have to start thinking cosmically, buddy."	In a somewhat typical scene, a preteen boy, perhaps 11 or 12, moodily stares up at his father. He's at his table of rocks, selling little rocks he's found or bought from shops to others at the Faery Human Relations Congress gathering. I didn't catch the beginning of the interaction, so I'm not sure what behavior his father is correcting. My ears perk up, because one of the interesting things about this camp is the number of children and the effort by parents to shift cultural norms around parenting. The father puts a hand gently on the boy's shoulder and looks down into his glaring eyes. He quietly says, "When you say you don't care, it really upsets me. You have to start thinking cosmically, buddy." The boy's gaze softens. He looks down at the rocks, which for this cultural group, are thought of as persons. He looks out at the big grassy meadow, the woods, and the mountains. He looks back at his father and heaves a big sigh, and nods. The father gives him a hug.

Discussion

Try your hand at making jottings of your everyday life the way you would in the field. Then try your hand in the evening at writing detailed field notes entries that include both sketches and episodes. The more you practice, the better you'll become! What do you notice as your strengths and weaknesses as a budding ethnographer?

Writing Choices

As you write sketches and episodes, you'll make a number of decisions as a writer that will shape your representation of the people you are studying. These include not only selection, which we've covered before, but also subtle ways you shape your narrative through choices in your writing style. The first of these is to select who your primary **audience** will be. While you are primarily writing for yourself, as the field notes become your data, some researchers (especially once they have had more experience) prefer to edit and polish their field notes as they go with an eye for eventually publishing portions of them in their ethnographic works. In these cases, they might consider whether their audience is primarily academic (and, in turn, if it is primarily for colleagues or for students) or broader—for dissemination through public channels or in blogs. In the beginning, you should write primarily for yourself, which takes some of the pressure off the writing process and allows you to focus on the most important function of field notes: to record your memories as data. Writing for yourself should allow you to shift writing styles, such as point of view, over the course of your fieldwork. Do not feel as though you must select one single style and be consistent; inconsistencies in your writing style can be edited later. The main thing is to select writing styles that feel comfortable and that assist you in accurately representing your observations, interactions, and social contexts. Simply take one day's entry (or even each sketch or episode!) at a time.

One of the big decisions you will make as a writer (which can change day to day) is which **point of view** you choose. Your point of view structures your reader's perspective of your experiences. There are two primary points of view used by ethnographers: **first person** and **third person**. The first-person point of view ("I saw," "I heard," "I felt") lends itself easily to reflexivity, which is when you turn the critical gaze back on yourself and explore how you feel and think in the context of your observations and examine where your feelings and thoughts come from. The first-person point of view is especially common for the observing participant, where the researcher is also a member of the cultural group they are studying. In this portion of her field notes from working with cattle ranchers, Kirner uses the first person to explore the physical, embodied experience of the weather and work:

> It was about four-thirty in the morning, and I sat on the back of a horse in frigid darkness. Autumn, with its golden leaves on the higher altitude aspen trees and the seemingly endless process of sorting, weaning, and shipping calves, had settled into the quiet of winter. I think it likely that every cultural anthropologist has a moment in the field when you wonder what in the world you were thinking when you created your research agenda, and it was that moment for me. The cowboys surrounding me were fuzzy charcoal shapes against the lighter gray of the desert and we rode in silence in a general direction of where someone thought the cattle might be. It would be understandable to assume that I was silent due to the early hour, or cultural norms, or something equally reasonable. In fact, I desperately wanted to ask questions of the cowboys, not the least of which was how they knew where to find the cattle and how to get there, considering I could scarcely see anything and heard no cattle whatsoever, but I was unable to form the words. My entire face was numb. It was before dawn, ten degrees, and a steady winter wind blew across my uncovered face, rendering me unable to even gauge my facial expressions.

Audience The people who will be the primary consumers of your writing.

Point of view Your position as the writer in relationship to the story being told.

First person The point of view in which writer tells the story with themselves inserted in it as the storyteller.

Third person The point of view in which the writer tells the story as if they're a camera recording events around them.

It's important to remember, when using the first-person point of view, that your overall focus is still understanding the culture you are studying. Your field notes aren't a journal of your life. They're a journal of your life *among this particular cultural group you're studying, with attentiveness to your particular research question.* It can be tempting when writing in the first person to wander off into a style that more closely resembles a personal journal. This is especially true if you are functioning as an observing participant. However, you must continually reorient yourself, both while making jottings and while writing field notes, to the observations that are relevant to your research question. In this way, you will balance writing about yourself and writing about others in ways that lead to acknowledgment of your biases and insights into the cultural group you are studying, thereby avoiding the problem of writing in a style too much like a personal diary.

Third person ("they saw," "he heard," "she felt"), the other common point of view that ethnographers use, is most frequently employed by participating observers (those who are not part of the cultural group). Third person is highly effective for describing others' actions and dialogue, and it tends to highlight what the researcher saw or heard without assigning internal states to the actors involved. Mills, in her autoethnographic work as an elementary school teacher, understandably employed first-person narratives to describe her own thoughts and feelings, but she also used a third-person point of view to describe interactions between her students:

> Well, this turned out to be a *terrible, horrible, no good, very bad day.* I will forever remember this to be the day I chose to ignore minor behavior interruptions. I chose not to intervene to see if I could pursue teaching academics instead of interrupting academics to teach yet another social skill lesson just to make it through to the end of the period. Today, when I refused to stop the lesson for Jeff's repeated burping, it rapidly degenerated into a scene from *Lord of the Flies,* with Sonia screaming and jumping off of her desk; Antonio belly-crawling across the floor underneath several student desks; Tye yelling, "Liar! Cheater! I hate this school!"; Peter covering his hearing aid as the noise level shot up; and Jeff and Nyles snapping rubber bands across the room, hitting someone in the eye. Jeff shouted out at the top of his lungs—"WWHHH-HOOOOOOEEEEEEE!" Ugh! A fifth-grade teacher from down the hall came into our classroom and complained, despite our closed door—my strategy for noise containment!

It's very important to remember that if you assign these internal states (feelings, thoughts, motivations) to others in your field notes, they should be carefully and consciously assigned, and you should describe what you're basing your inferences on: prior conversation or cultural norms, for example. One of the challenges in using third person, due to its offering a more distant and objective tone, is to remember to critically reflect on your own thoughts and feelings (to be reflexive from time to time) and to be sure you aren't assigning internal states to people without a very solid foundation from which to do so.

It is common to shift back and forth between points of view in your field notes (from first to third person and back), but these shifts should be intentional. For example, you might start a field notes entry in the third person, recounting observations of an interaction between three other people, but then shift to first person as you reflect on how the interaction made you feel. Or you might start in the first person, orienting the reader to what you were doing while observing and providing context for the interactions you will describe, then shifting to the third person to more aptly describe a large number of people's actions in a folk festival. What is important is that you critically select which point of view you use for each portion of your field notes narrative. Each sketch or episode should have one consistent point of view, and it should be thoughtfully chosen to most accurately represent your experiences in the field and the way you want to portray the people you are studying.

Discussion

When you reflect on your particular research question you selected in Chapter 1, what point of view do you think you'll use most? Why? How will that particular point of view help you accurately represent your observations? How will it help a reader best understand your field experiences?

Analytical Writing within Field Notes

Field notes aren't only descriptive; they are also analytical. Ethnography is social science, so it not only collects descriptive data but analyzes data for patterns and reflects on these patterns through the lens of social theory. There are various methods for data analysis, two of which we'll cover in Chapter 7. However, aside from formal data analysis (conducted as a stage of research, after data collection), many researchers have analytical ideas and hunches during their process of data collection. What do you do with these ideas and hunches? You write them down, of course!

There are three different kinds of analytical writing that can happen in field notes, more or less defined by how long and complex they are (see Figure 5.5).

Asides are brief comments in the margins (sometimes literally, in the case of hard copy field notes, and sometimes digitally, using the "comments" feature in Word). These very short notes clarify, interpret, or question field notes entries. Side by side with the descriptive narrative, they are very short (a sentence or briefer) analytical notes that provide analytical context for or deeper questioning of the observations made. Here is an example of an aside in an early field notes entry (set off from the entry in brackets and italics), in which Mills reconsiders her research question, based on data she is collecting:

Asides Brief analytical comments in the margins, related to specific short bits of field notes.

Monday [day 5] and Maggie continues to SHRIEK—SCREAM at the top of her lungs, bursting out loud at any moment throughout the day with a high-pitched shrill squealing that hurts my ears! She is out of her seat almost every one-to-five minutes all day long, every day so far. . . . Jules screams, shouts, spins, crawls on the floor, talks non-stop (even to himself), hits, and calls other students "stupid" throughout these first five days of school. . . . I have, again, come to experientially understand the importance of student cooperation in the partnership they must be willing to build, for it will take the two of us working together to reach

Figure 5.5 Three Forms of Analytical Writing in Field Notes

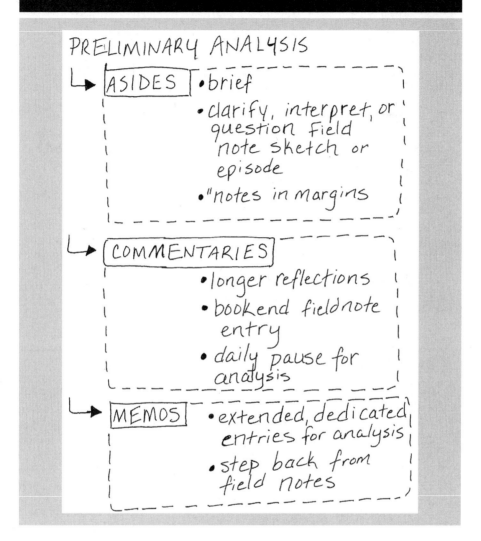

PRELIMINARY ANALYSIS

ASIDES
- brief
- clarify, interpret, or question field note sketch or episode
- "notes in margins

COMMENTARIES
- longer reflections
- bookend fieldnote entry
- daily pause for analysis

MEMOS
- extended, dedicated entries for analysis
- step back from field notes

the finish line—learning to read and gaining number sense—yet I am one with twenty-four highly active students, all trying to work together!

[Though initially I entertained many challenging thoughts and ideas and had gravitated towards a focus on literacy, after the first two weeks of this school year I find that my research interests are changing.]

Asides differ from commentaries in that they are shorter and more integrated with specific, limited portions of descriptive narrative.

Commentaries are longer reflections that, rather than being notes in the margins, are more like bookends to descriptive writing, occurring at the beginning or end of a field notes entry or portion of an entry. Most frequently, commentaries are written after the day's field notes entry, after a pause for deeper reflection. Commentaries are one or several paragraphs that might include extended reflexive writing or notes about changes to one's methodology in response to the data. Following Kirner's exploration of the embodied feeling of the weather and land (provided on page 98 of this chapter), she continues in her field notes with a weaving together of the descriptive passage and a commentary:

> It was all very romantic the first time or two, but as winter set in, a certain nagging remorse built in me as I left my bed in the wee hours to drive an hour or more, climb on a horse, and head out into the pre-dawn valley. The ranchers and cowboys did this most of their days. Why? What was the draw for them, day after day? What was the draw for me?
>
> We neared the cattle; I could hear their lowing in the distance. The night sky gave way to the first rays of sunlight that peeked over the White Mountains to our southeast. The desert turned pale green and ghostly, frost shimmering on the Great Basin wild rye and salt grass. The White Mountains began to turn gold as the snow caught the sunlight, while the Sierra Nevada Mountains kept their austere appearance, with Mount Whitney rising above the rest, its dark purple base still stark against the silver of the snow. As dawn gave way to cerulean sky, I knew why. It was the land. It was the life, a life unknown now to most Americans, that fluctuates with the seasons and weather, pulls you from your warm bed, and reminds you to watch the sunrise.
>
> In that moment, it was easy to understand why all the sacrifices, risks, and hard work are worth it to the ranchers to be here on this land. I found myself falling in love with the wide, flat sea of salt grass and rabbit brush rimmed by the rocky crags of the Sierras and the sparse heights of the Whites. Each night, I looked out my window as I wrote and saw the deep purple of the high Sierra, capped white with snow, and breathed in the heavenly air. I stared at the deepening blue of the desert sky at nightfall, and I too wanted to make the sacrifices to live there. I imagined all this beauty, combined with the pride of self-ownership and the depth of community that the ranchers have, and I felt a sense of longing for that life. I caught a glimpse of what they must feel . . . that all the sweat, blood, and tears are worth the scent of the rye grass in summer and the spectacle of each sunrise and sunset as it comes over the mountains, the dust kicked up by the cattle turning to burnished gold.

Commentaries
Longer analytical comments (one or more paragraphs) related to a particular episode, sketch, or entry in your field notes.

Analytical commentaries, rather than formal analysis and longer analytical writing, are more reflexive and intuitive discussions of significant patterns and insights noted by the researcher as they continue to do participant observation. It is relatively common to begin field notes (at the start of field work) with predominantly descriptive narratives and to introduce more analytical commentaries that flank these narratives as time goes on. As you continue to participate and observe, you'll begin to have reflections that unite your research question, your theoretical orientations, and insights you derive from your day's experiences and observations. These are not set in stone; these are your first *ideas* for analysis, not the final analysis itself. As you have these ideas, recording them is a way of generating hypotheses or further research questions when you get to the formal analysis stage of your research, as well as a way of chronicling your inner thoughts and feelings over time (including initial mistakes that you make).

We'll talk more about analytical memos in Chapter 7, but for now, we'll discuss these in relationship to a more informal process of reflecting on your field notes. **Analytical memos** are extended entries that reflect on your analytical asides and commentaries. While asides and commentaries are analytical notes on specific portions of descriptive narrative, analytical memos are analytical notes that transcend specific portions of descriptive narrative. To write an analytical memo, you'll want to block out extensive dedicated time specifically for this form of writing. Take a day off from participant observation and regular field notes writing, and instead read and review the asides and commentaries you've written over a portion of time—perhaps several weeks (or the first few months when you first begin a year of fieldwork). You'll want to reframe your asides and commentaries as you read them, in light of your research question and theoretical perspectives. Search for insights that arise as you reflect on them, and then write these insights down as their own entry—as an analytical memo. Here is an analytical memo from Jan Mills's research:

> In reflecting on my students' needs, I go back to Glasser's Choice Theory (Charles, 2005, p. 75, 82–85). He states student needs as security, belonging, power, fun, and freedom. I need to teach these students to TREAT OTHER PEOPLE THE WAY YOU WANT TO BE TREATED! We are in this class together. I want to help them be their best. My job is to teach them and help them learn. If they have a question, ask me. If they need more time, I'll give it to them. If they have an idea about how to do what we're trying to do better, tell me and I'll listen. I must clarify what a quality existence would be like; plan choices that will help achieve that existence. WARM, TRUSTING STUDENT-TEACHER RELATIONSHIPS! Humans control acting and thinking, but not feeling and physiology, in choosing Total Behavior.

Analytical memos that arise from this kind of periodic reflection are a form of preliminary analysis that can provide you with direction for further research. This may include connections you notice between observations, connections between theory and your field notes, or reinterpretation of your field notes based on the more complete knowledge you have later in your fieldwork period.

Discussion

You can use your own daily journaling about your life as a way to practice not only descriptive writing but also analytical writing. Try your hand at reflecting critically on your own life experiences, trying out each of the forms of analytical writing: asides, commentaries, and memos. Try to notice your strengths and weaknesses related to analytical writing. What feels difficult or uncomfortable, and how can you improve?

Analytical memos
Extended field note entries in which you reflect on a number of asides and commentaries.

Common Problems with Field Notes

While some choices are yours to creatively make with regard to your field notes, there are standards for assessing the quality of field notes and a variety of common problems that occur (see Figure 5.6). These problems not only reduce the accuracy of your data (and therefore your study's conclusions); they also can cause your own biases and assumptions to get mixed up with your observations, coloring the way in which readers perceive the culture you are studying.

Figure 5.6 Common Problems in Field Notes

Mistake: Paraphrasing Dialogue

Poor quality: The teacher told Johnny to sit down in his seat.	*High quality:* "Johnny," the teacher said, raising her voice, "you have until the count of three to sit down in your seat. One, two . . . thank you."

Why it's important: Ethnography should capture your participants' voices, in their own words, as much as possible. Furthermore, when you paraphrase your participants, you often skew the tone of what they said or miss key details for analysis, because you're filtering their words through your own assumptions and voice.

Mistake: Disembodied Characters

Poor quality: Maria was a middle-aged woman of Mexican ancestry, whose mother had emigrated here when Maria was only twelve years old.	*High quality:* Maria was a small, middle-aged woman with long, thick black hair up in a tidy bun. She wore a beige business skirt suit and low pumps, having come straight from work to the interview. However, she had a Mayan hair sash tied around her bun, and she spoke with warmth and a smile when she described her mother's heritage from the Yucatan in Mexico and how she came to the United States when Maria was twelve years old.

Why it's important: The participants in your study are characters in your ethnography. The people in your ethnography should be whole characters, with descriptions of their dress, gestures, facial expressions, and other characteristics.

Mistake: The Missing Anthropologist

Poor quality: The elderly couple seemed to be arguing with one another, with raised voices and angry expressions, but abruptly stopped.	*High quality:* I watched with interest from across the reception hall as an elderly couple began to raise their voices. Their facial expressions seemed angry, and I surmised they might be having an argument. I walked toward them along the edge of the room in an effort to better understand how they would deescalate the situation in this socially visible space. As soon as they noticed me, they stopped.

Why it's important: If your notes routinely leave you out of the picture, there is a problem. You are a data collection instrument when doing participant observation, and your actions and characteristics shape the ways in which participants respond. Your field notes need to account for the ways in which your own actions, assumptions, feelings, and phrasing of questions shape the ways in which your participants respond.

Mistake: Caricature

Poor quality: The group was obnoxious.

High quality: The group spoke very loudly and occupied a lot of the public space.

Why it's important: When you write caricatures instead of field notes, you are filtering your observations through your own ethnocentric assumptions. This is very problematic, because your participants may not interpret the behavior or words you are recording the way you do. Remember to *show, not tell.* Question your assumptions and biases, and don't cloud your observations with them.

Mistake: Misusing Concepts

Poor quality: Wiccan covens are usually facilitated by a High Priestess, and I observed that in Druid groves, one or two people also fill this role.

High quality: Wiccan covens are usually facilitated by someone they call the High Priestess. In Druid groves, there is also frequently a person who organizes and facilitates ritual, but this person is called a Chosen Chief.

Why it's important: It's tempting, usually out of laziness, to use words you know from one social group to describe a key concept in another social group. However, this poses multiple problems. First, the two concepts are rarely identical. Second, part of your work as an ethnographer to is find out *insiders' (members') meanings.* That is, in your ethnographic research, you should attempt to find words that people in the cultural group you are studying use for core concepts. If you think that the concept is similar to one in another culture, you can explore this both theoretically and through discussions with participants. But even if the two concepts are similar, you should maintain the rich detail of your field notes by using the appropriate terms and concepts from inside the group.

Mistake: Dismissive Stance

Poor quality: Many Pagans use magic alongside traditional biomedicine when faced with a serious or chronic illness; as Malinowski's work points out, why not try everything in a high-risk situation?

High quality: Many Pagans believe the universe to be interconnected, so one's attitude and will are important factors in the healing process. In order to ensure the patient's focus on healing, rather than accepting anxiety and negativity, Pagans will encourage one another in magical practices that impose the (positive) will on the universe, believing this strengthens the chances that traditional biomedical treatment will work.

Why it's important: When a researcher dismisses insiders' (members') meanings, values, and assessments—treating them as flawed, contradictory, false, or commonsensical—they impose a judgment on their participants that is both ethically and analytically problematic. These judgments usually arise from the researcher's own ethnocentrism and bias and need to be critically reflect on and deconstructed. Such judgments can be very helpful for building a researcher's awareness of their own assumptions and biases but have no place in actual representations of data.

(Continued)

Figure 5.6 (Continued)

Mistake: Ideal versus Real Culture

Poor quality: Family ranchers never assume debt, except for the annual farm operating expenses loan; to do so easily leads to losing the ranch in a "bad year."	*High quality:* Family ranchers agree that whenever possible, a ranch should not assume debt, except for the annual farm operating expenses loan, because other debts may lead to losing the ranch in a "bad year." However, there are some circumstances in which this might occur, such as family medical emergency. Also, recent tycoon ranchers may have a mortgage and personal debt, using a more normal business model due to lacking the experience to see the family ranch and family economies as intertwined.

Why it's important: Beginning researchers sometimes struggle to differentiate between ideal culture and real culture in their field notes, but the distinctions are very important. There can be substantial gaps between what people think *should be* and *what is*. These gaps are important areas of research, because they point out certain contingencies, imperfections, or other mechanisms at work in translating cultural ideals to cultural norms of behavior. If the researcher fails to address the difference in their notes, they've failed to capture a very common and important part of social life.

Remember, at the heart of ethnography, you're trying to capture emic (insider) meanings: your participants' terms, routines, descriptions of their own actions and processes, concepts and categories, explanations and theories, and perceptions of local and wider forces at play. While you will ultimately analyze these notes as data, within the context of theoretical perspectives you select, you don't want to preemptively assign your own interpretations to what you observe, hear, and experience. Try to write field notes that let your participants speak for themselves!

Discussion

Reviewing the common problems in field notes, can you identify one mistake that you think you'd be most prone to making? What strategy might you be able to employ when writing field notes to avoid that particular problem?

Autoethnography
A combination of ethnography and autobiography, connecting personal experiences with cultural ones.

Autoethnography

Some anthropologists use their own life experiences, as members of a specific cultural group, to critically reflect on their lives as data within the context of a research question (of course, informed by theoretical perspectives). This is **autoethnography**, which is grounded in **phenomenology**—treating the subjective, lived, and embodied experience of the researcher as data to analyze. Phenomenology doesn't have to be autoethnographic in nature. To some extent, it informs participant observation generally, and it also can be used in cases where the researcher *becomes* a member of the cultural group they're studying (when that is possible). However, phenomenology can also be used when the researcher is already a member of a particular cultural group, through a process of reflecting deeply and critically on their own past experiences.

In both phenomenological and autoethnographic studies, internal switching back and forth between the insider's point of view and the outsider's analysis forms the framework of the study. It's critically important (and challenging) that the researcher doesn't identify as an insider to the point that they lose track of bringing analysis to bear as a social scientist. In such cases, it can be very helpful to talk with a colleague regularly about the issues that arise in doing such research—in theory, method, and emotional investment. This process reminds you, the researcher, that you are more than the phenomenon you're studying and that you are *both* anthropologist *and* insider.

Autoethnography, then, is a combination of ethnography and autobiography, connecting personal experiences with cultural ones. It uses the researcher's own life experience as a starting point for studying something, combining your observations with the world around you with your own internal perceptions and feelings. Generally speaking, the goal of autoethnography is not accuracy or validity, but rather a communication of a complex emotional truth. It's a way to engage and open readers to a conversation with someone, rather than focusing on definitive conclusions from data. By intensely marrying your life experience and your social commentary, your encourage the reader to empathetically relate to your life (and, by extension, you as a representative of an entire cultural group), and this helps the reader become the social scientist, analyzing your story and drawing their own conclusions. In the case of autoethnography, generalizability has to do with the stories resonating with an audience, rather than specific conclusions or interpretations being applicable to an entire cultural group. The purpose is to help readers relate to people seemingly unlike themselves and deeply question their own assumptions and biases, rather than to definitively represent the cultural norms or processes of a group.

Because of this very different purpose, autoethnographies are often written stylistically differently than ethnographies are. They usually use a literary style to draw in readers, making the work more accessible and like one or more stories. They are, obviously, usually written in the first person (because they are about a single individual, the researcher), and they can take a wide range of creative literary forms, including novels, short stories, photographic essays, or poetry. While they may read like other literature, what makes autoethnographies remain firmly works in the social sciences is bringing in commentary that, while sometimes subtle, brings complex and nuanced understandings of social theory to bear on the researcher's lived experiences. Through these more subtle, internal discussions the researcher has with themselves, making meaning out of their own life, the readers are drawn into a more complex and critically thoughtful way of engaging with their lives and the lives of others.

Phenomenology Treating the subjective, lived, and embodied experience of the researcher as data to analyze.

If you were to select a single event in your life that is emotionally charged and worthy of social science examination, what would that event be? Why do you think that event is particularly significant for unpacking through autoethnographic writing? What research question might that event relate to? What do you think a reader could learn from engaging with your autoethnographic story about this event, if you wrote one?

Pairing the Textbook and Workbook

You've now learned how to move from "doing" participant observation, to making jottings, to unpacking jottings into field notes and beginning preliminary analysis! It will continue to be a very helpful practice to use your daily life to build your ethnographic skills—not only for observational memory but also in developing a writing practice. The more you practice, the more comfortable you will become, and the easier the culminating assignment for this chapter (Activity 5.6 and/or 5.7) will be. Continue to use daily journaling to build your capacity to remember the details of your observations and experiences and to critically reflect on these.

Reflective Prompts

1. Am I practicing my new skills, such as writing analytical memos in the margins?

2. How deeply do I understand the concept of inscribing my own reality through selection and presentation?

3. What are my thoughts as I consider audience, stance, style, and perspective when writing narratives?

Case Study

Anderson, E. N. 2005. *Political Ecology in a Yucatec Maya Community.* Tucson: University of Arizona Press.

Anderson, E. N., and Felix Medina Tzuc. 2005. *Animals and the Maya in Southeast Mexico.* Tucson: University of Arizona Press.

The Project

Basically, I was interested in how well the Yucatec Maya manage animal and plant resources and how they manage to get everyone on board with sustainability. My big thing is sustainability. First, the Maya are really consummate managers of plant and animal resources. Second, they do it by letting kids help out and absorb the knowledge, wandering through the forest and doing all kinds of stuff. Until recently these were tight-knit, jointly run, owned, and governed communities. Everyone knew what was necessary to keep the system functional, and there was a lot of pressure to keep everyone doing that. Everyone knew what you had to do, and everyone was willing to informally police everyone else. They represented this system religiously through helpful forest spirits and gods. They're always there to watch you, too.

I figure out the way the Maya classify and categorize biological and ecological stuff, and question them and watch what they do until I'm pretty sure I've got it right. And I compare it to Western scientific classification. It's closest for birds; plants are a pretty good match. You have these generic terms and specifics attached to the generics. But, of course, you're interested in how the local system is different from the Western Linnaean system, and this means you have to know the local system of classification the way it is. That takes a long time, to see how they use terms in the field. So we patiently slogged through the Maya forest until we saw every bird and plant and asked everyone what things are called and why. Otherwise, you run the risk of projecting your own system onto them erroneously.

I've done a lot of frame elicitation and decision-making studies. In decision making, people go back and forth and reconsider the issue from several viewpoints. They're doing this under social influences. They're not doing it alone. I had to look at decision making under social constraints. This is different from the idea that people make rational decisions that can be understood as flowcharts. The nice thing is learning the flowcharts and rational choice theory and then learning how the world works differently. Because you have to see how far people are from the ideal process and why they're so far from it. I got books out of that! Now, no sane person thinks people make choices rationally, but it spun off into tons of work on what people really do. There are very rational reasons people do things, but there's also a lot of craziness.

How would you describe your own process as a researcher for integrating participant observation and writing ethnography?

Long ago, even before I started anthropology (just from my biology background), I learned to journal and make extensive notes, to make a record of everything you observed and to organize my notes. This changed over time, to change from hard copy journals to computer files for specific information. Every day you write up field notes. In the old days, you spent hours handwriting by candlelight, but now you can do this much more easily. I keep 3 × 5 cards in my pocket, which is the advice I got from my graduate adviser (and still use!). You record everything on these cards, and then the minute you get back to where you are staying, you record it in the computer. You want to keep the hard copies and use cloud storage so if your computer fails, you're OK. I think the thing that's essential to point out is that the way everyone learns stuff in the world, except crazy Americans and Europeans, is that they learn by doing. They mostly learn by guided imitation and apprenticeship. This is also participant observation. You watch, you imitate, you play at doing things the same way you did as a little kid. You start doing the real thing under guidance of parents and siblings, and in the field it's under guidance of key informants. You get verbal guidance

(Continued)

(Continued)

as you do it: "No, not that way; do it this way!" and even stepping in, making your hands do it right. You've probably learned this way before, and it's like that in the field. But in the field, we jot notes throughout this process.

What kinds of writing do you do in the field— when, how often, and how was your writing process shaped by your field conditions?

I sure learned to write tersely! When you have to write up field notes under dubious lighting and uncomfortable circumstances, with little time to do it, you learn to be very telegraphic. You want the maximum information in the fewest words.

What writing style choices did you make in writing the ethnographies related to this specific project? Why did you make these choices?

My writing style is a very standard ethnographic style. However, I coauthored with a field assistant for one of the books, because about a quarter of the book is his own words. This key informant told me much of the information, and so it's his book as much as mine. Some of my other books are in a more popular style for a broader audience. I've also sometimes lapsed into a more formal style, such as for edited books. Writing ethnography is often a sort of genre: write accessibly but scholarly, which isn't always the best writing style in the world, but it gets the stuff out clearly. Some people have beautiful writing, but I don't feel I'm there yet. I do know writers who are wonderful stylists, but they work terribly hard at it. They usually write very little, but when they get it out, it is really good. And then some people produce floods of verbiage with little content. Every researcher-author is different.

What advice do you have about ethnographic writing, based on your research career, for beginning researchers?

Count everything countable and write everything down. Don't think you'll remember it later; you won't. Learn techniques from journalists to remember speech for later. You need to get a lot of data and sort it out the best you can. You need to figure out how the people you're studying think about things: their ways of linking one thing to another. You have to see how they think about the data. It's a good idea to move back and forth between how the people you are studying think about the data, and how classical ethnographers would have thought about it (categorically by kinship, economy, religion, and so on). This classical method was worked out over the course of years, and it is good for some things, but then you have to integrate that with how the people you're working with actually see this stuff—how they classify, use, talk about their own lives. That's something ethnographers in general have picked up from ethnobiologists. All good ethnography is now concerned with how local people think about stuff, use words, and classify things.

Case Study Reflections

1. How did Anderson's specialization in ethnobiology merge with his concern for emic approaches in writing ethnography? Why should we be concerned with an emic approach in ethnographic works?

2. What are some strategies you gleaned from this case study for writing in the field: doing jottings and field notes?

3. How is participant observation a learning process that parallels how young children typically learn their culture? How does writing notes factor into the difference between that early developmental process and the researcher's process?

4. Anderson has written and published more than a dozen books. But he says that he doesn't have beautiful writing . . . yet. What does this tell you, as a future ethnographer, about how you should approach your own feelings of imperfection as a writer?

STUDY GUIDE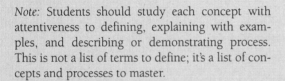

Note: Students should study each concept with attentiveness to defining, explaining with examples, and describing or demonstrating process. This is not a list of terms to define; it's a list of concepts and processes to master.

Orientation

Reactivity

Selection

Presentation

Sketch

Episode

Audience

Point of view

First person

Third person

Reflexivity

Aside

Commentary

Analytical memo

Autoethnography

Phenomenology

FOR FURTHER STUDY

Berger, Leigh, and Carolyn Ellis. 2007. "Composing Autoethnographic Stories." In *Doing Cultural Anthropology: Projects in Ethnographic Data Collection*, edited by Michael V. Angrosino, 161–76. Long Grove, IL: Waveland Press.

Bernard, H. Russell. 2018. "Field Notes and Database Management." In *Research Methods in Anthropology*, by H. Russell Bernard, 308–22. Lanham, MD: Rowman and Littlefield.

Emerson, Robert M., Rachel I. Fretz, and Linda L. Shaw. 2011. "Writing Fieldnotes I," "Writing Fieldnotes II," and "Pursuing Members' Meanings." In *Writing Ethnographic Fieldnotes*, by Robert M. Emerson, Rachel I. Fretz, and Linda L. Shaw, 45–170. Chicago: University of Chicago Press.

REFERENCE

Emerson, Robert M., Rachel I. Fretz, and Linda L. Shaw. 2011. "Writing Fieldnotes I," "Writing Fieldnotes II," and "Pursuing Members' Meanings." In *Writing Ethnographic Fieldnotes*, by Robert M. Emerson, Rachel I. Fretz, and Linda L. Shaw, 45–170. Chicago: University of Chicago Press.

Visit **study.sagepub.com/kirner** to help you accomplish your coursework goals in an easy-to-use learning environment.

Interviewing

Orientation

One of the most common pairings of methods in ethnographic research is participant observation with interviewing key informants. Why is this? The two methods complement one another: Frequently, participant observation provides data on *real culture* (what is actually happening) and gives the research greater experiential insight into these events, whereas interviewing is a means to understand both *ideal culture* (what people think should happen—the patterns they recognize as normative) and the ways in which people understand their own lives, including meanings, emotions, and knowledge. Interviewing has an advantage as a method for when we wish to know another person's thoughts or feelings, because we can't get at this information through observation or even our own experiences without a significant amount of assumption and bias. Generally speaking, interviewing is talking to people with a purpose, and it is an integral part of many (if not most) qualitative research designs.

Types of Interviewing

Interviewing, in general, makes intuitive sense to many students. It's natural that when we want to know things about someone's experiences, thoughts, or feelings, we'd ask them. But there are a variety of types of interviews and specific ways that make interviewing different from an ordinary conversation. **Unstructured interviews** are the most like a normal conversation. They happen everywhere, at any moment when we can have a chat with someone, and they're generally like ordinary conversations, except that we have research questions in mind

Chapter Learning Objectives

Students will be able to do the following:

6.1 Describe various types of interviews and their advantages and disadvantages

6.2 Analyze interview questions to ensure they are clear, open-ended, and nonbiased

6.3 Describe different probing techniques

6.4 Describe the ways inaccuracies can be produced in interview data

Unstructured interviews: The type of interview most like a normal conversation, which happens anywhere and at any time, without prior scheduling, but focuses on the research question.

Structured interviews A highly structured type of interview in which people respond to a set of stimuli that is presented as identically as possible to each participant.

Interview schedule The highly structured guide to introductory and follow-up questions for a structured interview.

In-depth interviews A type of semi-structured interview that is designed to gather a lot of information in great detail on a narrowly defined subject area.

Oral histories A type of semi-structured interview that is designed to help a participant tell their life story in detail.

Semi-structured interviews Logically structured but relatively open-ended interviews that schedule a time and location for each interview in advance.

as we're chatting. Unstructured interviews are usually embedded in participant observation. As we participate and observe, it brings to mind questions we have—such as "How often does this happen?" or "What does this mean?" or "How did you learn how to do that? Who taught you?" Like children would while learning their own culture, we often voice our questions to those around us when we have an appropriate time to do so, seeking answers. However, we have no standardized, uniform set of questions we're asking every informant—instead, the questions we pose are generated by the immediate context.

Structured interviews are at the other end of the spectrum. They ask people to respond to a set of stimuli presented as identically as possible—in the same order from participant to participant. This uses an **interview schedule**, which guides not only the questions and order but also complex chains of questions ("if . . . then" structures). Structured interviews structure not only the questions but the order of questioning and sometimes the potential answers as well. In between these two poles are semi-structured interviews. These types of interviews are designed to elicit the maximum amount of information from an informant (often someone who was specially chosen because they have a lot to share on the topic and/or are known as an expert in that area). Common types of semi-structured interviews include **in-depth interviews** (which are designed to elicit a lot of information about a narrowly defined subject area) and **oral histories** (which are designed to help an informant recount their life story).

Semi-structured interviews are, unlike unstructured interviews, scheduled activities that usually take place apart from the everyday tasks we might partake in during participant observation. Unlike unstructured interviews, semi-structured interviews follow an **interview guide** that has a list of open-ended prompts or questions that will be posed to all participants. This list of questions, however, allows for a wide range of responses and is designed more to open up a deep and complex conversation, as opposed to structured interviews, which move participants through a set of questions in a highly structured order. Generally speaking, the set of questions that are posed to the participant may shift based on how the conversation goes—not only in order but also in terms of follow-up questions that the interviewer uses to get more information on key topics, contextualized by the conversation at hand. This chapter will focus on semi-structured interviewing as a method, because it is one of the most common to pair with participant observation and unstructured interviews. This is because semi-structured interviews are highly efficient ways to acquire a lot of deep, rich information in a relatively short amount of time, and they produce data that are difficult to generate through participant observation, in ways that consistently collect information from a number of different participants. See Figure 6.1 for a summary of the types of interviewing.

Aside from the degree of structure of interviews, researchers have to make decisions about whether interviews will involve only one participant at a time or more than one. **Group interviews** occur when more than one person at a time are involved in the interview process. This can happen because a researcher chooses this as a method or because participants simply gather and start having a conversation during the interview. For example, a researcher may be interested in the ways couples negotiate household chores, so they might ask both partners in a couple to be present for the interview—in part, looking (by design) for points of agreement and disagreement in response to questions. On the other hand, perhaps the researcher is really interested in how wives in heteronormative marriages think about their roles and responsibilities. They might begin the interview with only the wife present, but experience the husband getting home

Figure 6.1 Types of Interviewing

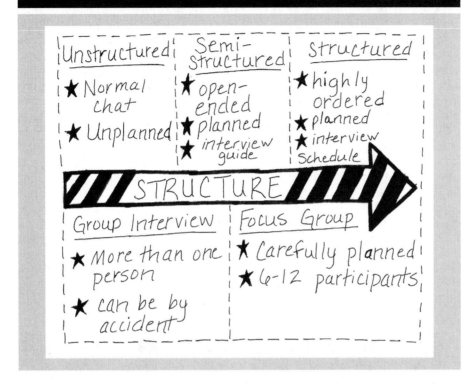

Unstructured	Semi-structured	Structured
★ Normal chat	★ open-ended	★ highly ordered
★ Unplanned	★ planned interview guide	★ planned interview Schedule

STRUCTURE →

Group Interview	Focus Group
★ More than one person	★ Carefully planned
★ can be by accident	★ 6-12 participants

during the process of the interview and then staying and dynamically interacting with both the researcher and the wife throughout the rest of the interview. Group interviews can be helpful by generating greater dialogue and illuminating negotiated, contested, and manipulated ideas. However, they can also be unhelpful or more challenging by providing opportunities for distraction, by reducing the honesty one person may otherwise have in their responses (if not under the social pressure of the group), or by having shy or marginalized people in the group dominated by others.

All group interviews are not focus groups. **Focus groups** discuss a particular topic in a group format, with a specific goal to capitalize on the dynamic conversations that occur in the group as questions are posed. Focus groups are generally selected with a lot of attentiveness to who is invited to the group—either trying to forge similarities to generate greater camaraderie and comfort for participants or by trying to ensure that a diverse and representative sample is chosen. Unlike informal group interviews, focus groups are planned and generally have a target size of six to twelve individuals (which usually means you will invite more participants than this, because a number generally do not show up). A focus group is designed to be (at best) like a lively dinner party. With fewer than six people, conversation often lags. With more than twelve people, the group typically splits into two or more subgroups who have conversations at the same time (very difficult for a researcher to record or moderate!).

Interview guide
A list of open-ended questions or prompts that guides a semi-structured interview.

Group interviews
A type of interview in which more than one person participates in the interview process at once.

Focus groups A type of interview that is specifically designed, through both selection of the participants and construction of the interview guide, to elicit dynamic conversations among a small group of people on a narrowly defined topic.

Focus groups and larger group interviews require significant skills in addition to good interviewing skills (which are established in one-on-one settings). The researcher must be a strong moderator as well as a very good note-taker. Even when a focus group is recorded, because multiple interactions often happen at the same time, it is very difficult to completely grasp the group dynamics (their interactions, expressions, etc.) and everything that is said. The researcher should be a strong note-taker and observer in order to capture this. At the same time, the researcher must be able to moderate the group—to make space and time for those in the group who are noted as being less talkative, to rein in those who are domineering or treated deferentially (and therefore speak a disproportionate amount of the time), and to keep track of the time and move people through the questions (because a lively group will often go into tangents and take up all of their time in this way). Because this is a tall order for any researcher, it isn't uncommon to have a team of two or more researchers run focus groups—taking turns moderating and note-taking, so that each of these tasks is done with a person's full attention, and so that no one becomes excessively fatigued.

Decisions the researcher makes about the number of people to interview at once and the type of interview they will use come back to their research question, as well as how they conceptualize the interviews fitting with other data collection techniques. As you consider different ways to structure your interviews, keep your research questions in mind and let these guide you toward the optimal plan for this critical task.

Discussion

Consider the research question(s) you developed in Chapter 1. What type of interview would work best to address your research question? Group or individual? Do you think semi-structured interviews would be helpful? Why or why not?

The Semi-structured Interview

Semi-structured interviews, then, follow an interview guide: a set of questions that will guide your conversation with your participant. The interview guide should be relatively brief—ten questions is often plenty if you plan to ask follow-up questions about each one. Questions should be open-ended and constructed in ways that do not pressure or lead the participant to respond in particular ways. The examples in Figure 6.2 demonstrate how to frame a good interview question.

Unlike unstructured interviews, for a semi-structured interview, you will create a calendar and schedule ahead of time. While a variety of locations can be comfortable—sitting outdoors in a public space, meeting at a coffee shop, or talking around the dining table at a participant's home—you'll need to consider several issues in making these

Figure 6.2   Good and Poor Interview Question Framing

Closed Question	Open Question
"Have you ever left your child home alone?"	"How many times in the past have you left your child home alone, if you've done so, and what were the circumstances?"

Why it's important: Closed questions (especially yes/no questions) truncate conversation and lead to short, unproductive interviews—or require a great deal of follow-up on the part of the interviewer. Open-ended questions encourage participants to consider more options, to discuss subtle nuances and details, and to provide longer and more complete answers.

Leading Question	Nonbiased Question
"You've never left your child home alone, have you?"	"How many times in the past have you left your child home alone, if you've done so, and what were the circumstances?"

Why it's important: Leading questions embed social expectations into the question, making participants feel inner social pressure to respond in particular acceptable ways. Often, the question is worded to indicate that a particular response would be shameful, less appropriate, or wrong. When an interviewer asks leading questions, they jeopardize the participant's truthfulness and openness by putting social cues into play that prompt the participant to respond in specific ways rather than others.

Vague Question	Clear Question
"Have you or would you leave your child home on their own?"	"How many times in the past have you left your child home alone, if you've done so, and what were the circumstances?"

Why it's important: When we ask vague questions—either conflating ideal and real culture prompts or failing to define critical specifics (i.e., Is "on their own" the same as "alone"?)—we fail to give the participant enough information to answer the question clearly. That is, a vague question produces a vague response—or different participants will interpret the question differently, leading to fuzzy data. In this case, for example, a participant may answer affirmatively, but you may not know whether they have left their child alone before or they are merely speculating that they would under new conditions. While some participants will ask for clarification, others (often due to shyness or social norms) will not. This means that the interviewer has to do a lot of unnecessary extra work through follow-up questions to gain clarity. Further, if the interviewer does not do this, the data are generally ambiguous and difficult to interpret reliably from participant to participant.

plans. First, issues of safety and convenience: If you'll be audio or video recording someone, you'll need to consider issues of background noise, visibility, and other practical matters. You should plan for minimal distractions (and definitely somewhere that you feel safe and that will make your participants feel safe), but you should balance your desire to avoid distractions with a need to create a comfortable atmosphere for your participant to relax and talk. Sometimes a little ambient noise and a familiar setting allow for much more openness and rapport than, for example, if you ask someone to come to an office. Many semi-structured interviews take between a half-hour and two hours to complete, so there should be comfortable seating and a lack of time pressure for both you and the participant to be interviewed.

The first step in interviewing is to acquire informed consent. Remember, informed consent is a process that informs the participant of their rights to anonymity, confidentiality, and exiting the study process when they choose. It ensures they know how much time you are requesting, the topics you will cover, any risks they incur, and the purpose of your research. After introducing yourself (if the participant doesn't know you), you should go over the informed consent form. This involves more than simply handing someone the form, even if they read the language the form is in fluently (by the way, you should have forms in the participants' native language whenever possible). Rather, you will review each of the major parts of the form in a conversational way, prompting the participant to ask any questions they have and giving them the time to do so. After all their questions have been answered and they agree to participate, you should collect the signature on the form. They should receive a copy of what they have signed, and you keep the signature page for yourself.

The informed consent process tends to be one of the most awkward and difficult parts of interviewing for a student. While other parts of the interview feel more familiar—a bit like a conversation combined with note-taking, which are both common tasks for students in their everyday lives—informed consent is new and uncharted social interaction territory. However, it's very important. Try not to rush through it. Practice this critical part of social science ethics dutifully until it becomes easier and less uncomfortable for you.

After this introduction is finished, you can begin the interview itself. The first step is a broad, very open-ended introductory question. The question should be selected to help people build trust and openness—so it should not be too nosy, emotionally challenging, or narrow. The idea is that you want to move in the interview period from general and broad to narrower and more specific questions. Starting with general questions not only frames up a logical sequence of responsive questions to probe for more details but also makes it easier to develop rapport between yourself and your participant.

In the interview, you'll bounce back and forth between addressing the questions on your interview guide (questions you'll ask of all your participants) and asking specific follow-up questions to gain more detail or clarity in participants' specific responses. You'll want to keep an eye on the time as well, making sure that you get through your list of questions on your interview guide but also asking sufficient follow-up questions to have clarity. Periodically, especially when you're about to move from one question to another, or when you're not sure that you understood your participant's response, you should ask a follow-up question that asks the participant to confirm what they said. Read them a bit of your notes, summarizing what you wrote down about that particular point, to ensure you got it right. This allows them to correct misunderstandings or gaps in what you recorded. Finally, when you near the end of the interview, be sure to debrief your participant. Thank them for their time and remind them of how they can contact you if they have questions or concerns.

One of the decisions you'll have to make is whether or not you will audio or video record the interview. Advantages to doing so are primarily that you increase your accuracy in data recording. You can review your notes later and compare them to the recording, filling in anything you missed. You should always take notes in addition to recording, both in case technical difficulties arise and because sometimes recordings miss things if a participant moves away from the microphone. Disadvantages of recording primarily have to do with the level of comfort and openness of your participant. Some people feel awkward or uncomfortable while being recorded, and some social groups feel mistrustful of recording devices. Transcribing interview recordings is also very time-consuming. Unless you pay a transcriptionist to do it for you, you can plan to spend seven hours of transcription (typing) time for every one hour of interview recording time. Select your recording option with these issues in mind, choosing recording when it is appropriate. If you are recording, always include this information in the informed consent process, and ask outright if the person minds being recorded, assuring them that they can decline recording if they choose. Once you've acquired recordings, be careful to store the data carefully until you are able to transcribe and anonymize the information, especially if the subject matter poses risk to the participants.

Ultimately, what produces successful interviews? First, assurance of confidentiality and anonymity: If participants believe their identities will be protected, they'll be more open and forthright in their responses. Second, you should encourage your participants throughout the interview. You're learning from them—periodically give them the same sorts of encouragement ("mmhmmm," "I see," "that makes sense") as you would in any interesting conversation. As much as you can, let your participant lead in the conversation. Let them talk about details that most interest them or that they feel are most necessary to impart. While you do need to keep track of the time and ask your questions, as much as you can, make this like a normal conversation—but one that gives more time to your participant to provide their insights and experiences. That said, interview guides should be relatively short. With much more than ten questions, you'll feel rushed and have little time for following up on details or letting the participant lead the conversation. Keep your questions clear, succinct, and necessary—if the question doesn't really address your research question, it shouldn't be asked.

As you listen to your participant, listen to what isn't said along with what is said. When you ask a question, are there glaring gaps in the response? Does your participant take a long pause, look upset, stare into the distance, take in a sharp breath? Body language and what isn't said—either because it is absent or because it is nonverbal—matters. Sometimes, it matters more than the words people use. This is also true for tone and volume of voice. What we mean is a combination of the words we say, our tone, and our body language all at once. It's important to capture the subtle nuances in people's responses and not only their words. Finally, ensure that you're sensitive to cultural norms. These include norms about what you should wear and how you should present yourself, how formal or informal the conversation should be, and whether recording is appropriate or not. Take time before you start the interview stage of your research to understand the cultural rules around such conversations, and find ways to make the process as culturally appropriate and familiar as you can.

Discussion

Based on your research question you've been developing, try writing four or five interview questions to get started in the planning process. Try to write one or two general questions to start the interview and two or three more specific, narrower questions that you'd use later in the interview. It's always a good idea to share with a friend or colleague in class to get feedback on each question itself—whether it is clear or not, whether people feel pressured to answer in certain ways or not, and so on. You can then use this feedback to improve your questions.

Interactions during the Interview

You've probably surmised that getting the participant to comfortably converse freely and with ease is a key factor in successfully collecting data through interviews. Participants vary considerably in how easily they adapt to the interview process and begin to provide greater details. They also vary a lot in how clear their responses are. Some people have a gift for clarity in their discussions, and some don't. The interviewer can facilitate clarity through follow-up questions and repeating back to the participant what they thought was said for confirmation. The interviewer can encourage free-flowing conversation (and plenty of it!) through probing. **Probing** stimulates a respondent for more information while not leading them too much. Probing is essential and sounds simple, but it's actually hard to master timing, use, and variety so that the conversation feels natural but produces more detailed information than an ordinary conversation would. Popular probing techniques include the following:

- *Silence:* In many cultures, long silences in a conversation are awkward and prompt someone to volunteer more information. (But if you wait too long, it will be extremely awkward and may compromise the participant's comfort level too much.) The technique of silence during an interview is highly effective but also rests on the ability of the interviewer to overcome their own socialization that prompts them to talk when the other person is not. Silence is crucial as a probing technique because frequently someone will have a long pause when they're gathering their remaining thoughts on a topic. If we preemptively move on to the next question, we haven't given the person adequate time and social prompting to think more carefully about the details of the response and provide all the relevant information.

- *Echo:* Echoing is when the interviewer repeats back to the participant, in new words, what the participant just said. This not only serves as confirmation in cases where the interviewer needs greater clarity or assurance that their notes were adequate but also facilitates the conversation. Frequently, participants will respond with confirmation and then remember other things they wish to

Probing Interview techniques that stimulate further detail or conversation without leading the participant.

impart related to that point—reopening the conversation and offering greater detail to the interviewer.

- *"Uh-huh" and nonverbal responses:* If you pay attention to conversations with friends or colleagues, you'll find that many people foster ongoing discussion through a variety of encouraging noises, expressions, and body language cues. As an interviewer, you will also need to master these in order to facilitate the interview. Understanding or encouraging noises, such as "uh-huh," "yes," and "wow," move the conversation along without prompting the participant to focus on any specific topic. Expressions and body language should be encouraging and mirror emotions that the participant demonstrates—a difficult story of grief should be received with a different facial expression and body language than a humorous story about a bureaucratic system. While for many people this is intuitive, in an interview, we have to remind ourselves to be in the facilitator role constantly and to encourage our participants, because they are less likely to do so for us (because it is a strange sort of conversation).

- *"Grand tour" questions:* Grand tour questions are longer questions that are used in particular ways to prompt responses to more nuanced or difficult topics. Usually, the grand tour question provides a specific situational context or set of information, to which the participant responds. The interviewer may use a grand tour question to open a sensitive topic that otherwise would prompt withdrawal and social pressure on the part of the participant. For example, they might ask, "If a person were really broke this month, and had to pay rent so they weren't on the street with their kids, would it be understandable if they sold drugs to maintain their apartment?" If your study is on the black market economy in a specific town, this question would allow you to lead into challenging questions without making them personal. Other uses of the grand tour question include clarifying what you're studying through providing a situational context to which a participant responds or expanding on a prior question.

Many students find that one of the harder situations to face as a new interviewer is what to do when a participant responds, "I don't know." Far too often, a new interviewer will simply give up and move on, taking this response literally. However, "I don't know" means all sorts of things. For some participants, it means "I don't care." That is, the person is bored with the question, or they've never considered it before because they never had the motivation to do so. These participants may have something to share with you if they are re-prompted and assured that anything they know and could share would be valuable to you, and they can have time to think about it if necessary. For some participants, "I don't know" means "It's none of your business" or "I want to change the subject because I'm uncomfortable." In these cases, the participant actually has quite a lot of information but is resistant to sharing it. With assurances that would build trust, or perhaps by shifting to a related grand tour question, this participant may open up with valuable data. Very frequently, participants respond with "I don't know" when it would take them some time to think of their response, and they don't want to waste your time or appear stupid. Assuring them that you (and they) have time, and that you're genuinely interested, can prompt them to give that thought to the question and provide you with information. Interviewers need to work on becoming adept at reading the nonverbal (body language, tone, facial expression) cues of their participants so that they can probe in appropriate ways when participants initially shut down the conversation. This opens the door to further response, and the participant can always assure you and clarify if they really do not know an answer.

While many of these techniques come intuitively to some people, for others, they're more difficult. Because boys tend to be socialized to facilitate conversation less than girls (in the United States), beginning male interviewers often find it more challenging to adapt to the facilitator role (and often must practice more, rather than intuitively producing lengthy interview data). Some cultures are more reticent than others, and, of course, all interviewers have to adapt to cultural norms around conversation in the culture of their participants—including such things as how far away to be from the other person during a conversation. As is generally the case, practice is key to becoming a good interviewer. Facilitating conversation, active listening (being fully present for the conversation and listening for understanding), and note-taking are all important skills to practice regularly.

Discussion

In the next conversation or two you have with someone, bring your role in the conversation to mindfulness. Do you facilitate or not? How do you facilitate? Begin trying out, in ordinary conversations, techniques of probing and facilitation. Practice active listening and full presence. Use your everyday life to become a better listener and conversationalist, which will make you a better interviewer.

Interviewing and "the Truth"

Once you get participants talking and the data come rolling in, it is tempting for new researchers to think their interview data reveal "the truth." They don't. Interview data are one piece of a broader puzzle. Interview data are also stories told to you by your participant. They're the participant's interpretation of their own experiences, thoughts, and feelings in light of your prompts. As such, they're subject to a variety of drivers that produce a particular set of responses at a particular time, including your participant's agenda and identity, your identity (and the participant's perception of it), and problems that frequently plague interview data accuracy.

One of the biggest challenges with interview data is that while people may think they are telling you the truth, they are often inaccurate. Why? There are lots of reasons this happens. Participants generally want to be helpful to the interviewer, as well as to appear intelligent. This means that they will often try to answer questions for which they really haven't had clear thoughts until you've asked them. They'll generally try to answer those questions almost immediately after you've prompted them, because this avoids awkward pauses in the conversation and because many people feel stupid when they ask for a moment to think. This means that your participants will sometimes try to answer even when they don't understand the question; they don't have clear memories in order to craft an accurate answer; or they haven't sufficiently considered such a question before, so they use rules of thumb rather than take time to reflect on the "real" answer. In addition, some participants may consciously manipulate their response to serve their own needs—those needs can range from wanting you to like them to wanting the outcome of your study to be a certain way. Again, the interviewer has to use subtle cues to intuit whether or not the participant is responding without adequately understanding or considering the question, or if they have a specific agenda, and use follow-up questions to assess these issues further. Because of this, as researchers we should be mindful that interview data don't always portray everything we are asking about accurately. At the same time, these data provide valuable insight into participants' own thoughts and feelings and the ways in which they craft their stories—and this kind of data is not easily acquired through other methods.

Finally, there are various interactions that usually occur in the interview process that often make the interview data less than optimally accurate (see Figure 6.3).

Response effects are differences in the responses of people being interviewed based on the characteristics of the interviewer. These characteristics might include ethnicity, age, and gender. Essentially, participants will respond to different interviewers differently—not only because of their differing conversational styles but also because of assumptions participants will make about them vis-à-vis the participant's identity. A man, for example, will often respond quite differently to a male interviewer than he would to a female interviewer. At times, these different responses depend somewhat on the research question and the interview guide itself. In some cases, where the questions are threatening, such as questions about illegal activity or trauma, these response effects are heightened. In other cases, if the participant perceives the interviewer as inappropriate for acquiring knowledge in a particular domain, they won't share information that they otherwise would.

Expectancy results in the interviewer getting a response they expected because they shaped the response. This can be because they wrote leading interview questions, but responses can also be shaped by subtle cues when you're actively interviewing someone—such as leaning in closer to them, crinkling your nose in disgust as you ask a question, or laughing at the end of a question. We have to be careful about how we ask questions, as well as the words we use to ask them. **Deference** happens when people tell you what they think you want to know. People like to be helpful, as a general rule. We have to be careful that we curb the tendency for participants to assume that they know what we want to hear and to offer this to us.

Social desirability happens when participants tell you what makes them look good. This is a huge issue in accuracy, because it often subconsciously affects people's memories and self-reflection. People regularly underreport or over-report all sorts of behaviors—for example, how frequently they eat fast food or how much they give to charity in a year. They often tend to bend their self-assessment of their emotions to fit with socially acceptable feelings. Thus, a man asked about his feelings about a recent loss may say he is angry, when he is also afraid. Social desirability effects increase even more when combined with **third-party effects**, which occur when a third party is present during the interview. This not only complicates the dynamics of interactions but also brings up more complex, multilayered desires in the participant to be viewed as socially desirable. In being aware of social desirability as a factor in the construction of data, interviewers can take greater actions toward assuring participants that there are no right answers to questions and building rapport.

Response effects Differences in the responses of people being interviewed based on the characteristics of the interviewer.

Expectancy When an interviewer gets a response they expected because they shaped the response.

Deference When the interviewee tells you what they think you want to know or hear (rather than answering truthfully).

Social desirability When the interviewee tells you what they think will increase their social standing or status.

Third-party effects When the presence of a third person during an interview changes how the interviewee responds, usually due to issues of social desirability.

Figure 6.3 Pressures that Produce Inaccuracies in Interview Data

Pressures that Produce 😞
Inaccuracies 😞

1. RESPONSE EFFECTS...
because of your identity

2. EXPECTANCY...
because of your actions

3. DEFERENCE...
because they want to
help too much

4. SOCIAL DESIRABILITY...
because they want to
look good

5. THIRD-PARTY EFFECTS...
because they are
responding to someone
else present

Discussion

Think critically about topics, questions, and/or interviewer characteristics that might cause you to respond in ways that aren't entirely accurate. Try to get into your participants' shoes through doing so. What could the interviewer do or say that would help you be more accurate? Given the questions you've constructed so far and your positionality vis-à-vis your participants (based on their and your characteristics), what response effects and accuracy issues do you expect to find in your interview process? How will you respond to minimize these effects?

You've now learned about the two biggest methods of data collection in ethnographic research: participant observation and interviewing. These two are usually paired in ethnographic fieldwork because participant observation allows us direct data collection on human behavior, while interviewing people allows us to collect data on people's thoughts and feelings. You've tried your hand at participant observation and writing field notes, and now it's time to try interviewing people and transcribing interview notes! You should continue to build your skills as a researcher in your everyday life as you work toward the culminating assignment for this chapter in the workbook (Activity 6.7). Try to build mindfulness in how you interact with others while having conversations, and build your skills at probing and active listening as you talk with your peers, family, and others. Remember to reflect on your internal thoughts and feelings as you become more aware of your conversational skills and style.

Reflective Prompts

1. What kind of plan and commitment can I make to improve my weaker skills?

2. Can I select and justify an appropriate interview method for different research questions?

3. Am I comfortable with analyzing interview questions to ensure they are clear, open-ended, and nonbiased?

Case Study

Vélez-Ibáñez, Carlos G. 2017. *Hegemonies of Language and Their Discontents*. Tucson: University of Arizona Press.

Vélez-Ibáñez, Carlos G., and Greenberg, James B. 1992. "Formation and Transformation of Funds of Knowledge among U.S.-Mexican Households." *Anthropology and Education Quarterly* 23, no. 4: 313–35.

The Project

The question we started with was "How have Mexican households changed over time?" For us, this included changes to language, income, wealth, roles, migration, occupation, education, and generational changes and shifts. From that beginning, we created a questionnaire. In part, this was based on the work I'd done in Central Mexico, where I did a stratified random sample study of 1,026 households asking basically the same questions. But that was only after spending about a year in intensive ethnographic observation and experience, and then generating the questionnaire. We knew that basically the questions I was asking in Central Mexico were probably also pretty good for our study in Tucson, Arizona. The difference was in Central Mexico, about 95 percent of the population was unemployed or underemployed. In Tucson, we

(Continued)

(Continued)

had an entirely different stratified random sample of Mexican households, defined by where they were located, because Tucson itself is distributed in a stratified way. We then generated a stratified random sample of seventy-five households to be treated intensively with interviews as well as the questionnaires. This is how we went beyond what sociologists would do. We had a lot of room for open-ended questions, depending on our observations while conducting the project.

What is something that you learned that you couldn't have known if you hadn't done interviews?

When we looked at both the questionnaire responses in terms of occupation, education, areas of information, and knowledge they had, and the follow-up open-ended questions in interviews about what they were interested in, we saw in their interview responses that they had skills and knowledge tangential to their questionnaire responses. For example, there was the official job and income someone had, such as a man who was a carpenter and built houses. But in interviews, we'd learn he was also building toys on the side, and his wife is selling them at a swap meet. There is a lot more skill and knowledge there in that household than what's official in their occupation. So our focus moved from an occupational response to a knowledge response. We also had a person who did nothing but take photographs of the households outside and inside. The photographs tell you a lot about what the household values. We took pictures of their pictures. Everything is important; there's nothing that isn't. Even, maybe especially, what you don't see—what is missing—is important.

How did your findings integrate collegial relationships with other academics?

When we analyzed this and charted it all up on the wall, we saw so much depth in these different forms of knowledge. I was chatting to Jim Greenberg about it, and he said, "This is like Marxist notions of funds of rent," and I thought, "Wait, they're more like funds of knowledge." On top of it, we saw that the children would go to Mom while she makes these toys, and they'd go bother her. And then Mom might say, "Juanita, help me sand this wheel." And then she might correct the child as the child is sanding that wheel, and that's transmission of knowledge. The interesting part is that my friend Luis Moll (an educational psychologist) recognized this (and he's more of a cognitive person than me—I'm a materialist type), and he said, "Maybe you should look at Vygotsky [a famous developmental psychologist]." So we put together a proposal to apply this notion of funds of knowledge to the public schools, so that teachers could become anthropologists of their students' households and use it in the schools to increase parent engagement and student learning outcomes.

This was picked up by Luis Moll in education, who worked with one of my graduate students and a third-grade teacher (who went on to her own doctorate after applying it in her classroom). There are over five thousand citations of that work. It became highly circulated. The last generation of the funds of knowledge concept for me was in the last book I wrote, where I expanded the idea to hegemonies of knowledge. I detail in the pre-Hispanic period to the present how language gets imposed on populations who don't want it, which is tying studies of dual-language programs to the funds of knowledge concept.

We started in 1982 with a scientific project on the ways Mexican households changed over time, and I ended up discussing dual-language programs in 2017.

How did you gain rapport with the interviewees?
We pre-contacted each household, and we sent them a follow-up letter as well. This was before e-mail. We oversampled because we knew we would get denials. So in this way, we could generate the right number. Always oversample! That's the trick. And if something gets interesting in the oversample, we leave the oversample as it is.

What advice do you have about interviewing, based on your research career, for beginning researchers?
Know yourself first. If you don't know why you're doing what you're doing, you'll filter your questions and project on the people you're working with through your feelings about yourself. That skill comes from training. At University of California, San Diego, we had a dual anthropologist and psychologist, and we were given a client for a year. During that year, you could only ask questions as the aftermath of their response, not any question you generated ahead of time. So your first question was "Can you tell me everything you remember between ages zero and five?" That question then led over the year a whole series of questions generated from their responses. We taped all of these, and so we would listen to our questions, their responses, and our questions following up on their responses. We'd gauge how many of our follow-up questions were really based on their responses, versus what was in ourselves and not related to their responses. This gave us a strong and useful lesson in being mindful about projecting ourselves into our interviews.

Case Study Reflections

1. How did participant observation (ethnographic fieldwork), interviewing, and questionnaires (surveys) work together in the study design? Why were each of these methods important to answer the central research question?

2. What did Vélez-Ibáñez and Greenberg specifically learn from interview data that did not arise in the survey data? Can you imagine another example where interviews and surveys might produce different results?

3. What do you notice about the importance of talking to colleagues (including across disciplines) when interpreting the results of a study?

4. What are some key lessons you can use from this study in your own interview research to gain cooperation with representative participants and collect data skillfully?

STUDY GUIDE ●━━━━━━━━━━━━━━━

Note: Students should study each concept with attentiveness to defining, explaining with examples, and describing or demonstrating process. This is not a list of terms to define; it's a list of concepts and processes to master.

Unstructured interview

Structured interview

Interview schedule

Semi-structured interview

Interview guide

Group interview

Focus group

Probing

Response effects

Expectancy

Deference

Social desirability

Third-party effects

FOR FURTHER STUDY

Bernard, H. Russell. 2018. "Interviewing I: Unstructured and Semistructured." In *Research Methods in Anthropology*, by H. Russell Bernard, 163–94. Lanham, MD: Rowman and Littlefield.

Pelto, Pertti J. 2013. "In-Depth Interviewing: Case Interviews." In *Applied Ethnography: Guidelines for Field Research*, by Pertti J. Pelto, 157–68. Walnut Creek, CA: Left Coast Press.

Visit **study.sagepub.com/kirner** to help you accomplish your coursework goals in an easy-to-use learning environment.

Introduction to Coding and Analysis

Orientation

You've participated and observed, and you have some field notes you've written up based on your jottings. You also have some interview transcripts from conducting your in-depth interviews. Now what? How do you go from notes to conclusions? What comes in between? Qualitative analysis can be messy, but there are methods to the madness. Just as there are many types of methods for data collection, there are also many for **analysis**. In this chapter, we'll explore just two common methods for analysis to begin with: one deductive form of coding (deductive latent content analysis) and one inductive form of coding (grounded theory). This will provide a foundation from which you can analyze many types of data and identify patterns in your data that are worth writing about.

What Is Coding?

When you have high-quality field notes or interview transcripts, they serve as a dataset for analysis. Participant observation and interviewing are the ways you have collected data, but then you still need ways to interpret those data and reach conclusions. A good place to start is to read your field notes and interview transcripts from start to finish. As you do so, don't try to analyze specific pieces of your notes or transcripts yet; simply allow yourself to reflect on your notes as a complete dataset. As you read, if you have thoughts on your notes, you might write these down in a separate notebook (not directly inserted in your notes) as a series of analytical memos. Often, when first reading their field notes as a complete dataset, researchers begin to truly appreciate how their relationships with participants and their own understanding changed over the course of their fieldwork. You may also

Chapter Learning Objectives

Students will be able to do the following:

7.1 Determine the difference between abbreviating and coding and between summarizing and analysis

7.2 Make decisions about approaching data through inductive versus deductive coding and justify decisions

7.3 Distinguish between manifest versus latent content and understand how to perform deductive latent content analysis

7.4 Understand how to perform grounded theory analysis

7.5 Understand how to categorize coded data to identify themes that shape ethnographic writing

7.6 Describe a process for outlining and writing ethnographic narrative using excerpts from field notes and interviews

129

recognize some patterns that recur in your notes. You should record these thoughts as you have them.

Once you've read your notes to refresh your memory of your time in the field as a whole, it's time to start finding patterns, themes, and variations in your notes regarding settings/contexts, behaviors, and participants' thoughts. The way that we do this is through coding. **Coding** is an analytical process by which you identify important bits of information that recur in your data and keep notes on what these are. Coding can be done inductively and deductively. If you remember, your first step of analysis was writing your field notes. Through your choices in selection and presentation, you completed your first conscious iteration of analysis, deciding what was important to write and how to write about it. Coding is the second step of analysis.

Many students confuse coding with abbreviating or summarizing. Abbreviating is using a shortened form of a word or a phrase. Coding is the process of assigning a code to something for the purposes of classification or identification. While codes are generally short (under seven letters) so that they can help you remember them, they are not abbreviations for the portion of data itself. Nor are they abbreviations of a summary of the data. Instead, they are short, often abbreviated words (codes) that stand for a category of analysis related to your research question or a pattern you notice in the data. Note that in the non-example of coding in Figure 7.1, the researcher has merely abbreviated the data points themselves. There is no analysis happening.

If you find, over ten pages of field notes or several pages of interview transcripts, that you are generating new codes constantly but are never reusing codes, you might look carefully at whether you are really coding or you are only abbreviating. If your codes always summarize or shorten your data but never transform them into analytical categories that describe bigger patterns you're finding, the chances are good that you're

Analysis Detailed examination of the elements or structure of your data, typically as a basis for interpretation and drawing conclusions.

Coding An analytical process by which you identify important bits of information that recur in your data and keep systematic notes on what these are.

....

Figure 7.1 Non-example of Coding (Abbreviating)

SRSINC
Unfortunately, more serious incidents that occurred today include Victor resorting to name- NAMES
BULLY calling and bullying other students throughout the day; we walked our way through the school
PROCES discipline process and he was sent to see the counselor. The day ended with him choking Tye-- CHOKE
OFFICE and I sent him to the office.   COUNS.

Figure 7.2 Example of Coding

REP.   Unfortunately, more serious incidents that occurred today include Victor resorting to name- SRSNEG
COMDISC. calling and bullying other students throughout the day; we walked our way through the school
         discipline process and he was sent to see the counselor. The day ended with him choking Tye- SRSNEG
         and I sent him to the office. → OUTHELP

Figure 7.3 Example of Codebook

Code	Full Title	Definition
SRSNEG	Serious Negative Behavior	Student behaviors that cause problems for learning or social functioning at a serious level, such as violence or aggression
REP	Repetitive Behavior	Behavior that repeats throughout an extended period of time (over the course of two or more hours of the day, or on multiple days)
OUTHELP	Outside Disciplinary Help	Disciplinary actions that involve resources other than the teacher/classroom, such as going to the counselor's or principal's office
COMDISC	Communication of Disciplinary Process to Student	Teacher or other staff member communication with a student about the disciplinary process as an intervention

still stuck abbreviating and haven't actually started data analysis yet! Instead, you want your codes to speak to significant recurring patterns you see in the data (see Figure 7.2 for an example).

As you code, you'll keep track of your codes in a **codebook**. This records the code, the full title of the code, and the definition of the code (see Figure 7.3 for an example). Sometimes, you'll also include examples of data that show how the code is applied.

Additionally, you'll write analytical memos to yourself as you have ideas for further analysis, such as noticing patterns between codes (for example, relationships, similarities, or two codes that show up in the data together frequently).

Inductive versus Deductive Coding

There are two main types of coding: inductive and deductive. (This should sound familiar from when we covered induction and deduction in research design.) **Deductive coding** is when you start with your theoretical lens, create labels or categories that make sense for using this theory, and then attach labels to your field notes in appropriate places. In deductive coding, you set up a codebook in advance of coding based on your research question and theoretical framework. For example, let's say you've conducted

Codebook An organized record of your codes and their definitions.

Deductive coding Coding in which you start with your theoretical lens, create labels or categories that make sense for using this theory, and then attach labels to your field notes in appropriate places.

forty interviews with people in the United States who self-identify as Pagans (people who practice a form of nature-centered spirituality), and you're interested in whether their history of religious identity (in childhood and now) affects how they think about the relationship between humans and animals. You read about a classification system for such conceptual relationships created by Philippe Descola (2013) and decide to use his four-category classification system to code portions of the interview transcripts. You create four codes (animism, naturalism, totemism, and analogism), using his definitions. You also create codes for a variety of religions your participants may have had in childhood or earlier adulthood, as well as codes for current Pagan religious traditions. Before you turn to coding your transcripts, you've already created a codebook to use, based on your theoretical framework and research question.

Inductive coding, by contrast, is when you start with your data, create labels that make sense for important pieces of information in your field notes, and then pile those labels into larger categories that make sense. Inductive coding is also called **grounded theory**, which is an approach where you develop theory from the data, rather than selecting specific theories to apply to the data. In both cases, after your data have been coded and you have analyzed the relationships between the codes and identified themes, you'll then craft a story about the data using these themes. Overall, this process allows the researcher to move from a large set of field notes to a small number of significant themes that relate to their research question and that outline the ethnographic narrative that they'll write.

Discussion

When you consider these two basic kinds of coding, deductive and inductive, what seems more appealing to you, and why? What do you think you'd be better at doing? Can you identify your initial strengths and weaknesses in how you approach the analytical process? In becoming aware of these baseline patterns in how you think, you'll be more capable of addressing your weaknesses through practice.

Analytical Method 1: Deductive Latent Content Analysis

There are different types of **content analysis**, which looks for patterns in the meanings of documents, communications, or media. Content analysis, like grounded theory, allows you to code qualitative data in ways that transform the data into quantitatively articulated patterns. You use the codebook to code the qualitative data, and then you can count how prevalent a code is across your participants or periods of participant observation and how frequently it shows up related to another code. One of the popular ways to use content analysis is to apply it to various forms of media as data, such as films,

Inductive coding
Coding in which you start with your data, create labels that make sense for important pieces of information in your field notes, and then pile those labels into larger categories that make sense.

Grounded theory
An approach in which you develop theory from the data, rather than selecting specific theories to apply to the data.

Content analysis
An analytical method that looks for patterns in the meanings of documents, communications, or media.

television shows, advertisements, or memes, in order to understand the **latent content** of these data. However, it can also be applied to oral communications (such as dialogue or interview transcripts). **Manifest content**, by contrast, is the tangible or concrete surface content (data). See Figure 7.4 for an example of both types of content.

Figure 7.4 Example of Manifest and Latent Content

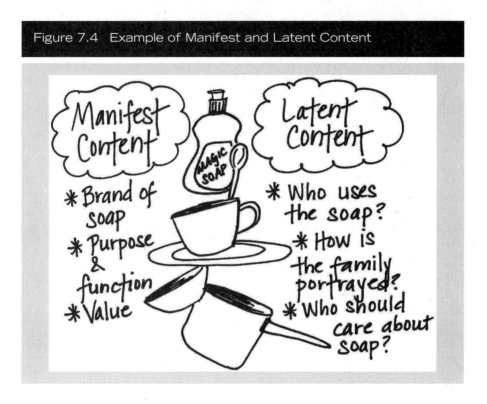

Latent content analysis focuses on investigating the manifest and latent content of interactions, media, or artifacts to understand the complex layers of meaning in culture. In this process, you take qualitative data and, by using a research question and theoretical framework, deductively build a codebook used to code the data. This process transforms the qualitative data into a quantitative analysis: counting each time in the data that a specific latent meaning arises. Let's take a look at a simple example of how this works. Suppose you are interested in how children's movies shape the ways they think about gender expectations. The manifest content would be the films themselves, particularly their storylines, characters, and settings. The latent content would be the messages the films send about gender roles and relationships. Before coding the films (the data), you'd start with generating a codebook that anticipates key dimensions of gender roles and expectations that you will want to look for in the data. These might include things such as who cleans, who cares for children, who cares for the elderly, who initiates a romantic interaction, who is shown compassion when they express fear or sadness, who is praised for their skills, who is praised for strength, and who is praised for beauty or physical attractiveness (see Figure 7.5).

Latent content The underlying meaning behind the surface content of a communication.

Manifest content The tangible or concrete surface content (data).

Figure 7.5 Example of a Codebook for Scoring Children's Movies

CODES	Female/Girl/ Woman	Male/Boy/ Man	Other/ Unclear
Cleans house, clothes, etc.			
Takes care of children			
Takes care of elderly			
Initiates romantic interactions			
Gives up/sacrifices something of personal value for romantic interaction or relationship			
Shows fear or sadness			
Is given compassion or sympathy when showing fear or sadness			
Shows anger			
Acts with violence or aggression			
Is praised for skills			
Is praised for strength			
Is praised for beauty or physical attractiveness			

In this method of analysis, based on your research question and your preexisting research on gender roles and expectations in the society in question, you've built a codebook that you'll use to score the data.

Once you code the data (for example, twenty children's movies), then you'll look for patterns in the codebook across all the films (see Figure 7.6). Aggregate (add) the codes that were counted for each of the films and then look for patterns across all the films. This process of categorizing and analyzing codes should include looking for prevalence (how often a code shows up across the data) and relationships between codes (whether certain codes show up together across the data).

Ultimately, deductive latent content analysis doesn't have to stop with just one kind of data in a study. Perhaps after finding some strong trends in gender expectations across children's films, you become interested in whether and how these emerge in young children's interactions with one another in imaginative play. You could record interactions of children playing together, or you could interview young children about what they choose to "make believe," and then code the resulting data using the same codebook you built before. You could then compare the two sets of data (the children's films as a form of ideal culture and the children's interactions as a form of real culture) to examine how the two might be correlated. This form of content analysis is particularly useful for

Figure 7.6 Example of Comparing Coded Data for Identifying Patterns

CODES	Female/Girl/Woman	Male/Boy/Man	Other/Unclear
Praised for skills	2	5	0
Praised for strength	(1)	(4)	0
Praised for beauty or physical attractiveness	5	2	0

CODES	Female/Girl/Woman	Male/Boy/Man	Other/Unclear
Praised for skills	3	4	1
Praised for strength	(3)	(5)	1
Praised for beauty or physical attractiveness	4	1	0

Memos:
Clear patterns –
♂ more praised for strength
♀ more praised for beauty
Lack of presence of androgynous or genderqueer characters.

addressing such aspects of culture: where ideal culture is communicated to those in the social group, as well as where it may differ from other communications of ideal culture (in this case, for example, parents' communications to their children), and where it may differ from real culture (behavior).

Discussion

Considering the research question that you've been working with since Chapter 1, do you think deductive latent content analysis might be useful as an analytical method? Why, or why not? What kinds of data related to your research question might be best approached using this analytical method?

Analytical Method 2: Grounded Theory (Inductive Coding)

As we discussed earlier in this chapter, in grounded theory, you begin with your data, rather than one or more specific theoretical perspectives. Instead of building a codebook first, you'll start with rereading your field notes and interview transcripts and then begin coding everything significant you see in the data. Your codebook is built as you code in grounded theory, rather than as a separate step prior to coding. As you begin coding, remember that writing your field notes was the first step in attentive analysis. You used the processes of selection and presentation to determine what was important to record and how the story would be shaped. Because of this, coding is actually your second step in the analytical process. To begin **open coding**, you'll read through your field notes carefully, recognizing points of significance or interest (without yet looking for specific themes or frameworks to apply to the data). When you find a section that you think is important, you'll highlight it. Then you'll create a code attached to this selection. As you code your field notes, you'll build a codebook. The codebook should contain the code (usually fewer than seven characters) and your operational definition for the code (that is, what the code means and what it describes), and you may also wish to provide one or two examples.

Many students find getting started in coding to be a daunting task. But start first with the small decisions and introductory chores. All your notes need to be written up into a digital format, then organized. You'll want to have an organizational system that allows you to easily locate and store a variety of notes—many researchers create folders by type of document (interviews vs. field notes), by informant (identified by a code, not their name—remember that data should always be anonymized), or by date or week. (See Figure 7.7 for an example.)

However you organize your files, be sure to do so throughout the time you assemble them so that you don't find yourself in a confusing pile of accumulated data. Your files should be stored in a secure fashion (with password protection) to protect the

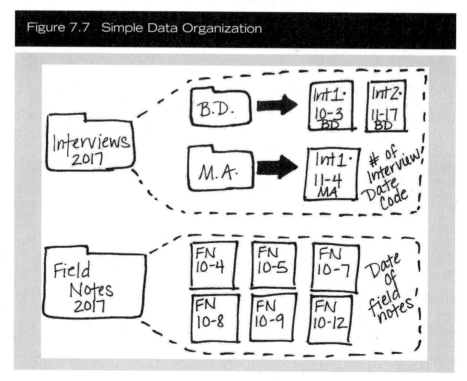

Figure 7.7 Simple Data Organization

Open coding
A form of coding that assigns codes to every part of the data that seems significant, without yet looking for specific themes or frameworks to apply to the data.

confidentiality of your participants, and you should back up your files daily to secure cloud storage and/or an external drive. Multiple copies—three or more—are great insurance. The last thing you want to do is suddenly lose months' worth of research because you made only one copy!

Once you have assembled an organized set of notes, it's time to select a strategy for coding. Coding involves some way of attaching codes to your field notes combined with your codebook (a document that details each of the codes, their meanings, and examples of their use) and a way to draft analytical memos as you code (notes to yourself as you have ideas for analysis). There are high-tech and low-tech ways to code. High-tech ways include qualitative analysis software or web-based interfaces. There are several widely used qualitative analysis software packages (such as NVivo), as well as a web-based interface (Dedoose) that will assist you with coding and analysis in a variety of ways (see Figure 7.8 for an example).

Such technology not only will allow you to select and dynamically code (with a built-in codebook) but also will offer various automated analytical tools, such as the ability to compare code frequency by type of participant (say, by gender) or to examine which codes show up together. Each of these technologies has a unique set of tools. The software packages tend to be more robust, with options for word frequency searches, cluster analysis (which helps you identify words or codes that group together across the data), and the ability to code not only text but also photos, audio, and video. However, the software packages tend to be the most expensive coding option (and the most complicated to learn), so students often don't use them unless they have access to a lab.

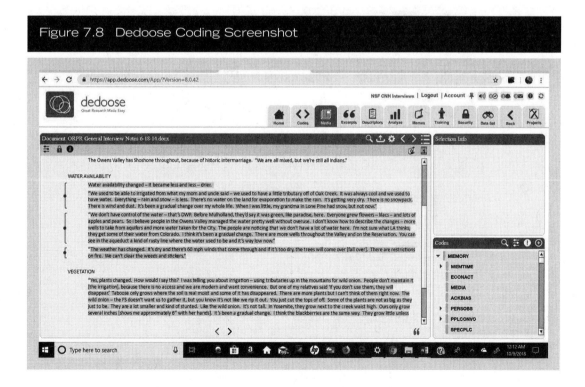

Figure 7.8 Dedoose Coding Screenshot

Dedoose provides a less robust but user- and budget-friendly option that many students find to be a helpful middle-of-the-road choice.

Medium-tech ways include using Microsoft Word for coding long transcripts and using Microsoft Excel for coding qualitative survey data. We'll discuss ways of using Excel later in this book, but let's focus for a moment on Word. Students sometimes find Word useful for coding because they usually already have access to it, and because it allows a cleaner and more easily saved way of coding (see Figure 7.9 for an example).

One way to code in Word is to use the highlight function (with colors) to select relevant text, then tie the color to a code in your codebook, kept as a separate Word document. Another way is to code in the text itself, highlighting a selection and then putting a code before or after it in caps lock or another formatting indicator. Analytical memos can be entered directly on the document using the comment function.

Low-tech coding uses hard copies of your notes. Essentially, you gather up highlighters of various colors and your notes, and you highlight relevant sections and write codes in the margins, keeping your codebook in a separate document (see Figure 7.10 for an example).

Later, you can also cut up your document with scissors and group quotes under the same code together. The disadvantage of the low-tech option is that it is quite messy and prone to the loss of data, as these become bits of paper. On the other hand, a pile of quotes that are in hard copy are the most easily manipulated (for most people) in the writing process. It is easy to take a stack of index cards, each with a coded quote on it, and arrange them in order for writing. It is more difficult for most people to do this with computer-based

Figure 7.9 Coding and Memoing in Word Screenshot

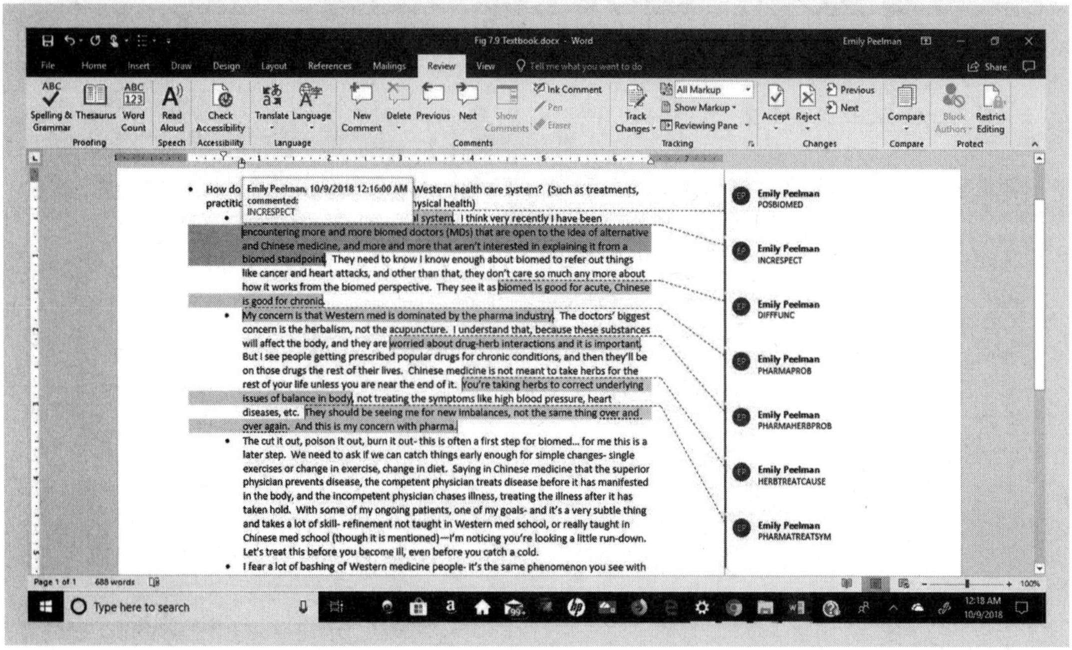

Figure 7.10 Hard Copy Coding

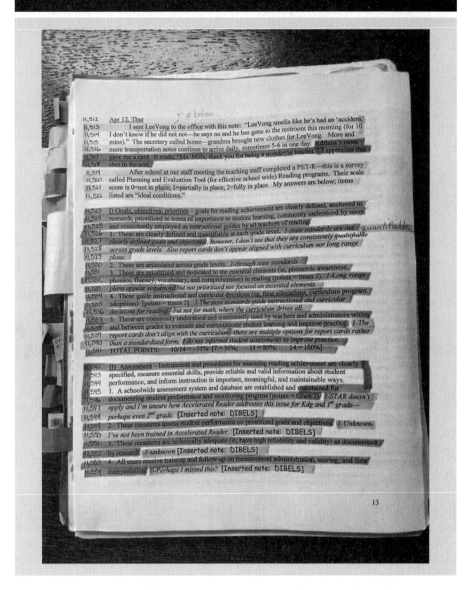

methods. While you might start out with low-tech coding, you might try a variety of ways to see what works best for you. Every researcher (and project!) is different, and some people find the advanced functionality of a qualitative analysis software indispensable, while others find it to be a distracting nuisance. Try out coding as a process—practice, practice, practice—and note your own personal preferences as you develop as a researcher.

Codes should make logical sense and, optimally, they should help you remember them. While you'll build a codebook, your coding speed will be faster if you can retain many of your codes in your memory at once. You'll use codes again and again. Generally speaking, your field notes will have recurring events, interactions, feelings, settings, and so on—so you'll reuse codes many times as you analyze the text. If you find that you rarely reuse codes, be sure that you aren't falling into that common trap for new researchers: abbreviating rather than coding. Remember, you aren't trying to abbreviate your notes, but rather are sorting them into conceptual categories that make sense. If you don't find yourself doing this, you need to start the process over again and push yourself to attach meaningful concepts and labels to your notes. You should continue open coding (grounded theory) until you are nearly always using the same codes that you've already created and you aren't noticing any new patterns in your data. This usually takes a long time. You might open-code all your interview transcripts if you have only twenty or thirty of them. If you're coding shorter qualitative narratives, such as in response to survey questions, but more of them, you might hit this saturation point after a couple hundred responses. You may find that you hit a saturation point in your field notes, but if your participant observation changed substantially over time or by season, you might find that you have to open-code all your field notes before moving on. Be patient and stick with it. Reorganize and rewrite your codebook as you realize the need to combine codes or split them apart. Remember to keep the integrity and validity of your analysis first and foremost. You want your conclusions to be meaningful and valid, so thoughtfully and carefully coding your data is critical.

Discussion

How do you feel about starting the process of coding? Does this sound easy or difficult? Exciting or boring? What do you lean toward in terms of using technology (or not) for coding, and why?

Analysis: Identifying Themes in Your Codes

As you code (whether deductively or inductively), you'll likely begin to notice patterns and have ideas about how the data relate to your research question. You should write these analytical memos down. They are spontaneous ideas that you have as you do the initial work of sorting your data into conceptual categories. After you've coded a significant portion of your data and hit a saturation point, take a look at how the codes fit together. At this point, instead of looking at your data, you'll look at your codebook. The idea is to begin to see if some of the codes fit together into larger conceptual categories that describe a relationship between the codes (and, therefore, between the interactions, events, settings, etc. in your notes associated with those codes). See Figure 7.11 for an example.

At this point, you may want to organize your codes into categories of codes that fit together in some way: They are related as types of the same interaction or pieces of the same process, for example. Essentially, you're conceptually identifying why certain codes should be understood in relationship to one another. If you're using qualitative analysis software or interfaces, this is where the exploratory analytical tools they offer are really useful. They can be used to very easily review which codes most frequently intersect in your notes. As you discover these categories, you'll want to write more analytical memos that consider the meaning of these relational categories and their context.

Once you've coded your data and identified categories that lump codes together, it's time to look at the categories and identify key **themes** that emerge from the data (see Figure 7.12 for an example). Themes articulate how the most significant categories fit into your research question. There are usually only three to five significant themes that

Figure 7.11 Analyzing the Codebook

Color	Title of Category	Description of Relationship or Similarity
GREEN	Herbalism versus Pharmaceuticals	All codes that describe the functions or purposes behind herbs and pharmaceuticals; critique either category or both, or describe their mechanisms for working
BLUE	Health Care Choice	All codes that describe specific choices with regard to treatment for health issues
RED	Poor Past Experience of Biomedicine	All codes that describe negative past experiences with biomedicine, including prejudice, discrimination, inaccurate diagnosis, and dismissiveness

Figure 7.12 Identifying Themes from Codebook Analysis

Themes
Categorizations that articulate how the most significant patterns in your data fit into answering the research question.

a student will find. In fact, it is common that professional researchers may find only a few strongly significant themes relevant to their research question. Common overarching types of themes in ethnographic writing include the following:

- What your participants thought was important

- What you discerned was important in practice

- What engaged a lot of time and energy for participants

- How a theme might be related to other themes

- Personal commitments and feelings from researcher to participant community

Theoretical orientation will also influence your themes. For example, if I use political ecology as a theoretical approach in one of my studies, I will be likely to focus on themes about power and environment. After this point, you'll return to coding—usually with a focus on the themes you've identified (this is **focused coding**). Focused coding has a different goal than open coding does. Rather than trying to identify *all* potentially significant patterns in your data, it locates *every instance* of specific, pre-identified themes in your data. When have finished focused coding, you will be left with a pile of quotes that directly relate to the trends, patterns, or relationships that you identified as the most important and relevant ones for speaking to your research question.

You can think of themes as the future headings or chapters of the story about the data. When you get ready to write this story, you should begin by rereading all the highlighted sections of your data that are associated with a particular theme (through their codes). Select particularly relevant, articulate, or interesting portions of your data for elaborating on each theme. When you've finished this process, you should have only a few themes (at most) and quotes from your data that you can use as a springboard for writing.

Discussion

For many students, coding and analysis are difficult topics at first. Many students are very unsure of themselves when they first begin the process of data analysis, because it is a lot less familiar to them than the types of skills we use in participant observation or interviewing. You might try a few critical reflection techniques to identify any uncertainties you have about the process so that you can tackle these with peers and your instructor in class. Try drawing a diagram you'd use to explain the process of deductive latent content analysis versus grounded theory. Or try explaining these processes to someone who doesn't know what they are. Then jot down the parts of the process you feel you understand and could help a peer with, as well as the parts of the process you feel uncertain or anxious about and any questions you have. Use these to seek out ways to fill in the gaps of your understanding.

Focused coding
A form of coding that looks specifically for data that relate to pre-identified themes.

Crafting an Ethnographic Story:
The Recipe Box Method

You've analyzed your data, and you have a pile of quotes that relate to a few themes. Now what? The first step is revisiting your data and initial impressions that you'd written about in memos. Reread any analytical memos that you wrote related to the themes, both from your coding/analysis process and from your field notes (the asides, commentaries, and memos you wrote during your participant observation). Reread all your data that related to the themes. Then select particularly relevant, articulate, or interesting portions of your data (field notes excerpts, quotes from interviews) for elaborating on and providing examples for each theme. You'll want to mark your most relevant and exemplary analytical memos and selected data. If you're working with hard copy notes, Post-its of various colors are great for this. If you're working with digital notes, using the comments function with a different font from other comments can help you flag selected text.

Next, you're going to get a lot of index cards. Yep, hard copy index cards. There is a method to this madness, and it's a method that helps students overcome their two biggest enemies in writing: disorganization and writer's block. If you've ever planned a party that involved food, then you probably searched for ideas for what to include in categorical stages of the evening: beverages, snacks, appetizers, perhaps a meal, and dessert. You'd sift through recipes and sort them into short lists of food that fits together at a certain time of the party. The recipe box method collects your conceptual "stuff" in a similar way and helps you organize it into one manuscript that weaves one coherent story out of your citations, data, and thoughts.

Why index cards? They are easy to visualize—you can literally see and touch them, and you can see all of them at once. They are easy to manipulate—you can stack them, fan them out on the floor, and so on. They are easy to change—it requires almost no effort to reorganize them, which means you're more likely to actually do it. They're cheap. They get you away from the computer and into the present moment, where your mind can be more creative and less anxious, by involving your whole body (reaching, stretching, touching); giving your eyes a break from screen time, which can trigger eye strain and headaches; and avoiding "blank page" syndrome—now you start off with stuff to sort, and it feels like your paper is almost done!

So how do you employ the recipe box method for writing? Put *everything* on an index card! Use *one card* per literature citation, informant quote, statistic, or analytical memo. Cards can refer to longer annotations with direct quotes elsewhere, but the card should be succinct and describe what information is in that particular source (or provide the direct quote). This avoids plagiarism and also ensures that your paper isn't choppy. Make sure every card identifies where the information came from (i.e., analytical memo, Informant 2, field notes Sept. 22). New analytical thoughts can be put on index cards as you work.

Then brainstorm using a mind map. The main point of a mind map is for you to map out the connections or relationships between your themes and ideas related to these themes. The point is to spur *creativity* and discover *all the ideas* that link to your paper, not to organize them logically. While you can do brainstorming on a computer, it is much easier and often better spurs your creativity to do it the old-fashioned, low-tech way with big pieces of paper and markers. (See Figure 7.13 for an example.)

Figure 7.13   Example of a Mind Map

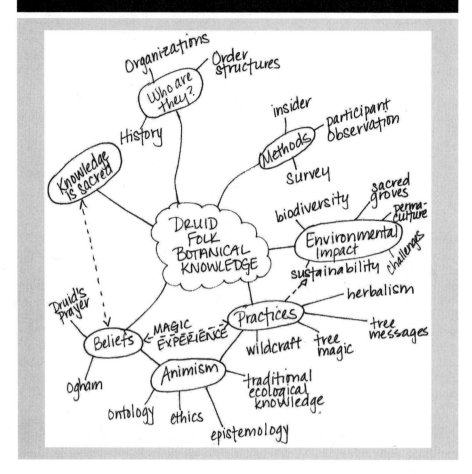

Why? This method works well for all the same reasons why using cards can help you overcome the kinds of blocks you get when you try using the computer to organize and integrate different types of sources and ideas. We tend to freeze up, associating the blank page with being forced to write. The more we can use a variety of embodied techniques in our writing process, the more we give our mind a little break from the anxiety the blank computer page can give us.

Now you'll move from brainstorm to outline. The outline is meant to give you a *logical, linear progression of ideas*. It organizes your creativity that you generated in your mind map. Look at your mind map as a guide and open up the computer . . . time to face the blank white page. What ideas go together in your brainstorm? List these one after another, each on a new line, in your computer (don't worry about sequence yet). Now play with the flow of these main ideas. In what order do they make the most amount of sense leading to concluding thoughts? Rearrange the order until they form a logical sequence.

Once you have a solid sense of the sequence, look at the main ideas you are presenting and try to identify your overarching main points for the introduction and the conclusion. *Your introduction should answer these questions:* What is the paper about, and why did you select this topic? What does your research do to contribute to the topic? *Your conclusion should answer this question:* If someone asked you to tell them, in a nutshell (let's say, one minute), what your research found out, what would you tell them? It is important to identify what major thoughts you will put in the introduction and conclusion. These parts of a paper are some of the hardest to write, but together they frame up the entire arc of your thoughts. Frequently, readers go to these two things first to get a conceptual understanding of the rest of the paper. So it is important to give thought and attention to them. Finally, identify subthemes and main supporting points from your mind map or that arise as you look at the progression of your thoughts. Write these into your outline below each of the major themes, and put each of those in logical sequence. See Figure 7.14 for a comparison of an ineffective outline versus an effective one.

A good outline will provide you with a road map for writing. It's a tool that allows you to break up your writing sessions into smaller portions (so that you're not doing the ever-popular method of cram writing all weekend). This is absolutely critical when you get to writing longer papers (the length of a published article) or thesis- and

Figure 7.14 Example and Non-example of an Outline

Ineffective (Non-example)	Effective (Example)
I. Pagan Model of Healing and Care-Seeking Behavior	I. Pagan Model of Healing and Care-Seeking Behavior
a. Goal of Healing	a. Goal of Healing
i. Example	i. Well-being rather than cure
ii. Citations	ii. Dissatisfaction with big pharma
iii. Conclusions	iii. Critique of biomedicine (holistic view)
b. Care-Seeking Approaches	b. Diversity of Care-Seeking Approaches
i. Example	i. Dual approach (biomed + CAM)
ii. Citations	ii. Vulnerable populations and CAM
iii. Conclusions	iii. Chronic illness and CAM
c. Spirituality and Healing	c. Spirituality and Healing
i. Example	i. Spiritual healing
ii. Citations	ii. Healing as a theme in Pagan spirituality
iii. Conclusions	iii. Pagan worldview reflected in care-seeking behavior (empowerment/agency)

dissertation-length manuscripts (sixty to three hundred pages). You can't hold all that information in your head or organize it efficiently without a good outline. So it pays off to do this now. Make sure that your outline uses an alphanumeric system of organization (not a bulleted list). You'll need this format to move on to the next step in the writing process: The sequence of letters and numbers forms codes that you can use to identify where index cards go. They form categorical "buckets" into which you place your index cards.

It's time to put the cards into categories based on the outline. You can color-code your outline if that works better for you, or you can just use the number/letter code system from your outline (i.e., IIA; IIIB2). Sticky notes let you do this and reuse the cards later (a handy tip if you plan to keep researching the same things over time). Hooray! Your mess of thoughts rolling around in your head has been transformed into a logical sequence of ideas and tidy piles of details! Your paper is now in many small, bite-size pieces, each with multiple sources to include as you tackle these pieces. This is much less overwhelming to most people than simply starting with a blank page, as well as more organized. It also ensures that you integrate multiple types of sources (field notes excerpts, quotes from interview transcripts, analytical memos) around each idea that holds them together. Now you're almost ready to write. You can take things bit by bit. Pick up one pile, mapped onto one theme in your outline. Put all the cards for this pile out on a flat surface. Organize your cards for this theme into a logical sequence: What sources or thoughts do you want to present first, next, and so on? You can do this with one theme at a time.

Write from the cards—you have a logical sequence of sources/materials, so now ask yourself these questions:

- What's the point of this paragraph? (introductory sentence)

- What's my first supporting material/source/point? How does it support the point of this paragraph? (transition sentence)

- What is the evidence, or the first supporting material/source/point? (detail sentence)

- What's my next supporting material/source/point? How does it relate to the last one? (transition sentence)

- What is the evidence, or the second supporting material/source/point? (detail sentence)

- When I close a paragraph or a section of my outline, how would I summarize the point I just made with those supporting materials/sources/points? (concluding sentence)

Don't forget to add in your own original thoughts, commentary, and analysis—some of this will come from analytical memo cards, and some will arise as you weave together sources/materials into one narrative. Between each "pile" or "chunk" of ideas, after you've written them, make sure you transition between main ideas (piles/chunks). You're writing ethnography!

Think about your process you've used for writing research papers in the past. What does your process usually look like? What happens, first, next, last? What obstacles or challenges do you feel you routinely face in the writing process? What kinds of criticism do you receive from your instructors? Try to identify your strengths and weaknesses in your writing process, and then think about how these will affect your ethnographic writing. How will the validity of your interpretations and discussion be shaped by your writing process, style, and ability? How can you improve in areas where you are weak? Can you identify specific steps in the recipe box method that can help your weaknesses?

Pairing the Textbook and Workbook

You've explored two different methods for analysis that work for a wide range of data: one deductive method (deductive latent content analysis) and one inductive method (grounded theory). You've also learned how to analyze your codebook to identify themes that you can use to outline your ethnographic writing and organize your data. And you've been given a process to help you efficiently prepare your data and thoughts for writing. Following these processes allow you to transform, through hard work and a lot of critical thinking, the messiness of qualitative data into valid, relevant interpretations that speak to your research question, and then to communicate these in writing to an audience. Coding, analysis, and writing, like every other methodological skill, will improve the more you practice. As much as some students find the processes of analysis and writing anxiety-producing, frustrating, or confusing at first, there is no way out but through it. Keep working on it. Don't feel bad about erasing codes and starting over. Don't feel bad about asking for help to identify what goes wrong in this process. Most students require feedback and a number of attempts before they "click" with the process of analysis and ethnographic writing. Remember, practice is the main thing! We all started here at one point in our careers. You will get better in time!

Reflective Prompts

1. Do I identify a main thread and connect the most important details to support it?

2. Can I describe the difference between manifest versus latent content?

3. Do I have questions regarding content analysis or grounded theory?

Case Study

Moses, Yolanda T. 1975. "What Price Education? The Working Women of Montserrat." *Council on Anthropology and Education Quarterly* 6, no. 3: 13–16.

Moses, Yolanda. 1977. "Female Status, the Family, and Male Dominance in a West Indian Community." *Signs* 3, no. 1: 142–53.

The Project

I'm reflecting back on my doctoral work, on my dissertation. The reason this is interesting for me, looking back, is I started out wanting to do one project in the field, and I had to switch gears and do a different one. I had no one immediately around me (this was before the internet and texting), and I thought: "Wow—what do I do?" The original research was to interview people in the political class in Montserrat, a small island in the Caribbean. Everything I'd read in preparing me to go to the field said the island was going to switch politically from a British colony to an independent nation. I could study the whole island because it was only fourteen thousand people. Other islands around Montserrat, such as Jamaica and Antigua, had gone through this process. I thought being present while this happens and documenting this as an ethnographic experience is something that had never been done in the anthropological research on the Caribbean. So that was my idea.

The reason I chose the political class as a focus was that the people were educated politicians who were the ones negotiating the independence processes on the islands. There were formal and informal political movements for independence, and there were people you could interview as active political players. I had my initial set of questions and theoretical framework, planning to combine looking at the written documentation and interviews, to understand the key factors that pushed the political class to start seeing their nation as independent. My committee had approved it all, I had IRB approval, and I went to the field. I had letters of introduction from the chair of my committee, Dr. Michael Kearney. The first person I talked to when I got there was the prime minister, because in a colony like that, there is a prime minister elected by the people and the governor who represents the Crown of England. And the prime minister said, "Oh, no. We're not going to become independent." I was stupefied. I said, "Why not?" And the prime minister said, "We're a poor island, and it's too expensive. All the services we get for free now, we'd have to pay for." He pointed out that other islands, such as Jamaica and Antigua, were more complex in their economies, and Montserrat was much smaller, and the market for their one crop (Sea Island Cotton) was getting smaller.

I had to figure out what I was going to do, since my original project wouldn't work. This took a while, because the only means of communication back then was through the mail and through one long-distance phone conversation. My adviser said, "Look around and see what's going on. See what's making people not want to make the shift to independence." I spent a lot of time looking at the data and talked to the minister of education, the minister of labor, and so on. It was a small place, so you could talk to these people. I thought, there is a lot of out-migration of people who go and work off-island.

Through trial and error, I shifted my research to looking at the impact of out-migration on the social fabric on the people left on the island, and I decided I was going to focus on women. Now, there was a big ripple that went through the anthropology department back at UC Riverside, because my committee wanted to know if I could do an entire dissertation just focused on women. This was just the beginning of the feminist movements and the rise of feminist scholarship in anthropology. I decided that there was a lot going on there, and I was trying to see if the absence of men in the hierarchy provided opportunities for women to become leaders in the family and public sphere in their own right. After much convincing of the committee that I could do a whole dissertation on women, I became the first gender-focused dissertation in our department. I did this because women's stories had not been told in their entirety. They were statistics, they were numbers, and they were a part of charts and graphs. I wanted to get past this and know who these women were and how they were coping. Clearly, they were not only making do, but their families were thriving. They were doing something in the absence of the "male head of the household" who was keeping food on the table and creating opportunities on the island that they had not had before. The questions then became more about how to get at how they lived their everyday lives. Having had that opportunity to be there and observe what was happening, I could not just base my research on my own assumptions and what I wanted to do. The people I initially wanted to interview and what I wanted to ask them were all the wrong people and all the wrong questions. I initially went about it the wrong way. I ultimately realized

that had to have the island's people speak to me in their own voices. People's voices needed to be there—not my interpretation of them, but their voices, needed to be out there. They can tell their stories a lot better than I could.

How did you select methods for analyzing your qualitative data? Why did you choose those specific analytical methods?

Because my focus was originally on the political elites, I was missing a whole lot of voices, and the analysis would have been very incomplete. In the revised version of what I did, I looked at two different groups of women to show that their voices were not monolithic. I could look at two sets of voices side by side—those of working-class women and those of middle-class women—and dispel the myth that women in the Caribbean are monolithic, as if there were one model for womanhood and those who deviated were aberrant. When I got back to the United States, this posed similar research questions about other poor women: How did they deal with economic precarity? Were their coping strategies recognized as innovative and cutting-edge, or were they stereotyped? And in the United States at the time, these poor women were stereotyped as loose (promiscuous), because some of these women had kids out of wedlock. So then I could compare women, class, and racial issues across cultures and nations, and in the United States as well.

Back in the 1970s, I didn't use computer software. Data analysis and sorting was done by hand. I did it by sorting and resorting. I had lots and lots of cards [of data] and boxes to find the themes that ran through them. I looked at my notes and highlighted things I was seeing in different colors. By the time I got halfway through the interviews, I was seeing some themes

(Continued)

(Continued)

emerge. I waited until the end of the interviewing process, and then I sorted the data for big themes, and after that I went back to see what people said about the themes. It was so much work! Then I did a network analysis, because the island was small enough. The network analysis told me if there were connections between the women across class and within class. I also did a discourse analysis on language that was used by the women, looking for their words that expressed agency. For working-class women, they would say things like, "Oh yes, I'm looking for stability," but their actions were just the opposite. They took more risk and more chances and were more entrepreneurial and opportunistic. They'd even try working off-island because they had a safety net in their social network of family and girlfriends. Even though they talked about wanting the traditional family and husband, their actions belied that. People will tell you one thing, but then you have to figure out: Is this true? Can I triangulate what they tell me with their behavior?

What advice do you have about qualitative data analysis, based on your research career, for beginning researchers?

Be flexible. You need to see what is happening versus what it is that you want to study. That may be two different things. If you do that, then there may be some way to tie what you see with how you will more effectively be able to study what you want. Sometimes anthropology is about seeing the ordinary in a different way. You don't need an exotic topic. At first, don't do any interpretation; just write it. Write what you see. Then start analysis later, thinking what the anthropological interpretation could be, when you return from the field. We automatically put our spin on it; that's how humans operate. We evolved as a species to do that automatically. We sort things out quickly to make decisions about what is next. But to be an anthropologist, you have to be able to go into that other mode to gather data. We need to destabilize that urge for automatic interpretation—slow down and listen and observe instead of assuming we know something!

Case Study Reflections

1. How did the unfortunate challenge that Moses encountered in the field—that her research proposal and questions were not going to work, after all—lead to innovative advancements in anthropological research and knowledge?

2. How was the comparative analysis Moses did of different classes of women instrumental in advancing feminist theory and questioning dominant cultural assumptions about poor women across cultures?

3. How does the process for analysis (without a computer) described in the case study help you understand how to conduct coding and analysis?

4. Why is it important to leave analysis and interpretation for later in our research cycle, rather than doing it while we are in the middle of collecting data?

STUDY GUIDE

Note: Students should study each concept with attentiveness to defining, explaining with examples, and describing or demonstrating process. This is not a list of terms to define; it's a list of concepts and processes to master.

Coding

Abbreviating

Codebook

Deductive coding

Inductive coding

Grounded theory (including the process/steps)

Latent versus manifest content

Deductive latent content analysis (including the process/steps)

Technology options for coding

Open versus focused coding

Themes

Recipe box writing method (process/steps)

Mind map

Outline

FOR FURTHER STUDY

Bernard, H. Russell. 2018. "Text Analysis II." In *Research Methods in Anthropology*, by H. Russell Bernard, 459–90. Lanham, MD: Rowman and Littlefield.

Emerson, Robert M., Rachel I. Fretz, and Linda L. Shaw. 2011. "Processing Fieldnotes: Coding and Memoing" and "Writing an Ethnography."

In *Writing Ethnographic Fieldnotes*, by Robert M. Emerson, Rachel I. Fretz, and Linda L. Shaw, 171–242. Chicago: University of Chicago Press.

Pelto, Pertti J. 2013. "Analysis of Qualitative Text Data: Basic Steps." In *Applied Ethnography: Guidelines for Field Research*, by Pertti J. Pelto, 199–216. Walnut Creek, CA: Left Coast Press.

REFERENCE

Descola, Philippe. 2013. *Beyond Nature and Culture.* Translated by Janet Lloyd. Chicago: University of Chicago Press.

Visit **study.sagepub.com/kirner** to help you accomplish your coursework goals in an easy-to-use learning environment.

Surveys and Mixed Methods Design

Orientation

You should feel quite accomplished by now. You've learned about research design, collected participant observation and interview data, analyzed your data using grounded theory, and written a brief ethnographic narrative. This means you've used two of the three most common data collection methods in cultural anthropology. Now, we'll tackle the third: survey research. **Surveys** are different from participant observation and interviews in a number of key ways, but chief among them is that they're designed to collect data *from more participants but at a more superficial level* than either participant observation or interviewing. If you think back to the chapter on sampling, you'll remember that we discussed both nonprobability and probability sampling. Survey research generally uses probability sampling (and therefore a much larger sample size) and is especially useful for studying complex, large populations that have a lot of diversity between different subgroups. Survey research often generates a mix of qualitative and quantitative data, and it is often used alongside other methods (such as participant observation or semi-structured interviews) to generate a combination of broad, superficial data for a large population and narrow, rich data for a smaller subset of participants within that population.

Mixed Methods Design

Surveys, then, are frequently used alongside other methods in cultural anthropology to provide a combination of lots of data for a population but not much for each participant (the

Chapter Learning Objectives

Students will be able to do the following:

8.1 Explain how multiple methods work together in triangulation

8.2 Describe the difference between demographic, quantitative, and qualitative questions and why each type of question is useful in survey data

8.3 Explain how to construct survey questions and a survey consent page

8.4 Describe survey distribution methods and their advantages and disadvantages

8.5 Explain how to analyze survey data using qualitative and quantitative methods of analysis, including identifying meaningful filters or demographic categories for answering a research question

survey) and lots of data for each participant but not many participants (semi-structured interviews). They're often instrumental in mixed methods research, which combines elements of qualitative and quantitative approaches. Mixed methods research affords excellent potential for triangulation, which enhances the validity of your findings by using multiple methods at once to investigate your research question—allowing you to notice points of agreement and conflict among the data. Such research enhances the breadth and depth of our understanding, retaining both the depth of qualitative research and our capacity to assess how widespread the patterns we find are, as well as whether they are equally distributed across a population or whether they differ by cultural or social subgroup. Mixed methods research also is almost a necessity in certain kinds of research questions, which may demand a variety of kinds of data in order to address the questions adequately. For example, if you are studying Americans' food habits and how these are potentially linked to a set of health problems, you might want to pair interviewing with food journals and food receipts in order to capture how people think about and remember their dietary habits, the contexts around their food choices, and their actual behavior in purchasing and consuming food.

When conducting mixed methods research, additional work is necessary to put into the design stage. It's not enough to identify a few methods that will produce different kinds of data. You have to have a plan, from the beginning, in how you think these different data will be integrated in order to answer your research question. There are three main models of how you can integrate your qualitative and quantitative data in order to yield results: merged integration, embedded integration, and connected integration. **Merged integration** interprets the findings of separate qualitative and quantitative data, after these forms of data have already been analyzed (see Figure 8.1 for an example).

Through comparing the analysis and findings from both types of data, the researcher can identify where their analysis agrees and disagrees and then analyze why they think the differences between their findings occurred. For example, let's get back to our food study. You've collected interview data (qualitative), asking people about their overall dietary habits, such as how frequently they eat fast food, processed food, and junk food. You've also asked them to give you all their food receipts for a month. The qualitative data analysis yields results that, on average, participants report eating junk and processed food a few times a week and fast food only once per week. They also say that it is hard to eat better-quality, raw foods (such as fruits and vegetables) because these are more expensive. But when you analyze the quantitative data of what they bought and

Surveys Structured interviews that are often delivered online or via mail, rather than in person; also known as *questionnaires*.

Merged integration Integration of the findings of separate qualitative and quantitative data, after these forms of data have already been analyzed.

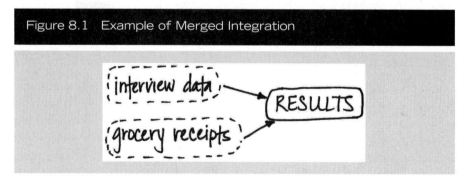

Figure 8.1   Example of Merged Integration

how frequently from their receipts, you find that, on average, they are eating fast food several times a week and processed and junk food every day and that they are spending more of their money (per meal) on these foods. This important distinction between the two datasets indicates a divergence of how people are thinking about and remembering their food choices when compared with their actual behavior. If you'd collected only one type of data or the other, your findings would be far less complex and interesting.

With **embedded integration**, your methods are addressing different sub-questions under one overarching research question. You may have primary and secondary questions, each of which are better addressed through either qualitative or quantitative approaches (see Figure 8.2 for an example).

As with merged integration, you'll analyze your qualitative data separately from your quantitative data. But unlike merged integration, you'll tackle different research questions with the two approaches, interpreting your findings to each of these sub-questions within the context of a larger, overarching research question. For example, let's return to diet-related questions. Let's say you're interested in how people choose to change their dietary habits, the sorts of resources they use, and the experiences they have in their attempts to learn new ways of eating. You formulate an overarching research question: How and why do people choose to change their dietary habits? You then break this into sub-questions: How many people in the population have tried to change their dietary habits at least once? Why did they make this choice? What new diets are people choosing? Do people struggle with learning how to eat in a new diet? What is that experience like, and what strategies do people use to help them? Then you assign some kinds of questions to a quantitative approach (such as questions about how prevalent this phenomenon is in the population, what diets people are trying to change to, and how frequently people struggle with the dietary shift) and some kinds of questions to a qualitative approach (such as people's decision-making process behind changing their diet, their experiences in trying to do so, and the strategies they employ to learn to eat differently). Each set of questions, under its approach, will be addressed through the analysis before you bring these analyses together in writing a response to the overarching question.

Finally, data can be brought together in a process of **connected integration**. Connected integration occurs when one type of data builds from another. This occurs when you're using one set of data and approach to define measurement tools (such as surveys

Embedded integration Integration of the findings from primary and secondary questions by framing the secondary question findings within the overarching research question.

Connected integration Integration of the data by generating only one type of data at a time, with the first dataset informing the formation of the second dataset.

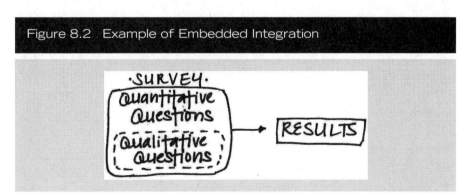

Figure 8.2 Example of Embedded Integration

or interview guides) or a future sample that you will use to generate a different set of data, using a different approach (see Figure 8.3 for an example).

For example, you might first use a survey to identify trends in the population in terms of people's health issues related to diet, and then based on these trends, select a sample of participants who are facing one of the two most prevalent health issues (let's say, high blood pressure and type II diabetes). This smaller sample could then participate in a qualitative study in which they maintain food journals (tracking what they eat, when, and why), which you'd study as qualitative documents.

Figure 8.3 Example of Connected Integration

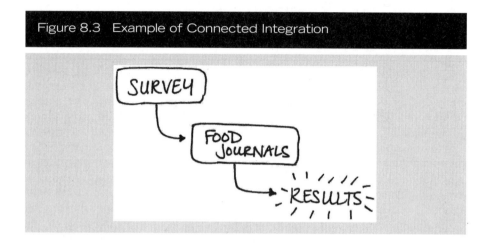

Mixed methods allows for not only multiple methods of integration but also multiple types of design (see Figure 8.4).

Remember how projects might be exploratory or confirmatory research? Mixed methods can help you do both in an iterative process. Consider how a mixed methods process can structure the hypothetico-deductive method in terms of data collection, merging quantitative and qualitative data in meaningful ways.

Figure 8.4 Mixed Methods Designs

Design	Data Integration Model
Convergent: Qualitative and quantitative data are considered together to answer a set of related research questions.	Merged *or* Embedded
Exploratory sequential: Qualitative data are used to explore a research question and develop a quantitative study.	Embedded *or* Connected
Explanatory sequential: Quantitative data are used to generate a list of more specific research questions that necessitate qualitative study.	Embedded *or* Connected

Thinking about your research question you selected in Chapter 1, try writing two columns: one for a quantitative approach and one for a qualitative approach. Then think of two or three sub-questions that fit best in each column. Which questions would work better with gathering shallow, numerical data from more participants? Which questions would work better with gathering deep, narrative data from fewer participants? Then try to identify whether these questions fit into one of the data integration models, and why. Try to also identify whether these questions are in a convergent, an explanatory sequential, or an exploratory sequential design, and why. Use this process to reflect on any part of this section that is confusing to you so that you can review with peers or your instructor later.

Survey Question Format

You've probably completed at least one survey in your life. Surveys are incredibly common ways to gather data in complex societies because they allow you to gather data from many participants without investing too much time or money. As you've realized from the earlier text, surveys fit best with particular kinds of research questions and particular stages of research. You can't build a survey, for example, without enough cultural knowledge and language savvy to know what questions to ask and how to ask them. But once you have the baseline information necessary to build a good survey, this method can be invaluable for generating a sufficient sample size to address research questions that are likely to have multiple, nuanced answers based on diversity between subcultural groups in a population.

Surveys usually ask three types of questions: demographic, quantitative, and qualitative questions. Sometimes surveys will leave out qualitative questions, but they almost always capture demographic and quantitative questions. **Demographic questions** are those that establish the attributes of individuals in a population, such as ethnicity, gender, age, sexual orientation, and income (see Figure 8.5 for an example). Demographic questions help you later sort your survey data by subpopulation so that you can compare different social and cultural groups and see if their answers differ along these descriptive lines.

Quantitative questions on surveys are those that produce numerical data without the researcher having to code the data. These can ask for a variety of types of information, such as household size (as a number of household occupants), rank-ordered preferences (such as asking participants to select their top three desired home energy programs from a list of ten options), and **Likert scale questions**. You've probably encountered Likert scale questions; they're the ones that ask you how strongly you agree with a statement on a scale of 1 to 5 (strongly agree, agree, neutral, disagree, or strongly disagree;

Demographic questions
Questions that establish the attributes of individuals in a population.

Quantitative questions
Questions that produce numerical data.

Likert scale questions
Questions that ask you how strongly you agree with a statement, on a scale of 1 to 5.

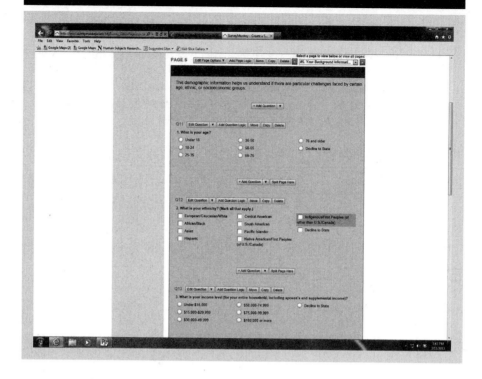

Figure 8.5 Example of Demographic Questions

see Figure 8.6 for an example). These transform information about people's opinions and preferences into quantitative data that can be statistically analyzed.

Qualitative questions, as you know from previous chapters, are questions that produce narrative text that you have to code in order to analyze. Qualitative questions are asked using **open-ended questions**, which, like interview questions, allow participants to freely respond in their own words. Contrastingly, quantitative questions are asked using **closed-ended questions** (or fixed-choice questions), which offer a specific list of options from which participants choose their answer.

Many questions can be asked in either format. For example, you could ask questions about health care decisions in a closed-ended format: "Please select from the following options where you first sought treatment when you began experiencing your chronic illness: (1) emergency room, (2) urgent care, (3) primary care doctor, (4) specialist doctor, (5) nurse practitioner, (6) acupuncturist, (7) Chinese medical doctor, (8) other, (9) decline to state." Or you could ask the question in an open-ended format: "When you began experiencing your chronic illness, where did you seek treatment first?" But just because you can ask the question in either way does not mean that the two ways of asking are the same. In closed-ended questions, you greatly reduce your time spent on analysis, because you don't have to code the answers (just count them). But if you don't have a fairly robust list of options that will make sense to your participants, you'll

Qualitative questions
Questions that produce narrative text.

Open-ended questions
Questions that allow participants to respond in their own words.

Closed-ended questions
Questions that offer a list of options from which participants select their response.

Figure 8.6 Example of Likert Scale Questions

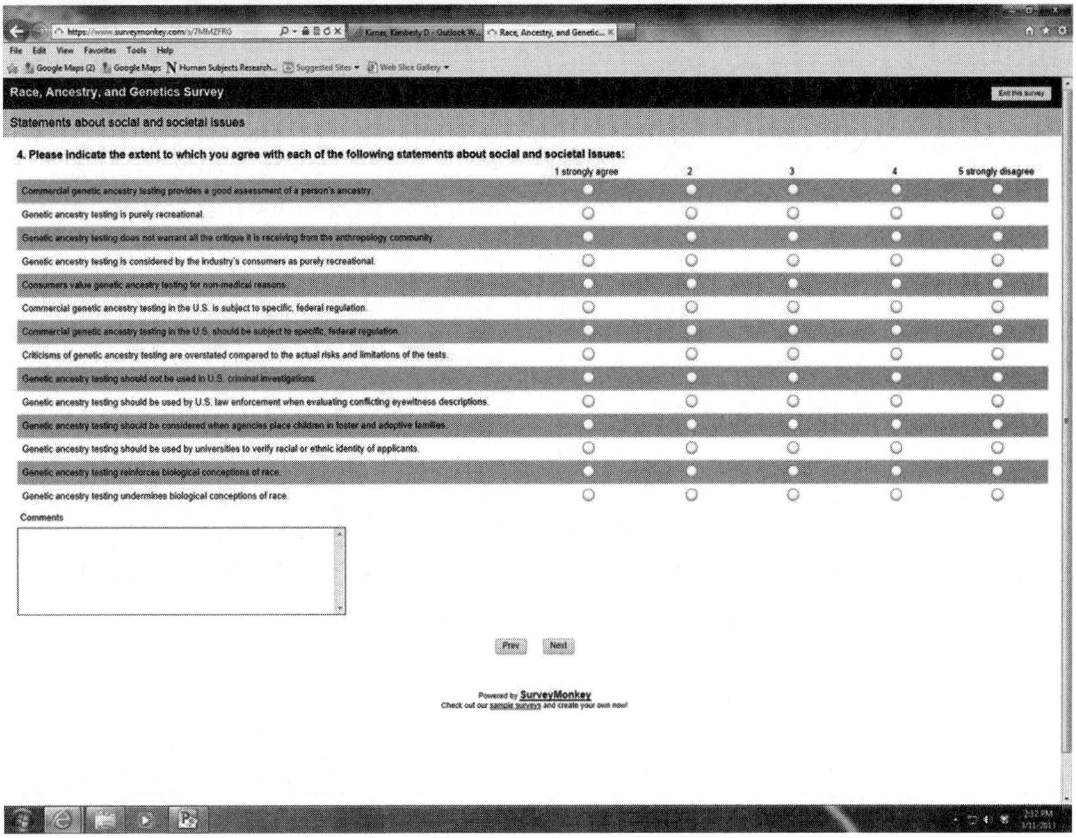

skew the data in ways that you may not even be able to anticipate. Choosing the ways in which you format and word your questions is important for maintaining the validity of your data. In some ways, it's even more important in survey research than in interviews, because the participant filling out your survey can't express their confusion to you and receive guidance on what your question meant or have follow-up questions tailored to their responses. You should consider a number of factors when deciding what format to use for a specific question:

- Do you want to "force" the respondent to quantify or clearly delineate their response? (If so, use a closed-ended question.)

- Does the response need to correspond to other large datasets (for example, the US Census)? (If so, use a closed-ended question with the same options the other survey offers.)

- Do you need to have an easy way to compare respondents and filter them by group for analysis? (If so, use closed-ended questions for demographic information.)

- Is the question possible to phrase in a definitive manner, with relevant and reasonably short lists of options? (If so, use a closed-ended question, because it will reduce your time spent on analysis. If not, use an open-ended question to ensure that data accurately reflect your participants' answers.)

- Are you exploring the topic or confirming prior research of it? (If you're exploring, you're more likely to use open-ended questions; if you're confirming, you're more likely to use closed-ended questions.)

For each of the pieces of information you'll request from your participants, think carefully about whether the information is really necessary to answer your research question (generally, surveys need to be short in order for participants to complete them—so choose questions wisely) and thoughtfully consider the type of format that each question should take in order to acquire that information.

Discussion

Think about your research question you've been working with since Chapter 1. Make a list of the information (data) you would try to collect by using survey research. Try to identify ten to twenty pieces of information that would help you answer your research question and that would be suitable for a short-answer format (i.e., rather than an interview). Then decide whether the question will be answered using demographic, quantitative, or qualitative data (and try to articulate to yourself why you made that choice). Finally, select whether you will therefore use a closed-ended or an open-ended question.

Rules for Wording Survey Questions

You now understand how to format survey questions, but how do you word the questions to maximize clarity for your participants? For ease of learning, we'll summarize this guidance as a series of rules. *Rule 1: Make sure your questions are clear.* This should be obvious, but it's actually difficult to do for many beginning researchers. If your questions are unclear, you'll get muddled data that aren't accurately representing your participants' thoughts or behaviors. For instance, "How much do you exercise?" doesn't tell the participant whether you mean frequency (three times a week), amount of time (five hours a week), or both. Clarity is absolutely the most important benchmark to strive for when conducting survey research. Along these lines, we have the next rule: *Rule 2: Don't use double-barreled questions.*

These sorts of questions ask two or more questions as part of one package. For example, "When choosing a child care provider, how much weight do you give to references and a background check?" This is really two questions in one: "When choosing a child care provider, how much weight do you give to references?" and "When choosing a child care provider, how much weight do you give to a background check?" Asking multiple questions at once is not only confusing to the respondent; it also undermines the accuracy of your data because you aren't sure what the respondent is actually responding to.

Rule 3: Use understandable vocabulary. The average reading level for US citizens is seventh- or eighth-grade. Be sure your questions are not too long, do not use vocabulary that assumes a high school or college education, and do not use jargon that is specialized in a field (unless your survey is going only to members of that specialized field, such as a survey about medical interventions going only to doctors). Be sure that your survey is produced in all languages that you want to capture in the study population. If your survey is specifically for recent immigrants, for example, you should translate it into several of the most common languages that recent immigrants in the region are speaking. The best option for translating surveys reliably is a process called **back translation**. First, you construct the survey in English (or your language). Then you have a bilingual person translate it into another language. You ask a second (different) bilingual person to translate the translation back to English (or your language). Then you compare the two English versions. Is this what you want? Are the questions an acceptable gloss of your original intent for them? This iterative process refines your translation in a way that ensures you ask what you really want to ask.

Rule 4: Respondents must know enough to respond. Some questions, such as hypothetical ones ("How would you respond if . . . ?") require contextual information that you provide in order for respondents to answer the question. Be sure that you're not assuming your respondents know background information that you do. For example, if you want to know whether someone would consider creating a fundraiser for expenses related to health issues they're having, as well as the threshold people have for doing so (in terms of need), it is not enough to ask, "Would you create a fundraiser if you had medical expenses?" This wouldn't fully answer your question because it doesn't provide nuanced context. Instead, you might say, "You had an extended illness that kept you out of work for a month and left you with $1,000 in medical bills. You're struggling to pay your bills. Would you create a fundraiser, like a GoFundMe, to ask your friends and family to contribute to your economic needs?" And then, because you're curious about thresholds, you might follow up with this: "If you said no, would your answer change if your situation weren't a shorter-term extended illness, but rather a long battle against cancer?" If the question requires background or contextual information to answer it, provide it. At the same time, keep this in mind: *Rule 5: Keep questions short, unless you are providing context or background information.* And if you do provide background information, visually separate the background information from the question. This will help your respondent not get lost while trying to determine what they're being asked.

Rule 6: Make sure your question asks what you think it asks. Look critically at the questions you write, asking yourself if the answers you might receive are what you're really trying to ask. "Are you married?" doesn't mean the same thing as "Have you ever been married?" or "Do you have a partner with whom you share a household?" Your word choice in questions should be deliberate and thoughtful, ensuring that you're asking participants for exactly the information that you need. This is also important to consider

Back translation
A process for reliable translation that involves two different translators to ensure that the translation asks the questions you really mean to ask.

for any scaled questions you ask, not only for the question but also for the responses you offer as options for participants to choose. Though your Likert scale questions may be assigned numerical values (1–5), your options for respondents should remind them of what this means throughout your survey: "Mark whether you strongly agree (1), agree (2), are neutral (3), disagree (4), or strongly disagree (5)." And this leads to the next rule: *Rule 7: Be sure to offer your respondents "decline to state," "no opinion/don't know," and/or "other" as options for closed-ended questions.* Respondents will become frustrated with your survey and either stop taking it or select neutral responses if you don't give them ways to express that they'd rather not answer that particular question, that they don't have an answer for it, or that their answer is not listed.

Additionally, take into account this rule: *Rule 8: If you ask a respondent to "choose only one response," be sure that your list of options is exhaustive and mutually exclusive.* Don't forget that such lists are often culturally grounded. It can feel uncomfortable and imposing for respondents to be forced to pick one response when their culture does not limit them in that way. For example, it is common in Abrahamic religions (Judaism, Christianity, and Islam) to view religious identity as mutually exclusive. That is, you generally can't be Christian *and* Muslim. In the Abrahamic religions, the common belief is that you are born into or convert to one religion, and that is your religious identity. A researcher who doesn't sufficiently examine their bias might phrase a question about religious identity as a closed-end question with a mutually exclusive list. However, in many religions of the world, religious identity is *not* mutually exclusive. If you're Buddhist, you can also be Shinto (the indigenous religion of Japan). Many new religious movements in the Western world allow for people to be multiple religions at once. You have to investigate your questions (and options for answers) for ethnocentrism and biased assumptions.

Finally, we have one more rule: *Rule 9: Avoid leading questions.* Just as you have to be careful about your assumptions in the answer options you offer, so too do you have to be very careful about asking leading questions, which, if you remember, are questions you phrase in a way that communicates your expected or desired response to the participant. This is particularly important in cases that ask about decisions the respondent makes or about their ethics and opinions. In Figure 8.7, can you spot what is wrong in this (unfortunately real) teachers' union survey from the early 2000s?

How might you rephrase these questions and responses so that they aren't leading the respondent and subtly socially shaming them for undesirable opinions? When you ask leading questions like these, the validity of your data is compromised. You haven't collected people's real opinions, because you haven't made an objective attempt to ask. Instead, you've asked people to respond to social pressure, and you have no way of knowing whether their response is authentically their answer or they're just trying to give you what they think you want.

How do you obtain consent for survey research, when you might not even be present with your respondent? Surveys don't usually require a signed informed consent form, unless you collect identifying information, such as a name or address. However, we still have to inform participants of what to expect, the risks, and the purpose of our survey. This is usually done using a cover sheet (for hard copy self-administered surveys), a brief explanation and handout (for face-to-face or phone surveys), or a landing page (for online self-administered surveys; see Figure 8.8 for an example).

The consent page reads as a short version of a consent form, and participants provide consent by starting to respond to the survey. When you build a survey, you should

Figure 8.7   Example of Leading Questions

15. **Which would you prefer: Our current health care system, in which most people get their health insurance from private employers, but are being forced to pay higher copays and some people have no insurance, OR a universal health insurance program, which reduces costs by covering everyone in a single program like Medicare, that's run by the government?**

☐ Current System   ☐ Universal Program   ☐ No Opinion

16. **Do you think the recent increase in gasoline prices is due more to gas companies charging artificially higher prices in order to increase profits, OR due more to existing market conditions such as a limited supply of oil in the world and the recent power blackout?**

☐ Artificially High Prices   ☐ Market Conditions   ☐ No Opinion

17. **When it comes to regulating the environment and safety practices of business, do you think the federal government is doing enough, should it do more, or should it do less?**

☐ Doing Enough   ☐ Should Do More   ☐ Should Do Less   ☐ No Opinion

18. **In general, which party comes closest to representing your political outlook?**

☐ Democrat   ☐ Republican   ☐ Green   ☐ Libertarian   ☐ Independent   ☐ Other _____

19. **How would you rate your union's efforts at...**

	Very Effective	Somewhat Effective	Somewhat Ineffective	Very Ineffective	No Opinion
communication between leaders and members?	☐	☐	☐	☐	☐
political action, getting out the vote, and lobbying?	☐	☐	☐	☐	☐
negotiations and grievance handling?	☐	☐	☐	☐	☐
organizing new members?	☐	☐	☐	☐	☐

Figure 8.8   Online Informed Consent Page

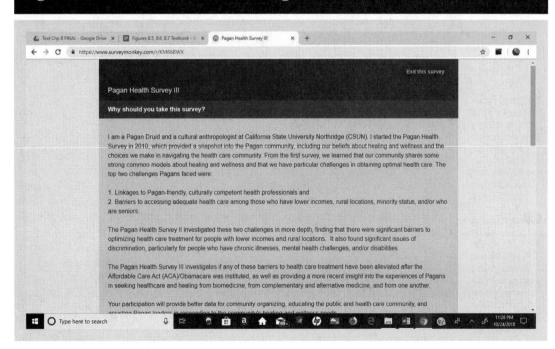

also build a consent page, being attentive to all the critical categories of information that you would provide in an interview. This ensures that your respondents know how you will use their data and what they might experience in the survey, as well as how long the survey will take.

Once you've written survey questions, you'll want to **pretest** them, which will assist you in designing an optimized survey. Before pretesting, you should have a completed, formatted survey, including a consent page. To pretest your survey, gather about a dozen people and sit with them as they complete a self-administered questionnaire. Their questions help guide your survey's clarity and improvement. You can also ask them questions about the survey, such as whether it was too long or whether certain sections were too long. You can ask them to think aloud, telling you their thought process as they fill out the survey. The whole point of this process is to refine and optimize your survey. You can't use the data you collect from the survey pretesting process for your research, but you receive valuable insight into how to make your survey clearer, more concise, and more user-friendly.

Discussion

In the previous discussion, you generated a list of research sub-questions and decided whether you'd ask for that information through closed-ended or open-ended questions. Try writing a few questions of each type (and answer options, for the closed-ended questions). Try to use the rules for survey question wording to develop high-quality questions and to check your own work. Jot down any questions that you have about the process to ask a peer or your instructor later. You might also consider asking your peers to volunteer for pretesting your survey questions!

Pretest A process of administering a survey to a very small sample while you are present, so that they can express areas that need clarity and improvement.

Self-administration A form of survey distribution through the mail or online, where participants take the survey without any assistance or guidance from the researcher.

Survey Distribution

You've written your questions, and you have a plan for formatting them. How do you get them to participants? There are three main options for survey distribution: face to face, by telephone, and through **self-administration**. There are advantages and disadvantages to each of these distribution strategies, and you should carefully assess, given your target population and your research question (as well as your resources in time and money), which of these distribution strategies is right for your research.

Face-to-face distribution, where the researcher conducts a structured interview directly with the participant and records their responses, has many advantages. Respondents can be illiterate, blind, bedridden, or very old and can still participate in the research. Your odds of failing to include people due to a variety of disabilities and age are lower than they are with the other distribution strategies. You can probe for more complete data, and the respondent can ask for clarification about a question. While the survey is conducted as a structured interview, it does allow the respondent to point out questions that confuse them and for you to clarify the intent of the question. You're less likely to have data that arise from respondent uncertainty about what you're asking them. You can easily use several types of techniques in one survey (for example, having respondents free-list based on images you provide then answer demographic questions—though advancements in online survey applications make it easier than it used to be to incorporate such questions in self-administered surveys). You can ask more questions. While respondents will rarely spend anywhere near an hour on a self-administered survey (they tend to get bored and fatigued and give up midway through the survey), they will routinely give you an hour or two for a face-to-face interview. You can hang out somewhere and do cluster sampling based on location (a mall, a clinic, a church), though usually these kinds of surveys need to be under fifteen minutes in duration because they are interrupting people's other activities. In face-to-face surveys, you get to control the order in which your respondents engage the questions. The respondent answers questions in the proper order without looking ahead, which is important for certain types of research questions. Additionally, you know who is answering and can sometimes get a sense of whether they are lying. In short, you have many of the advantages of interviewing.

However, these advantages come at a fairly significant cost, and the main cost is your time. Face-to-face surveys, like any interview, take a lot of your time. Even if you're only spending ten minutes per respondent, if you have to gather one thousand surveys (which isn't uncommon, given the necessity of a large sample size to ensure the data's reliability and generalizability), you're going to spend more than 160 hours on data collection alone (not including getting to and from the delivery location). When you consider that you could mail out the same survey and spend no more time than it takes to go to the post office or send an e-mail, you'll understand why so many researchers use self-administered delivery strategies, despite the advantages of face-to-face surveys. Face-to-face delivery strategy is expensive in both time and money, and it can be difficult to locate respondents and schedule them to take the survey. There are a few other disadvantages as well. Face-to-face surveys are intrusive and reactive. As in interviews, people may feel like they have less privacy, and they also might react to your characteristics and qualities. Subtle changes in your voice and posture can lead respondents to answer in certain ways, just as they can in interviews, and you'll find that your surveys are subject to response effects. This makes face-to-face surveys less standardized, especially if you have several researchers conducting them at once. Still, for certain kinds of research, face-to-face delivery strategies are nearly required. For example, if you wish to study populations who are very hard to reach otherwise, such as homeless people (who may not have a phone, e-mail, or a physical address—and who can be hard to find), it is far better to show up where they are to conduct surveys face to face. This is why many cities that conduct surveys of their homeless residents enlist the help of volunteers to deliver these surveys as structured interviews, conducted by canvassing the city in a logical way in which each researcher has a jurisdiction, so that as many respondents as possible are reached.

The second delivery strategy is the telephone survey. Compared to face-to-face surveys, telephone surveys are inexpensive and convenient. Researchers don't have to travel to show up on site somewhere, so while the time investment is similar, the scheduling demand and cost are much reduced. Phone surveys combine the impersonal quality of self-administered surveys with the personal quality of face-to-face surveys. By blending both, you soften the advantages and disadvantages both have around issues of reactivity and response effects. Random digit dialing, including mobile phones, captures almost everyone in the sampling frame for building your sample and automates what is frequently otherwise a difficult process of recruitment (for self-administered surveys). A researcher can oversee a central call location, monitoring interviewer quality to make sure that all interviewers are functioning similarly and reducing the differences in respondents' answers due to different interviewer skills or qualities. The lack of face-to-face contact also ensures interviewer safety (and interviewee security). Respondents feel they have more privacy and anonymity, which often frees them to respond more honestly.

The biggest problem with telephone surveys is that it doesn't work for much of the developing world. It is primarily a delivery strategy for industrialized nations, particularly those areas that are not rural and poor. It is much more challenging to find participants in regions that have insufficient mobile service, which still covers much of the United States (and, incidentally, both of your authors' homes!). Even in areas with good service, you'll have to make a lot of calls to get enough respondents. Many people simply don't pick up their phones for unrecognized numbers or refuse to participate because you've interrupted an activity, such as work, making dinner, or shopping. And while you resolve some of the issues that face-to-face surveys have with reactivity and response effects, you don't eliminate them. For example, while you won't have reactivity based on the appearance of the interviewer, respondents will still react to accents and speech patterns. On the other hand, you will maintain many of the advantages of the face-to-face delivery strategy, including allowing respondents to clarify questions that they find confusing. This is not possible in a self-administered survey. For example, in one of Kimberly Kirner's surveys of Pagans, she asked, "How long have you been a Pagan?" Respondents in her self-administered survey selected a number of years, which averaged seventeen years. But what did this number really represent? If it had been a telephone survey, she might have received a range of responses: "Do you mean when did I realize I was Pagan?" "I think I was always Pagan, but I just didn't know it until I realized other people believed this way in my twenties." "Well, I considered myself Pagan for ten years, but I didn't join any groups until recently." "I don't know if I consider myself Pagan, but I have a lot in common with Pagans, and I go to local Pagan workshops." Does this matter? It depends on the research question at hand. If the survey is on something different (in this case, health care treatment choices), it is fine to leave the question as it is, with the survey delivery strategy as self-administered. This is because it is being used only to contextualize the research findings with the demographic characteristics of the population. However, if the survey were explicitly about religious identity—how people viewed their own journey in their religion—then it'd be much more problematic.

With increasing frequency, researchers are using self-administered surveys. These largely used to be mailed through the postal service, which was costly and had relatively low response rates. But as you've probably noticed, online self-administered surveys abound, from entertainment "quizzes" that tell you which Harry Potter house you'd belong to based on your personal tastes to serious research projects that seek to locate hard-to-find populations, such as members of minority religious traditions or people who are LGBTQ+. One of the biggest advantages of the self-administered survey delivery strategy is that it allows a single researcher to gather data from a large, representative sample from a population at relatively low cost. There are data-related advantages as well. All respondents get the same question, and you don't have to worry about reactivity or response effects. Because respondents do not interact with the researcher, you can be sure that their responses won't be affected by qualities they perceive in the researcher or subtle cues a researcher might give that shift their response (such as tone of voice). They also feel more anonymous and private, which allows them to respond with more honesty and information on sensitive questions than they would if they were talking to an interviewer. You can ask more complex questions, such as respondents ranking long lists or providing answers to hypothetical scenarios (these types of questions get boring and hard to follow in person but are often interesting to respondents if they're reading them). You can also ask long series of boring questions that aren't like a normal conversation (tons of demographic information, for example), and respondents will find it less annoying than they would if you were asking them these questions face to face. For most respondents, the survey-taking process will also go faster in a self-administered survey, allowing you to ask more questions in less time.

Yet, as with all delivery strategies, there are also a number of disadvantages. The biggest problem is that online self-administered surveys work only for people with an internet connection, and all self-administered surveys work only for people who are literate. This means that your target population must be carefully considered for whether or not it is an appropriate population for this survey delivery strategy. Furthermore, if you're not working in highly industrialized nations, your response rate for self-administered surveys will likely be somewhat dismal (20 percent to 30 percent if you send it in the mail, and even lower online). This means you have to send surveys to a lot of people in order to get the number of respondents you're looking for. There are also some challenges with the ways respondents approach self-administered surveys. Unlike in the other delivery strategies, you have no control over how people interpret your questions, and it is impossible to give a paper-based survey that controls the order in which respondents answer the questions; rather, they can answer the questions in any order they choose. Finally, you can never be sure of who is answering your survey. Even if you send a survey to specific people, you can't be sure that the person you sent the survey to is the one who took it.

Still, it is very common for students (including graduate students) to use the self-administered survey delivery strategy (especially online), primarily because of its much lower time and money investment. Web-based applications, such as SurveyMonkey, are relatively cheap and user-friendly and allow you to format and deliver online surveys with minimal time investment (and even come with some analytical tools to use afterward). More broadly, even if there are not resource limitations, self-administered surveys are preferred when certain conditions are met: The population is literate and can access the survey. You're confident of a 70 percent or higher **response rate** (i.e., there are reasons to believe your target population or selected sample is invested in your project enough to respond). The questions you want to ask can be effectively asked without the presence of a researcher. You do not need a near-perfect **completion rate** (the rate at which respondents finish the survey). Online-only surveys are very helpful for certain populations, such as harder-to-reach groups (who are distributed across a large region) who congregate online and can therefore be located for marketing. In general, self-administered survey success is very much tied to marketing: People have to know about your survey and decide to take it!

Response rate The rate at which targeted people open and respond to your survey (e.g., if you send the survey to one thousand people and seven hundred of them respond, you have a 70 percent response rate).

Completion rate The rate at which respondents complete a survey (some respondents may open the survey and begin it but give up partway through taking it).

Discussion

Consider your target population for answering your research question you've been working on. What strategy for survey delivery would work best for your research, and why? How would you recruit respondents? What obstacles or challenges might you face in acquiring a large enough sample size, and how could you work around them?

Survey Analysis and Writing

The primary reason to use survey research is to collect demographic and quantitative data to use alongside your qualitative data. Once you have these data, what do you do with the information? Statistical analysis is a whole topic of its own, and while your authors have recommended some basic statistics resources at the end of this chapter, we'll cover only the most basic analysis here. This is a beginning point for the student just starting to think about how to use quantitative data in conversation with qualitative data. Many qualitative research students are rather intimidated by statistics. We'd encourage you to learn some very basic ways to think about your quantitative data and then take a statistics class or try using the resources at the end of the chapter. Basic statistics is like every other research skill: If you set aside some dedicated time to practice it and you find a peer or instructor to help you with parts you don't understand, you'll get better and more comfortable with it over time.

Once you've collected your survey data, there are several ways to work with the information. You'll want to enter the data into some kind of spreadsheet or data analysis application as the first step. Because some of your survey data will be quantitative, and you plan to use comparisons between demographically different groups to further understand patterns in your data, you need the help of a spreadsheet. The cheap and lower-tech way to do this is to use Microsoft Excel. This program is often available as a free download for students from their universities and has the basic functions you'll need, such as being able to automatically generate sums and averages and filter your data by demographic group. If you feel you can manage learning something a little bit more challenging but with a lot more utility for statistical analysis, you can use the Statistical Package for the Social Sciences (SPSS). This is also sometimes available for free to students in universities. It has more functionality for statistical analysis for social scientists, but it's also more complex. Finally, if you don't have too many surveys and your surveys aren't too long, you can use Dedoose for mixed methods analysis. Dedoose has a benefit that it has a lot of automatic functions for analyzing demographic combined with qualitative data, but compared to more robust data analysis software (such as NVivo), it has significant limits in terms of how many individual items of survey data can be easily uploaded to the application.

When using a spreadsheet such as Excel or SPSS, be sure to set up your columns in the spreadsheet as the questions in your survey and the rows as your individual respondents. Each respondent should have their own unique identifier that keeps them anonymous (see Figure 8.9 for an example).

Once your spreadsheet is set up, you can start with very basic quantitative analysis to help you understand your respondents. For example, you can characterize the demographics of your sample by counting how many people are in each demographic category and then dividing this number by your sample size. You can compare your sample's demographic profile to the profile of the larger population you are studying (if you have demographic information for the larger profile) to assess how closely your sample represents the larger population. A **representative sample** will have demographic characteristics similar to the larger study population. Remember, your sample must be representative in order to have your study findings be generalizable to the population you are studying. If your sample doesn't represent your study population, then your findings don't necessarily apply to that whole population (only to your sample).

After you've established your demographic profile of your sample and compared it to your study population, you'll start your quantitative analysis with simple averages across your entire sample. For example, let's say you ask a Likert scale question: "On a scale of 1 (strongly disagree) to 5 (strongly agree), how much do you agree that your university provides adequate tutoring resources?" You'll want to **average** the responses for the entire sample first (this is also called the *mean*). If you have two hundred respondents to that question, you'll do this by adding all their responses together, then dividing

Representative sample A sample that has the same demographic profile as your study population.

Average A calculation in which you add (sum) all responses, then divide by the number of respondents. This is meant to be a measurement that helps you understand how the most common person would respond, but it should be analyzed with comparison to the median and mode.

Figure 8.9 Excel® Spreadsheet Example

ID	HBSex	HBRace	HBAge	HBQ1	HBQ2	HBQ3	HBQ4	HBQ5	HBQ6	HBQ7	HBQ8	HBQ9	HBQ10	HBQ11	HBQ12	HBQ13	HBQ14	HBQ15	HBQ16	HBQ17	HBQ18	HBQ19	HBQ20
1	Boy	Hispanic/Latino	10-12	3	4	1	4	4	1	2	4	4	4	2	4	2	2	2	2	1	1	4
2	Boy	Asian/Pacific Islander	9 or younger	2	3	2	2	3	3	4	2	1	3	4	2	3	1	1		1	1	1	3
3	Boy	White	9 or younger	1	4	2	4	2	4	2	1	4	3	4	3	4	2	2	2	2	2	2	4
4	Boy	Black	13 or older	4	4	2	3	4	4	4	2	4	3	4	4	4	2	2	2	1	2	2
5	Boy	Other	13 or older	4	1	4	2	4	1	4	2	1	3	3	3	2	1	2	1	1	0
6	Boy	Hispanic/Latino	10-12	4	2	1	4	4	4	4	4	2	4	4	4	2	2	1	1		3
7	Boy	White	10-12	3	1	3	4
8	Girl	Hispanic/Latino	9 or younger	4	1	1	1	4	4	2	2	3	4	1	2	2	2	0	2	1	1	4
9	Boy	Hispanic/Latino	10-12	1	4	4	4	1	1	1	4	1	4	1	4	1	1	1	1	1	1	1
10	Boy	Black	9 or younger	4	1	1	1	4	4	4	1	4	1	4	1	4	2	2	2	2	2	4
11	Boy	White	9 or younger	4	4	4	4	4	4	4	4	3	4		0	2	2	2	0	0	4
12	Boy	Hispanic/Latino	9 or younger	4	4	3	4	1	2	4	4	4	1	4		0	1	0	2	1	0	4
13	Boy	Black	10-12	4	1	3	4	4	4	1	4	4	4	2	4	2	2	2	2	2	4
14	Girl		10-12	4	4	3	4	4	4	4	4	4	1	4	4	2	2	2	2	2	4
15	Boy	Hispanic/Latino	9 or younger	4	4	4	4	4	3	4	3	4	4	3	4	1	2	2	1	2	4
16	Girl	Hispanic/Latino	10-12	4	4	4	4	4	4	3	4	4	4	4	2	2	2	2	1	2	4
17	Boy	Hispanic/Latino	10-12	3	1	3	4	4	3	4	3	4	1	2	4	4	1	2	0	1	0	0	4

by two hundred (this might be different from your sample size if not all respondents responded to the question). You'll emerge from this process with the average response (let's say, 4 [agree]). It's important to note that the average doesn't mean that there are a lot of respondents with that exact response. You can emerge with 4 as the average response because many respondents selected 4 or because many respondents selected 3 and 5 (even if few selected 4). Therefore, you might also want to see what the most *common* responses were in the sample population.

The **median** is the number right in the middle of all the responses. The median is particularly useful to calculate when there are some very low or very high numbers that skew the average higher or lower than it otherwise would be. For example, if you ask about household size, and most people (in a small sample) say a number between two and five, but a small number of people have households that are ten or twelve, it will shift your average larger (even though most of your respondents had smaller household sizes). But when you calculate the median, you'll find that the household size settles between two and five. The **mode** is the most common response (for example, on household size, it may be three). The mean (or average), median, and mode may be the same number or numbers that are quite different, because they each speak to a different understanding of the sample as a whole. It's important, then, not to just calculate averages and leave it at that. You have to look for **outliers** and then decide whether you will remove those from the sample or whether you will include them, but then compare the average with the median and the mode. In all these cases, working in a spreadsheet helps because you can have functions that automatically calculate these statistics from the sample as a whole. That's a lot easier than trying to calculate long strings of numbers on your own with a calculator!

After you've characterized your sample as a whole, it's time to compare different subgroups in your sample to understand whether certain demographic characteristics influence the ways your respondents answer your questions. For example, let's get back to household size. You might be curious whether household size is influenced by respondents' age. To figure this out, you can divide your respondents into groups and compare their data. You might select all respondents ages eighteen to twenty-five, twenty-six to thirty-five, thirty-six to forty-five, forty-six to fifty-five, fifty-six to sixty-five, and sixty-six and older; generate average household size (and potentially mode and median) for each group; and then compare. Does age seem to have any patterns that go along with household size? If so, why do you think this is the case? There are ways to calculate correlation strength and whether or not it is statistically significant that you can learn by taking a statistics class. But for now, simply notice patterns that you find in the data.

Another type of pattern you'll want to look for is based on quantitative, non-demographic data. For example, let's say that your respondents on the university tutoring question we reviewed previously averaged a 4 response (that they agreed their university is providing adequate tutoring resources). However, when you review all the responses, you find that the students really split into three groups: a small group that strongly disagreed (1), a sizeable group that was neutral (3), and a sizeable group that strongly agreed (5). Very few students picked 4 (agree). Now, what might be going on with the split between these groups? Perhaps you try to look at demographic explanations first but find no patterns that link demographics to responses. But what about other quantitative responses? Let's say you ask survey respondents how many hours per day and how many days per week they are on campus. You might have the idea that their perceptions

Median The number that is the midway point in your entire set of responses for a question. If there is an even number of responses, you take the average (mean) of the middle two numbers to find the median. If there is an odd number of responses, the median is the middle number of the dataset.

Mode The most common response. You count the number of times each response is used, and the mode is the response with the largest number of respondents.

Outliers As a concept (rather than a calculation), an outlier is a response that is quite different from most or all of the rest.

of whether or not tutoring resources are adequate depend on whether they have sufficient time on campus to make use of them. To investigate this potential pattern, you'd sort your sample into three groups: your students who strongly disagreed, who were neutral, and who strongly agreed. Then you'd compare their averages in hours per day and days per week they are on campus. Alternatively, you could decide to group students together into categories of how much they are on campus based on your own predetermined groups for analysis: such as a "frequently on campus" group (five or more days a week, eight or more hours per day), a "moderately on campus" group (three or more days a week, five or more hours per day), and a "infrequently on campus" group (two or fewer days a week, four or fewer hours per day). Then you'd compare their average (and median and mode) response to the Likert scale question on tutoring.

As you can surmise, even with the most basic quantitative data analysis, there are potential questions you can ask and patterns you can find in the data that wouldn't necessarily be possible with purely qualitative data. This is the value of survey research: You can study larger, more diverse populations with accuracy and generalizability, and you can investigate certain kinds of questions with relative ease by making them quantitative responses.

In many cases, anthropologists conducting survey research choose to collect both quantitative and qualitative data in their surveys. As you learned earlier in this chapter, we can do this by asking open-ended questions. This allows respondents to answer using their own words. You can mix qualitative and quantitative methods through design (for example, combining a focus group and survey research), or you can mix them in one survey (using both closed-ended and open-ended questions). When you collect both qualitative and quantitative data in one survey, you'll have demographic information for your qualitative responses as well as your quantitative ones. When you conduct the analysis, you'll begin by coding your qualitative data (as you learned to do in Chapter 7), and then you'll compare the prevalence of codes for different demographically defined groups (similarly to how you learned to compare averages, medians, and modes across these groups). You can also compare your findings from the qualitative data with the quantitative findings, helping you better understand your quantitative findings and/or identify gaps between the two (which can indicate differences between how respondents think about and respond to the questions on their own versus the ways you've structured their responses in closed-ended questions).

After you've coded your qualitative data and you've analyzed your quantitative data (such as through calculating averages, medians, and modes), it's time to compare the two sets of findings. Where is there agreement in the data? Where is there disagreement? Why do you think the disagreements exist? How might you test those hypotheses? It's also time to compare the patterns in the qualitative data based on subgroups of your sample, usually along demographic lines. Do men say different things than women? Do older people say different things than younger people? Rather than investigating your codebook only once for relationships and similarities that indicate themes in the qualitative data, you'll want to do it several times for different subgroups in your sample and compare the patterns you recognize to see if these themes occur in the entire study population or if they are features of only some subgroups.

When you finish analysis for survey research, you'll have a lot of different types of findings: demographic characteristics of your sample and their comparison with the demographics of your total study population, statistical trends across your entire sample, themes you find across your entire sample, and detailed patterns you find that differ among subgroups of your sample. In the previous chapter, you learned about ethnographic writing. How can you integrate statistical evidence? Do not get lost in the numbers. Numbers should have a purpose that is clearly stated and relevant to the research question. Just because you have some analysis doesn't mean it's useful analysis. You have to use discernment to figure out which quantitative and mixed methods analysis is meaningful within the context of your broader research question, and then use only the findings that are relevant and significant: those that are actual trends (and not outliers) and that speak to the research question. Remember to tell a story with the data. Endless "results" are boring and not helpful. What is your point? If you continue to think of your data in terms of themes you'd like to address, you will find that there are both qualitative data (respondent quotes) and quantitative data (statistical trends) that can be used together to address these themes. While quantitative data provide a good starting point for an overview of your findings, you must remember to include your qualitative data. Quotes from participants add depth and richness to your study, as well as nuanced analysis about how qualitative and quantitative data were similar or different and why. Remember, there is a reason you're doing both!

Discussion

When you consider your research question you developed in Chapter 1, what sub-questions might be best answered through demographic analysis? Why? What sub-questions could be answered through asking questions that would produce quantitative data? Why? What sub-questions could be best answered using a mix of qualitative and quantitative data? Why?

Pairing the Textbook and Workbook

You've added surveys to your methodological tool kit and added basic quantitative and mixed methods analysis to the two qualitative analysis methods you learned in the previous chapter. Hopefully, you are beginning to recognize how some research questions are best addressed through qualitative-only methods and others are best approached with survey research, in which you will at least collect demographic data to pair with respondents' answers. For many students, the allure of quantitative, closed-ended questions is great, because it requires less time for collecting and analyzing such data. But be wary of shoving time-consuming, qualitative methods by the wayside. Many of the questions anthropologists ask are best approached, at least in exploratory stages, through qualitative methods such as interviewing and participant observation. However, especially in cases where you are working with a large, diverse population, survey research can be invaluable for collecting enough data to thoroughly understand the trends among subgroups and to generalize your findings to your study population. Especially if you plan to work with large, diverse populations or research questions in which individual attribute data matter, you might want to work more on survey research skills and take a quantitative analysis or statistics class. At this point, you can celebrate a bit of accomplishment! You've learned the three most common data collection methods—participant observation, interviewing, and surveys—and you've learned ways to analyze and write about your data. From this point forward in the book, you'll learn about more specific methods designed to address particular types of research questions.

Reflective Prompts

1. In what ways am I using my previous learning and applying those concepts toward understanding new information?

2. Can I explain how multiple methods work in triangulation?

3. Can I choose an appropriate survey distribution method for particular research questions and contexts and justify my choice?

Case Study

Magliocco, Sabina. 2018. "Beyond the Rainbow Bridge: Vernacular Ontologies of Animal Afterlives." *Journal of Folklore Research* 55, no. 2: 39–67.

The Project

My original idea was to survey modern Pagans about their attitudes, ontologies, and cosmologies about animals and whether this made a difference for the actions they took in the world (in favor of animals and sustainability). I was testing out the idea that cultures for whom other-than-human persons have agency and personhood have more ecological practices than those that don't. So I created a large survey and asked a number of questions about their religious identification growing up and in their current lives. I asked if people lived in rural, suburban, or urban settings now or when they were growing up, because I was testing a theory by Richard Bulliet that subsistence relationships to animals shift people's spiritual relationships to them. I also asked about spiritual experiences with animals. It's one thing to thing to believe that one's dog has a soul; it's another to encounter animals' spirits as lived experiences.

Why did you select survey research as your method for addressing your research question?
I wanted to try for a more representative sample than just my friends. I needed lots of data, not just twenty people willing to be interviewed for this. I wanted data that were more reliable. I think most of my contacts in the Pagan community are people who talk to anthropologists all the time. Many of the contacts have worked

(Continued)

(Continued)

with other researchers in social science and religious studies who have produced books about the Pagan community. So I didn't want just the people who always talk to the anthropologists. I wanted a wider group of people, especially to study issues of changing behavior. People who like to be interviewed are grassroots intellectuals; they're very reflexive and give insight into the way they see their own community. They're great for going into a community. But sometimes you need more data and broader data to understand the community as a whole.

What strategy did you use for recruitment? Why? Did you feel this generated a representative sample and, if not, how did you address this issue?

I sent the link out via social media and distribution lists. The link went viral, and this became a problem, because people who didn't identify as Pagan took the survey. So my data were all over the place. I had over five hundred respondents, and a significant chunk of the sample didn't identify as Pagan, which skewed the sample. One thing that was interesting about my results, however, is that Pagan attitudes and experiences toward animals were not unusual. People who identify as animal lovers shared a lot of their experiences and ideas, regardless of their religion. People from non-Pagan religions were willing to go against their religious teachings because they were animal lovers. I got a lot of answers of a certain type, such as "I know my religion says my dog doesn't have a soul, but I think that's BS, because I know she has a soul." So despite the sampling issues, the results turned out to be very interesting.

Thinking back to the first time you conducted survey research, what mistakes did you make? What strategies did you learn?

One reason that I was rejected for funding for this project was that reviewers said there were major sampling issues, and there were. This was the first big online survey I'd done on my own, the first survey I'd conducted since graduate school. My graduate school survey was part of a larger class project that my research institute was doing, and it wasn't my research project per se. The second survey project of my own I did recently was on fairies. One thing I learned from the animals survey was that social media has both pros and cons in terms of finding respondents. Both the animal and the fairy surveys filled up really fast. I practically had to instantaneously take the surveys down (after only a few days) because I exceeded the top limit of participants I told the IRB I'd have. But you can't control for certain things. I couldn't control that the animal survey went viral. In the second (fairy) survey, I said in the introduction that it was exclusively for people who identified as Pagans, and if they identified as part of another religious group, it wasn't for them. But to be honest, I don't know how many people read this stuff, because some people who took the second (fairy) survey did not identify as Pagan!

How did you prepare to analyze survey data, especially your quantitative and demographic data? Do you work with statisticians or do the work yourself? Why did you make the choices you did?

I didn't have the resources to pay a statistician, so I worked on my own. I followed up the survey collection with having my students collect interview data based on similar questions among animal practitioners and other non-Pagan people in specific religions and then compared the interview data to the survey answers. I had a fair sample of Christians: Catholics, nondenominational Christians, and an assortment of Christian denominations. I didn't have any Muslims, which is a problem. I did have Buddhists, Hindus, and representatives of other major religious groups. The quantitative data were easy to analyze, because the survey tool I used produced analyses of those data. I got results in terms of demographics very quickly: the percentage of people in different affiliations and geographic location. The qualitative data I had to code, and I coded based on themes: an initial coding process, and then I grouped narratives into broader categories, and finally looked at the themes within these categories. It was my first experience with a big survey. There were no desktop computers when I took statistics in the early 1980s, so I've had to learn how to work through data like these on my own later. But we can use a variety of approaches.

What advice do you have about surveys, based on your research career, for beginning researchers?

You need to think about your questions very, very carefully. Word them very carefully. Put yourself in the shoes of the person answering. Think about the kinds of answers you're looking for when you're asking the question. For the most part, I got the kinds of answers I was looking for because I was constructing the questions well. But having taught research methods many times and working with students on creating surveys, I've seen a lot of poorly worded, poorly thought-out questions. Bad questions get bad data. You have to really think about how the questions might be misread.

Case Study Reflections

1. Why did Magliocco need to use surveys as a method of data collection, rather than only interviews, in order to answer her research question?

2. What mistakes did Magliocco make in this case study? How do mistakes in our research sometimes afford new opportunities?

3. What are limiting factors to consider when conducting survey research and statistical analysis? What can we learn from this case study about a general attitude and approach toward these limitations?

4. What is absolutely essential, based on this case study, for producing meaningful data? What is the foundation for survey research that is accurate and useful?

STUDY GUIDE

Note: Students should study each concept with attentiveness to defining, explaining with examples, and describing or demonstrating process. This is not a list of terms to define; it's a list of concepts and processes to master.

Survey

Merged integration

Embedded integration

Connected integration

Convergent design

Exploratory sequential design

Explanatory sequential design

Demographic questions

Quantitative questions

Likert scale questions

Qualitative questions

Open-ended questions

Closed-ended questions

Back translation

Pretest

Self-administration

Response rate

Completion rate

Representative sample

Average (mean)

Median

Mode

Outliers

Process for mixed methods analysis

FOR FURTHER STUDY

Bernard, H. Russell. 2018. "Interviewing II: Questionnaires." In *Research Methods in Anthropology*, by H. Russell Bernard, 195–232. Lanham, MD: Rowman and Littlefield.

Salkind, Neil J. 2015. *Statistics for People Who Think They Hate Statistics*. 6th ed. Thousand Oaks, CA: SAGE.

Visit **study.sagepub.com/kirner** to help you accomplish your coursework goals in an easy-to-use learning environment.

Cultural Domains
Modeling Cognition and Knowledge

Orientation

In Chapter 6, we covered the basics of interviewing as a method. Interviewing can take many specialized forms, each of which constitutes specific data collection strategies that are appropriate for certain kinds of questions. In this chapter, we'll deepen our knowledge of interviewing and cover three methods from cognitive anthropology, each of which unites specific ways of collecting and analyzing data about cognition and knowledge. Cognitive anthropological research often focuses on cultural domains, specific areas of knowledge and action that exist within the larger cultural framework. The specificity of cultural domain research makes it popular in applied anthropology, because a researcher can relatively rapidly improve understanding of a wide range of social problems, including what people know about a specific topic, the cultural norms that govern their actions, and the factors that lead to the choices they make.

Cognitive Anthropology and Models

Cognitive anthropology is the study of the relationship between human society and human thought. At its heart, cognitive anthropology engages core questions about culture itself, such as these:

- What is cultural knowledge?

- How is cultural knowledge organized in the human brain?

- How is knowledge learned?

Chapter Learning Objectives

Students will be able to do the following:

9.1 Describe the major research questions driving cognitive anthropology and how models can be used in applied settings

9.2 Explain folk taxonomy study design and methods for data collection

9.3 Explain how to analyze data to derive a folk taxonomy

9.4 Explain cultural modeling study design and methods for data collection

9.5 Explain how to analyze data to derive a cultural model

9.6 Explain ethnographic decision-tree modeling study design and methods for data collection

9.7 Explain how to analyze data to derive an ethnographic decision-tree model

9.8 After reading the entire chapter, describe various cultural domain studies and justify which you would select for different research questions

- How does knowledge shape action?

- How do individual biological differences affect the organization, learning, and use of knowledge?

- How is knowledge shared and distributed?

Ultimately, it is after one of the broadly interesting and grand (BIG) questions: How do patterns in individuals and culture emerge in bidirectional and co-creative processes? At the same time, because cognitive anthropology frequently engages these theoretical questions through very specific, narrow areas of inquiry (for example, child care choices, or how people behave in restaurants, or ways people organize plant knowledge), it is also very popular in applied anthropology. It allows for rapid assessments of specific cultural domains with fairly high accuracy and reliability, specifically organized around how people think and act—and this makes it valuable for assessing and refining policies, programs, and products that are designed to help people make better choices and live improved lives.

Cognitive anthropology includes four primary specialization areas: semantics, ethnoscience, models, and discourse. *Semantics* is the study of meaning, and *discourse* is the study of how meaning and action are related to language and communication. Because this is an introduction to methodology, we'll leave aside these two specialization areas, both of which have specific methodologies related to them. We'll focus on the two areas that touch many research topics very broadly—especially in applied contexts: (1) ethnoscience and (2) models and systems. **Ethnoscience** is the study of the ways in which people classify and understand the world around them. Studies in ethnoscience provide us with a better understanding of the culturally constructed and transmitted knowledge structures that help people make sense of their social and natural environments, how widely these knowledge structures are shared, and how they relate to action.

Models are representations of emergent culturally constructed, shared, and transmitted patterns and include shared ways of ordering and engaging knowledge structures, decision-making factors, and motivational drivers. Rather than focusing on individual stories and meanings, models represent common frameworks that are widely distributed across a specific population. They provide a means to express theory about how information and action are organized in a given culture and to test this theory in iterations of observation. Models have practical uses that are difficult to obtain using descriptive methods, such as providing complex cultural information efficiently (in a diagram rather than a twenty-page descriptive paper), and this makes them valuable for communicating information to decision makers and policy makers.

Modeling can be done using complex and sophisticated statistical methods, but it can also be done ethnographically with fairly basic ways of uniting qualitative and quantitative analysis. Because this is a beginner's primer on qualitative methods, we'll focus on the most basic ways we can analyze qualitative data to produce models that take into account how to build models from interview data, assess the distribution of them in a population (how widely they are found in a population), and use iteration (multiple planned stages of research) to test models. We'll focus on three types of models: taxonomies, cultural models, and decision-tree models.

Cognitive anthropology The study of the relationship between human society and human thought.

Ethnoscience The study of the ways in which people classify and understand the world around them.

Models Representations of emergent culturally constructed, shared, and transmitted patterns.

Discussion

Can you think of a practical, applied topic that would be a particularly good fit for the construction of models? How might the model be used, and by whom?

Folk Taxonomies: Data Collection

Taxonomies are models that organize the relationships of entities within a domain. They model knowledge in which the relationship between concepts is "*X* is a kind of *Y*." Most of us are familiar with Linnaean taxonomy if we've taken biology—the way in which Western biological science, beginning with Linnaeus, ordered the life forms on Earth in nesting categories that describe the closeness of relationship between species. **Folk taxonomies**— or the informal (non-Western science) knowledge structures that organize information about all sorts of things, from plants to cars—are held for many domains by everyone in a given cultural group. This methodology arose from ethnobiology, which is a specialization that studies folk systems of classifying plants and animals. While individuals differ in the extent and content of their knowledge, the taxonomies as a whole are distributed widely across the cultural group and are understood by most of the people in it. Taxonomies are useful when we're attempting to understand how a culture organizes many items in a single domain—not just plants, animals, and other things in nature, but also technology, supernatural beings, human resources, and any other collection of related and categorically nested things or concepts. Theoretically, they're also helpful for improving our understanding of how people classify and remember information about things in their environments, including how much of this cognitive process is neurological as opposed to cultural.

There are two primary methods for data collection in folk taxonomies: pile sorting and frame elicitation. **Pile sorting** uses a set of stimuli that the researcher provides in order to understand how people categorize items in a domain. In ethnobiology, these might include pressed and mounted plants or animal skins. For other domains, the stimuli may be photos. While this can be done digitally, a set of hard copy stimuli is best. This is because it usually easier for people to manipulate actual objects and hold them all in their view at once than images on a screen. When conducting pile sorting, the researcher provides the pile of stimuli to the participant, and the participant sifts through the items and places them into categories that make sense. The researcher guides the participant only by asking "and then" sorts of questions—that is, after the piles are sorted, asking what each pile is called (requesting the native term for the conceptual category) and following up by asking, "And then can you make any smaller piles from this one that make sense to you?" or "And then do any of these piles belong together in a larger pile that makes sense to you?" You might also ask, "What is this pile of stuff called?" and "Why did you put these things in a pile?"

Note-taking should include what people call the piles (the emic language for these categories) and what is in each pile (see Figure 9.1 for an example); taking photos of piles that people make and linking the photo number to your notes on categories and information people give can be a helpful way of organizing the information.

Taxonomies Models that organize the relationships of entities within a domain.

Folk taxonomies Informal (non-Western science) knowledge structures that organize information about specific domains.

Pile sorting A method for data collection that uses a set of stimuli that the researcher provides in order to understand how people categorize items in a domain.

Figure 9.1   Notes on Pile Sorting

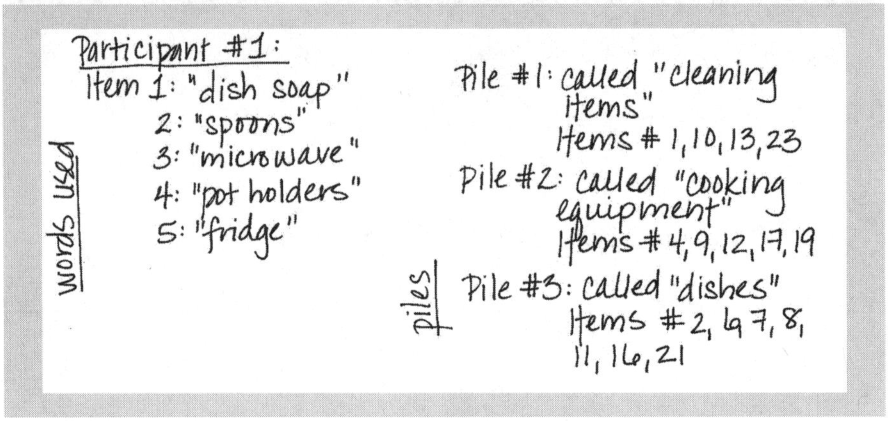

Participant #1:
Item 1: "dish soap"
    2: "spoons"
    3: "microwave"
    4: "pot holders"
    5: "fridge"
words used

Pile #1: called "cleaning items"
    Items # 1, 10, 13, 23
Pile #2: called "cooking equipment"
    Items # 4, 9, 12, 17, 19
Pile #3: called "dishes"
    Items # 2, 6, 7, 8, 11, 16, 21
piles

Pile sorting is easy to do for most people, but constructing the original set of stimuli can be challenging and time-consuming. Each stimulus must be carefully selected to be an adequate, normative representative of the item in question (i.e., you usually don't want outlier representatives), and the stimuli set as a whole must include sufficient items to truly represent the domain. If a researcher doesn't have prior knowledge of the social or natural environments of people in the culture, it can be difficult to construct an adequate stimuli set.

The other method for collection of taxonomic data is **frame elicitation**, which is a structured interview that follows this format:

- What is X?

- Is X a type of Y? Why?

- What types of X are there? How do you know the difference?

- What do you know about X?

Generally, such interviews are conducted during ethnographic field research. (See Figure 9.2 for an example.) This allows the everyday world around the participant to provide the stimuli set that prompts the researcher's questions and the participant's responses. In ethnobiology, frame elicitation is often paired with collecting samples or photos of particular items in the natural world during the interview process in order to better understand how the folk taxonomy overlays with Linnaean taxonomy.

Ethnobiologists are often dual-trained in botany or biology and anthropology, which allows them to analyze the differences between how Western science classifies a domain (say, grasses) and how a specific cultural group classifies the same species. The differences between the two often illuminate specific uses or meanings of the species in the culture in question and/or point out what is useful to practical field folk scientists as

Frame elicitation
A data collection method that uses a structured interview to collect folk taxonomic information on a specific domain.

Figure 9.2 Notes on Frame Elicitation

Participant #1:   [→ indicates participant response]

Item 1: What is X? [I hold up the photo.]
→ "dish soap"
Is "dish soap" a type of anything else?
→ "It's a kind of cleaning supplies"
Why?
→ "Well, it cleans stuff in the kitchen."
What are other kinds of cleaning supplies?
→ "Disinfecting wipes for the counters. There is Tilex for the sink & tiles. Oven cleaner for the stove."
How do you know the difference between the types of cleaning supplies?
→ "They're all for cleaning different things."

opposed to Western science. Ultimately, regardless of which method of data collection is chosen to produce data for constructing a folk taxonomy, the goal is a graphical display of the relationships between concepts or objects in the domain. There are particular ways of analyzing such data and then displaying the information so that the relationships are clearly and concisely depicted.

Discussion

When you think about your research question you developed in Chapter 1, can you think of an aspect of this question that might benefit from a taxonomic modeling approach? If so, what domain would be optimal for modeling, and how would it contribute to your research question? If not, why do think this method would be inappropriate for addressing your research question?

Folk Taxonomies: Analysis

When you've finished with pile sorting or frame elicitation, you'll have two types of data: (1) notes on what people called things, how they describe them, and the relationships they have to other things and (2) photos or samples of items. It's time to build a folk taxonomy of the domain: a visual way of representing the relationships between things, showing them from smaller groupings (and, depending on your research question, even individual species or items) to larger, more inclusive groupings. You'll want to start by organizing the individual things in your notes: Make a list of these. Then make a list of the smallest groups that were made and the items in these groups. Finally, make a list of the larger groups that were made and the items in those groups. You'll arrange the items and then groups in a visual diagram. The diagram describes the relationships between the items by showing increasingly large groups (at the top of the diagram) then smaller groups (in the middle of the diagram) and individual items (at the bottom of the diagram). Remember that the smallest groupings may still have many individual items in them, but they won't be diverse enough to make other groupings from them, and they'll be different enough that they won't fit into larger groupings.

Using the diagrams, you can communicate an entire emic classification of a domain through a single diagrammatic representation. This can be paired with narrative text that explains the auxiliary information you collected, such as why certain groupings were made and details participants shared with you. One visual diagrammatic representation is the "tree" structure (see Figure 9.3).

Here, the viewer can see that the native domain of "vehicles" includes four broad types: cars, SUVs, vans, and trucks. Cars, vans, and trucks have further distinctively different subtypes, whereas SUVs do not. The narrative text that is paired with this diagram could describe the sorts of representative items that fit in each of these categories and what distinguishes them from one another (such as SUVs having a large enclosed cargo space and vans typically having a sliding door into the seating or covered cargo area), as well as why people bother to distinguish between the types (primarily due to use). The other way to diagram the same content is the "box" structure (see Figure 9.4).

Figure 9.3 Tree Diagram of Vehicles

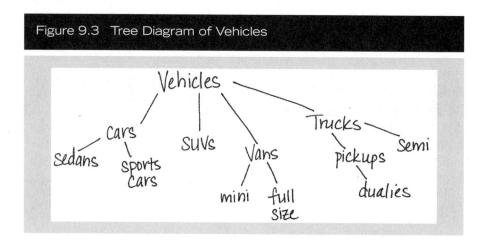

Figure 9.4 Box Diagram of Vehicles

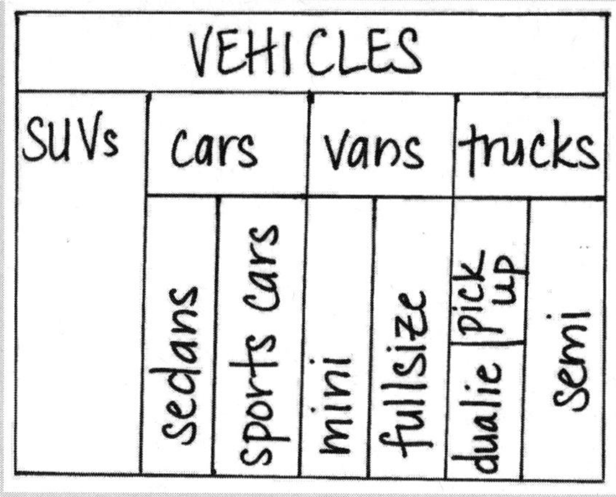

The type of structure that a researcher chooses typically depends on personal choice of aesthetic combined with ease of representing the quantity of relationships necessary. Overall, these diagrams convey a great deal of information about how a group of people understand a cultural domain and organize individual items into more complex structures in cases where narrative text alone would be long, hard to understand, and dull.

As you can imagine, it is easy to construct a folk taxonomy for one participant but more difficult to construct a representative taxonomy for an entire group of people. There are many reasons for this, which center around the issue of divergence (or disagreements) in taxonomic classification within cultural groups. First, people everywhere have two divergent tendencies when classifying things: **lumpers and splitters**. *Lumpers* see large, inclusive categories in everything, and *splitters* tend to see small, unique categories. Splitters often have many categories, while lumpers often have very few (but large) categories, for the same domain. When your participants have similar levels of expertise but differ in the complexity and depth of their taxonomy, you might be looking at the case of a lumper versus a splitter. The same pattern (one person with a complex, deep and rich taxonomy and another with only a few large and general categories) also exists due to differences in levels of expertise. Generally speaking, an expert in a field (for example, a car enthusiast for vehicle taxonomies) will have more knowledge of different types of items in the domain and more complex understandings of their relationships, so their taxonomy will be more complicated and rich (with more groups and more layers) than the taxonomy of a layperson.

At other times, subcultural diversity within a group (divergent smaller cultural groups within your larger population) will result in different views on a domain. In these cases, the divergence will track to identifiers in the participants (age, gender, ethnicity, location, etc.) rather than to individuals. Disagreements and conflicts may exist between

Lumpers and splitters A problem inherent to building group taxonomic systems in which some people tend to see fewer larger, inclusive categories and other people tend to see many smaller, diverse categories.

individuals and between subcultural groups about how a domain is to be understood. In all these cases, the researcher needs to assess how to best address their research question, while also representing the conflict that exists. In cases of idiosyncratic individual disagreements, the researcher should evaluate the total dataset (multiple individuals' taxonomic classifications of the same domain) and determine which are outliers and leave them out accordingly. However, in cases where there are patterned, meaningful divergences, it may be worthwhile to diagram multiple taxonomies and discuss the differences and why these disagreements occur.

It is worth noting that not all cultures will generate equally detailed taxonomies for the same domain. This is to be expected; after all, cultures will vary in terms of how useful or meaningful a domain is for them. A northern culture will likely have many different types of snow and ice, because communicating about the subtle qualities of this weather is inherently important for survival. A culture in a more temperate region that gets little snow rather infrequently may have a much simpler taxonomy of this type of weather. Taxonomies can tell us much about how a cultural group understands a domain: not only what is in it and the relationships between concepts or items but also how significant a domain is to the culture and why this is the case.

Discussion

Try diagramming a folk taxonomy for a cultural domain that you know something about. A good starting point is to select a domain, such as breeds of dogs, flowers, or food that you know well, and then to try to generate a folk taxonomic diagram for it. This will get you started with thinking about how to visually display cultural knowledge and help you identify steps or concepts related to taxonomies that are confusing or unclear for you.

Cultural Models: Data Collection

What about domains that aren't governed in those "X is a type of Y" relationships? How can we understand them? **Cultural models** organize knowledge that is used to plan for or understand actions—that is, how to act or think. Cultural models help us understand, predict, and choose actions in culturally appropriate ways. If you've ever played "Mad Libs"—a game in which a script has blanks that you fill in with words to make funny stories—then you have an idea of how cultural models operate. Cultural models function as scripts (for the most part) that have many fuzzy "blanks"—areas in them that are filled in with information from the environment around us. When we are faced with an environment, our brain selects the most appropriate, best-fitting cultural model (script) we have, and then it rapidly fills in all the blanks with the context we're in. This helps us interpret what is going on around us, predict what others will do, and select appropriate actions to take.

Cultural models Models that organize knowledge that is used to plan for or understand actions—that is, how to act or think.

Cultural models often have multiple **schemas** (more narrow models) embedded in them. For example, a cultural model of a restaurant will include schemas of waiters (including how to recognize one, how to interact with one, etc.). The model will have many blanks in it, such as whether you take food with you to go or sit down at a table at the restaurant, whether there are paper or cloth napkins (and whether they are already placed out for you or you need to get them yourself from somewhere in the restaurant), and whether you must go to a counter or speaker to order versus having a person come to your table to ask you what you want. Taxonomies can be associated with cultural models. In the case of restaurants, you have taxonomies of food. In all these cases, however, there is an overarching model that unites these blanks that you fill in with information from the context of your immediate restaurant. The model helps you interpret what is and isn't a restaurant and predict what will happen there so that you can behave properly. It's what allows you to recognize both McDonald's and a fine steakhouse as restaurants but not the sandwich counter at a grocery store.

Cultural models are never clear-cut, because they have to allow for creative use and expansion. And we must always remember that we are modeling cultural domains through this work. The cultural model is not exactly what is in someone's mind. It's an *emergent pattern* that represents a commonly held set of assumptions, concepts, and options associated with a domain. It's a *representation* of the shared, distributed knowledge and operating rules in a part of society.

Cultural modeling emerged from a wide variety of studies—in cognitive anthropology, psychology, and cognitive science—seeking to understand culture and how it is distributed and shared among individuals. Individuals are agents in this process (they dynamically manipulate, select, use, and develop cultural models), but they're also informed by the models they've learned as part of the wider social group. Cultural models are useful because they help us answer questions about how individuals learn and store cultural knowledge, including whether this is done consciously or not. Such models describe how cultural knowledge might be cognitively structured. Through understanding divergent models in a cultural or social group, we can gain greater insight into conflict within a culture—that is, we can better understand how different individuals in a given group may have differently patterned ways of thinking about and selecting available actions in a given scenario.

Because cultural models help us understand human actions and conflict, they're very useful in practicing anthropology. By contributing to our understanding of how decisions are made by individuals and how these emerge in patterns in groups, we can better comprehend how to change people's decisions, include them in programs or policies, or mediate conflict between stakeholder groups. For example, a popular development strategy is to try to increase the education of girls, because this often results in greater economic opportunity and therefore family income, as well as lower birth rates. In order to do this, it can be very helpful to understand how people in a culture perceive education (their cultural model of education) and femininity (their cultural model of womanhood). These can have clues for us as to why things are the way they are, as well as what would have to be addressed in policies or programs for things to change.

Cultural models also can help us provide the means to foster understanding among people in conflict. Let's say that you have a neighborhood trying to determine whether or not it should adopt a turf-reduction program (a program that pays homeowners to take out their lawn and put in drought-tolerant landscaping). There may be a stakeholder

Schemas
Subcomponents of cultural models that are themselves models of more narrowly defined domains that are nested within the larger domain.

group that is for turf reduction and another group against it. Starting with understanding the cultural model of landscaping for each of these groups can assist in fostering mutual understanding between them, and perhaps even compromise as policy is developed.

Free-listing is a really common method of data collection for developing cultural models. Free-listing is a structured interview or survey in which the participant is provided with a set of stimuli, then asked to spontaneously list a certain number of words or phrases (three to five is fairly common) in response to the stimuli. Participants are instructed not to think too hard about this task and not to take very long to do it. The goal is to have participants respond with the very first things that come to mind as being associated with the stimulus. The concept behind this is that the researcher is reaching into the category of concepts to which the stimulus belongs. These concepts are part of the cultural model of that stimulus, and the category as a whole (the domain) can be accessed through multiple iterations with different relevant stimuli.

Ethnographic research is necessary to have sufficient understanding of the cultural group in question and thus to select potentially relevant stimuli. The stimuli should make sense to the participants (unless selected as a control that is intentionally confusing or nonsensical), so a background knowledge of the domain in that culture is necessary to choose stimulus materials. The stimuli that are provided to participants could be written scenarios or storylines, videos, still photos, symbols, or objects, depending on the domain (see Figure 9.5 for an example).

For example, a study of romantic love as a domain could offer video clips from popular films, photos depicting couples engaged in different activities with different expressions, or stories that describe different ways that couples met and had a relationship progress. Participants would then list several words or phrases in response to each of the videos, photos, or storylines. Generally speaking, the type of stimulus (e.g., photo vs. storyline) should be consistent across the entire study to control for the medium affecting participants' responses.

One of the hardest parts of data collection for cultural modeling is selecting appropriate stimuli to begin with. As you can imagine, if you present participants with poor stimuli that are confusing, don't generate a strong response, or don't represent enough of a domain to make meaningful distinctions and extensive enough associations, you

Free-listing
A method of data collection for building cultural models in which a participant is provided with a set of stimuli and then, through a structured interview or survey, directed to spontaneously list a small number of words or phrases in response to the stimuli.

Figure 9.5 Example of a Stimulus and Free-Listed Response

Narrative 1 stimulus:
A man and a woman meet and immediately recognize that they have eyes only for each other. Their hearts beat excitedly when they are together, and each word of the other seems wonderful and deep—when all this turns out to be real, and not just brief infatuation, they then know that they will get married and live happily ever after.

Participant 01: Response 1	Love at first sight
Participant 01: Response 2	Romance
Participant 01: Response 3	Fairytale

will be unable to develop a cultural model from the data you collect. And because the interview is structured—that is, each respondent needs to be presented with the same stimuli, in the same order and in the same way, to ensure that you don't get effects from changes to the process (which can affect how people access their knowledge of a domain)—you can't clarify as you go through the interview itself (the way you might in an in-depth semi-structured interview). So as you think about getting started with cultural modeling, be very attentive to the choices you make in what you present to your participants. Refer back to field notes you've made while doing participant observation, conversations you've had with people in the population you're studying, and literature you've read about that social group and the domain in question. Use all this information to inform the way you structure your interview and the materials you select, so that you can acquire meaningful data.

Discussion

When you think about your research question you developed in Chapter 1, can you think of an aspect of this question that might benefit from a cultural modeling approach? If so, what domain would be optimal for modeling, and how would it contribute to your research question? If not, why do think this method would be inappropriate for addressing your research question?

Cultural Models: Analysis

Cultural model analysis starts with inductive coding of the free-listed data. This is done using grounded theory, as you learned to do in Chapter 7. However, you might find it easiest, for these very brief snippets of data, to code in Excel (alternatively, you might want to use Dedoose, if you wish to integrate this dataset with others—in-depth interviews, for example—or if you want to more easily explore relationships between codes). Why Excel? Excel's spreadsheet format makes it easy to alphabetize these short snippets of text and code repetitive associations all at once. Because cultural model research often uses a much larger sample size (sometimes more than one thousand participants) and associations frequently repeat from participant to participant, this provides a considerable time savings over individually coding each participant's responses. Excel can also hold demographic data in other columns, making later mixed methods analysis easier (remember, this is when you'll use quantifiable demographic data to better understand divergent patterns in qualitative data). So the first order of business, for doing the simplest cultural model analysis, is to enter the data into Excel format (see Figure 9.6 for an example). If you've used an online data collector, such as SurveyMonkey, the data can simply be downloaded into an Excel spreadsheet. If you haven't, you can enter the data in Excel from hard copy notes or free-lists. When you enter the data, if you plan

Figure 9.6 Example of Excel® Spreadsheet

	A	B	C	D	E	F
426	Naturopathic					
427	Toxin-free food, air, water, soil, body-care, cleaning products					
428	excercise	EXERCISE		111		
429	diet	DIET		65		
430	food	FOOD		49		
431	eat healthy	EATING RIGHT		35		SEE ALSO, DIET
432	nutrition	NUTRITION		23		
433	work	WORK		19		
434	my own responsibility	MY RESPONSIBILITY		14		
435	lifestyle	LIFESTYLE		10		
436	Organic	ORGANIC		9		
437	Fruit	FRUIT		8		
438	goal	GOAL		8		
439	choice	CHOICE		7		
440	hard work	HARD WORK		6		
441	Meditation	MEDITATION		6		
442	Taking care of myself	TAKING CARE OF MYS		6		
443	good food	GOOD FOOD		5		ALSO UNDER F(
444	healthy diet	HEALTHY DIET		4		ALSO SCORED L
445	healthy food	HEALTHY FOOD		4		ALSO SCORED L
446	Healthy lifestyle	HEALTHY LIVING		4		

to analyze the information based on participants' demographic or other characteristics later, you should be sure to associate each data point with a participant ID, so that all the responses will be linked to a unique identifier.

After you have a complete, aggregated (all participants together) free-list of all data, it is time to start coding. Use the data-sort function to alphabetize all responses. Select all responses that fit together (initially, the very obvious—misspellings or words with the same root and meaning) and code together. For example, "exhilaration," "exhilarating," and "exhilerating" (a misspelled response) would all be coded with something like "exhilaration." After all responses are coded in this way, you should look at your codes and sort them into categories of related codes based on similar or equivalent meaning. For example, you might then code all variants of "exhilaration," "excitement," and "elation" as "excitement" moving forward.

After you've settled on codes that adequately lump together similar responses, it's time to look for relationships among your most common codes. Cultural modeling is a numbers game—the most prevalent associations usually indicate a widespread cultural pattern, whereas rare associations indicate individual outliers. As is the case with taxonomies, models can differ by individual or subgroup—and unlike folk taxonomies, a single individual may hold a number of different cultural models for the same domain, each of which is considered valid and appropriate in certain circumstances or scenarios and not in others. Cultural modeling is about statistical probability, but sometimes a number of divergent models for the same domain will be more or less equally statistically prevalent.

What happens if stimuli produce non-responsiveness or confusion in the free-listing process? This is an indication that the stimulus itself is faulty. Examples of confused responses in free-listing could be "???," "Huh? LOL," or "What?" At other times, the responses will simply restate elements of the stimulus, because no association tied to a cultural model is actually available in the respondent's mind. When such results occur, it is important to return to the question of how to generate more appropriate, meaningful stimuli.

Codes may seem to fit together in terms of categories of significant concepts or categories of dimensions related to a particular domain. For example, a cultural model of health and healing might include concepts such as "balance" and "well-being"—each of which can be described by the codes (and associated responses) that you've determined belong to that category. A cultural model of romantic relationships might include dimensions such as emotion, judgment (i.e., moral, ethical, or positive/negative assumptions), and types of people. Models may be described by these categories and how they relate to one another. Alternatively, there may also be a number of different specific models that have names or phrases associated with them. For example, in the models of romantic

Figure 9.7 Pagan Model of Health and Healing

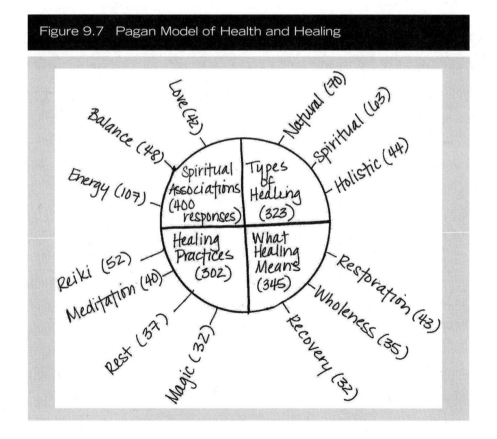

relationship, "fairytale," "gold-digger," and "player" are all labels of specific cultural schemas that integrate dimensions such as emotion, judgment, and types of people—but that vary considerably in the storyline associated with these commonly used labels.

Cultural models are often portrayed in a visual representation format with narrative text that unpacks the model, explains the relationship between its components, and provides examples of each component from participant responses (see Figure 9.7 for an example).

Cultural models can be tested through an iterative process, wherein they are translated to a series of statements, and respondents are asked to rate how much they agree with the statements (through a Likert Scale, a scale of 1–5 rated agreement, ranging from "strongly disagree" to "strongly agree"; see Figure 9.8 for an example). This allows the researcher to assess the model's accuracy in another representative sample of the cultural group in question. Accurate models will ultimately show a statistically significant set of common attributes from the free-listing process. They can be made even more accurate by incorporating very common associations from the free-lists so that they are more complete. These can then be tested on a new sample population from the same group.

The most significant challenge in cultural modeling is that it requires preexisting ethnographic and linguistic familiarity with a cultural group in order to begin to select

Figure 9.8 Likert Scale Confirmatory Research Survey Questions

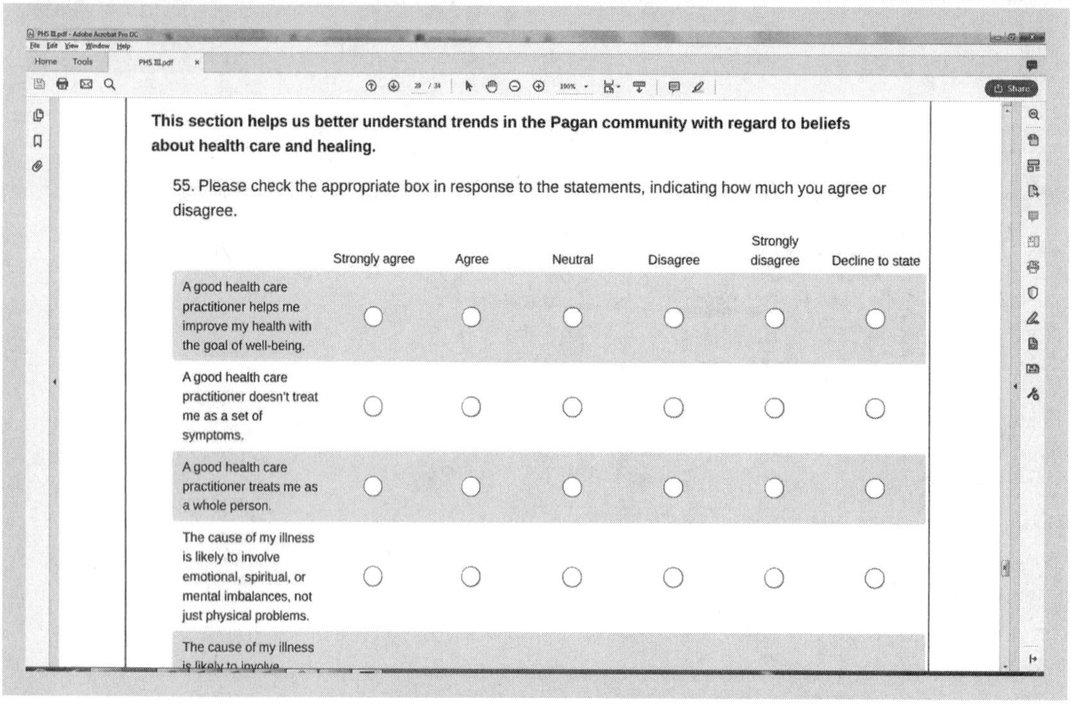

This section helps us better understand trends in the Pagan community with regard to beliefs about health care and healing.

55. Please check the appropriate box in response to the statements, indicating how much you agree or disagree.

	Strongly agree	Agree	Neutral	Disagree	Strongly disagree	Decline to state
A good health care practitioner helps me improve my health with the goal of well-being.	○	○	○	○	○	○
A good health care practitioner doesn't treat me as a set of symptoms.	○	○	○	○	○	○
A good health care practitioner treats me as a whole person.	○	○	○	○	○	○
The cause of my illness is likely to involve emotional, spiritual, or mental imbalances, not just physical problems.	○	○	○	○	○	○
The cause of my illness is likely to involve						

a meaningful domain and stimuli. The stimuli may not be maximally effective at first, which necessitates multiple iterations to more closely approximate meaningful prompts. Optimally effective stimuli may be difficult to produce—for example, in a case where video is the best type of stimuli. Finally, analysis of cultural models takes a combination of patience to wade through a lot of data and creativity in seeing the way patterns in the codes fit together to form meaningful clusters of information (schemas or cultural models). However, in patiently wading through these data, once an accurate and widely used model is constructed, it can be invaluable for communicating how a group thinks about a particular set of interactions and/or complex concepts, and this can be meaningful for mediating conflicts between groups with different models, planning for policy or programs, or understanding people whom an organization serves.

Discussion

Brainstorm several areas of your ordinary life that you navigate by engaging one or more cultural models (ones that haven't already been listed in the text here). For each one, create a mind map with what you think is the cultural model as the central focal point, connected to schemas that inform the model. Think about the relationships of how the schemas relate to one another. Once you feel that you have identified a cultural model and its potential schemas, list stimuli you think might be helpful to use in a structured interview. This process will help you assess whether or not you feel relatively confident in your understanding of what cultural models are and identify questions you may want to ask peers or your instructor.

Decision-Tree Models: Data Collection

We've covered how to model knowledge that is governed by relationships of "this is a type of that" and knowledge that helps people predict and understand social situations and interactions. **Decision-tree models** organize the use of knowledge in which people must choose between two or more options with constraints. While cultural models inform decision-tree models, they are different because they often operate in contexts in which action is either selected pre-attentively (subconsciously) or in which actions are not selected from clear "either/or" options. Many decisions that people consciously make, however, such as which car to buy or whether or not to look for a new job, are grounded in consciously chosen actions from a small number of options—and one way to investigate these is through decision-tree modeling.

Decision-tree models organize knowledge about alternatives based on aspects and limited by constraints. For example, a person might consider which college they will attend—they'll make a list of alternatives (possible choices). The potential colleges to attend will be considered by **aspects**, specific characteristics important to the decision

Decision-tree models Models that organize the use of knowledge in which people must choose between two or more options with constraints.

Aspects Specific characteristics important to the decision maker.

maker, such as distance from home, tuition cost, and amenities offered on the campus. The decision will also be governed by **constraints**, or specific limitations the person has in the decision-making process. For example, if a student wishes to study physical therapy, it's likely that they'll immediately eliminate all schools without a physical therapy program, regardless of whether or not the school is otherwise suitable. Decision-tree models emerged out of a variety of disciplinary interests but were particularly tied to research on how economic and development decisions were made in order to develop programs and policies that better spoke to ordinary people's decisions.

"Real-life" decision-tree models—those grounded in ethnographic or interview data rather than economic mathematical models—are attentive to how people actually make decisions (from the emic, or insider, perspective), rather than using mathematical formulas that achieve the right "answer" but may not explain how the answer is derived. Ethnographic decision-tree models explore how emotion and cultural values affect decisions, which may lead to "irrational" decisions that actually make sense. They remind us that ordinary people often put social standing (reputation), social relationships, and emotionally charged values ahead of optimizing outcomes. Further, these models point to the variety of constraints that affect the human creative response and therefore illustrate the intersection of individual agency and cultural knowledge in forming human action. Ultimately, decision-tree models generally include both *ideal culture* (values, ideal options, etc.) and *real culture*" (contextual modifiers that shift people toward decisions other than the ideal), and this helps us understand how culturally distributed knowledge is translated into individual actions.

Ethnographic decision-tree models—those that arise from qualitative and interactive methods—differ from economists' models because they acknowledge that "real" decision making is done to optimize a number of different goals (some seemingly unrelated to the decision at hand) and to minimize a number of different undesirable outcomes. Furthermore, the human mind simplifies the decision-making process because of our cognitive constraints. It is difficult for us to handle too much information at once in our minds, so we compensate for this through mechanisms that simplify the world and our perceived options to a reasonable workload. We do this predominantly through using our cultural knowledge to pre-attentively inform the way we see our options (through constraints) and to shape the aspects that we use to evaluate our options. Humans aren't necessarily logical decision makers, but the process isn't random. Decision making incorporates hallmarks of the human experience, such as emotion, desire or motivation, and belief, in ways that align the individual with culture.

Decision-tree models speak to theoretical interests about the interaction between the group and the individual, as well as how individuals view themselves and their actions. They're also very useful in practice. Policy makers and decision makers often need information about patterns in human action and reasons behind these actions, available in succinct and clear formats. They need information that details constraints on people's choices, provides references of cultural knowledge that informs people's choices, offers insight into how individuals come to different decisions, makes sense of irrational or unexpected choices, and predicts trends or patterns in human society. This type of information, especially if presented in a way that requires little to no background in professional social science for understanding, is very valuable in helping policy makers understand how to best shift the actions or choices that a constituency is selecting. In order to generate this information, the researcher starts on the individual scale and then tests on larger scales to confirm or deny a model that may be at work in a specific context and population.

Constraints
Specific limitations
a decision maker
is under that affect
their decision.
....

One way of doing so is through a methodological process advanced by Gladwin (1989). This researcher developed a method to study how people conceptually structure and process data in decision-making matters. She explained that the human mind chunks continuous variables (those that take place on a spectrum) into discrete categories (boundaried categories that hold specific information), that the mind makes complex calculations into sequences of simpler ones, and that it uses **rules of thumb** to predict outcomes and guide decisions. In short, the world itself is very complex, and the human mind reduces this complexity when making decisions so that it is less burdened by the process. Decisions are done in two stages (see Figure 9.9): First, **elimination by aspects**, which is often pre-attentive (subconscious), reduces a large number of alternatives to a subset of relevant alternatives to consider. For example, if you're buying a vehicle, your mind will likely pre-attentively eliminate semi-trucks and tanks, though these are vehicles.

Figure 9.9 Steps in the Decision-Making Process

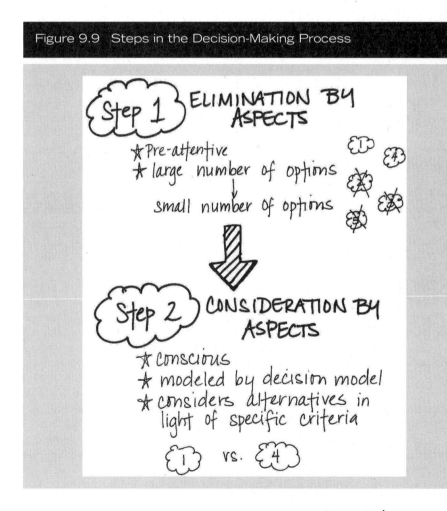

Rules of thumb Generally agreed-on principles or guides based on the collective experiences in a cultural group.

Elimination by aspects The first stage of decision making, in which a person subconsciously eliminates options deemed illogical or impossible by virtue of their cultural models, taxonomies, or other cultural knowledge.

In the second stage, people engage in **consideration by aspects**, which is the conscious, "real" part of the decision-making process. This is the stage that is modeled by a decision-tree model. In this stage, alternatives are considered in light of aspects. These aspects might be social (economic, cultural, or institutional), ecological or material, or personal (personality, desire). Aspects may involve sub-calculations, such as return on investment (what we consider we get out of investments of time, resources, etc.) or cost-benefit analysis (whether or not we think the outcomes are worth the inputs). Humans often work through their decision-making process through talking to others, considering various aspects of their decision with a friend or colleague (and sometimes even a professional, as when someone consults a financial adviser about retirement or investment decisions). Because of this, people are used to using discussion as a means to get at the conscious part of their decision-making process.

The researcher can get at this process in people's minds through structured interviews that use **comparison frames**: "Under what conditions do you do X instead of Y? Y instead of X?" To continue with our vehicle purchase example, you might ask, "Under what conditions do you buy a truck instead of buying a sedan?" You can probably already see that this type of interview is very similar to building a taxonomy, except that it isn't about kinds of things but rather is about decisions between options. Like frame elicitation, it's deceptively simple as an interview method. It's simple in the type of questions it asks, but it's deceptive because it actually takes a lot of skill on the part of the researcher to effectively probe for all the aspects being considered in a decision, rather than only those most conscious and obvious to the participant. Much of decision making is done at a subconscious level, and while a participant can become aware of it, it takes some digging on the part of the interviewer. If an interviewer glosses over the extensive probing that is typical of an ethnographic decision interview, they'll lose the detail they are seeking.

The ethnographic decision-tree model, the process developed by Gladwin (1989), is a highly effective way of understanding "this or that" decisions through interviewing relatively few participants. When we say *highly effective*, we mean that it will adequately explain the decision-making process for a group and predict outcomes of future decisions accurately—often at 90 percent accuracy, which is incredibly high for a qualitative-based model. How does the process work? In its entirety, it relies on iterative steps that refine the decision-tree model through interview data (see Figure 9.10).

Consideration by aspects The second stage of decision making, in which a person consciously weighs options based on a variety of aspects.

Comparison frames An interview technique in which the researcher presents sets of alternatives as a prompt.

It begins with asking ethnographic questions and collecting and analyzing ethnographic data, which yields better questions. The first stage, therefore, is refinement of the interview questioning process itself. This process is followed through ten iterations. That is, after ten iterations, the researcher generally understands a decision well enough to formulate a decision-tree model, which looks like a flowchart that guides a person through the decision process for a single "this or that" decision. The flowchart is essentially a compilation of all the interview data collected about how people make their decisions, combined with the refinement of the first stage. This decision-tree model is then tested through a new set of interviews, with a new sample of participants. The model is tested through asking people about their most recent decision or about a hypothetical decision and comparing their responses to the decision-tree model. The results can then be analyzed, and the model refined, if necessary.

Figure 9.10   The Ethnographic Decision-Tree Model Process

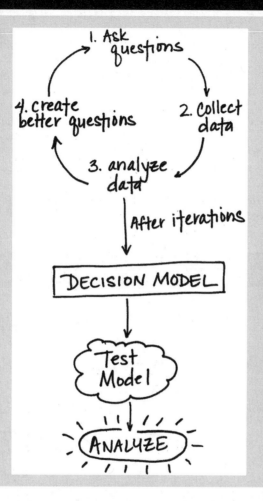

Discussion

When you think about your research question you developed in Chapter 1, can you think of an aspect of this question that might benefit from a decision-tree modeling approach? If so, what domain would be optimal for modeling, and how would it contribute to your research question? If not, why do think this method would be inappropriate for addressing your research question?

Decision-Tree Models: Analysis

Decision-tree models are usually presented as flowcharts. These are very useful for conveying cultural assumptions, interests, concerns, and views in a single at-a-glance representation for policy makers. First, the researcher should make decision flowcharts for each respondent. Very important aspects that are considered at the beginning of the decision-making process go at the top of the flowchart, while less important aspects that are considered later go at the bottom of the flowchart. Pre-attentive decisions are not represented—only those that are in conscious awareness. Each flowchart begins with the most important aspect related to the decision you are researching and ends with the various decision outcomes that might occur, given your research question (i.e., "this" or "that" outcome). Each decision leads to a "yes" or "no" decision, which then leads to another aspect question or to a particular decision outcome, depending on what participants describe in their interviews. The flowchart will look something like Figure 9.11.

This is a very simplified version of what a decision-tree model might look like for a person renting an apartment. Most decision-tree models, even for relatively minor

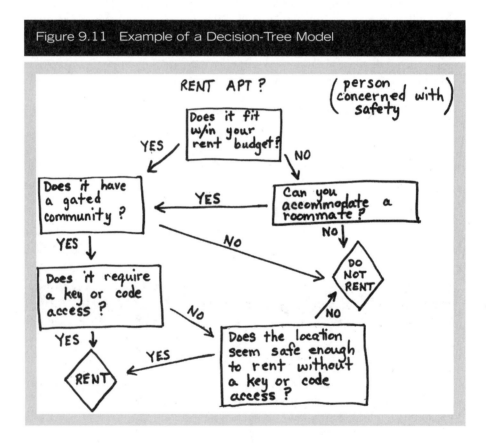

Figure 9.11   Example of a Decision-Tree Model

decisions, are actually quite complex if the researcher probes enough. For renting an apartment, a person may consider all sorts of features of the apartment itself (the number of bedrooms and bathrooms, square footage, closet space), issues related to the neighborhood (school ratings, crime rates, amenities and services), financial concerns (not only the rent cost but also commute costs and average utility bills), design features (paint color, kitchen tile, counters, cabinets), and security features of the apartment building (gated community, key or code access). A prospective apartment tenant may have long checklists of aspects they are considering. The researcher will note that aside from a great many aspects, there may be categories of these aspects, and the renter will likely prioritize these by importance.

After the researcher has drawn up flowcharts for each of their respondents, it is time to draft a decision-tree model that represents the common patterns among the respondents. In this case, as much as possible, even outliers' aspects should be included in the model. This is for two reasons: First, decision-tree models are frequently constructed with relatively few interviewees, which means that each participant is more likely to represent a broader trend, even if they seem unique in the sample. Second, many respondents, when prompted in interviews about decisions they make, do not have full conscious awareness of all the aspects they consider or find it challenging to recall them all on demand (without a decision needing to be made) and recite them to the researcher. Including as many aspects as possible helps ensure that more of the broader patterns from the culture in question are included.

The flowcharts for each respondent are compared, side by side. Commonalities are noted, such as very commonly considered aspects and common ranking of aspects (as more or less important). Then, as much as possible, the researcher forges ahead on a tentative flowchart model that represents all the respondents at once. This can then be tested on the respondents' data (to see if the model actually represents the data that have already been collected) and on another sample (to test the model itself and how strong it is against a new set of respondents). This can be done iteratively until the decision-tree model has a high degree of accuracy (more than 90 percent) among a sample population.

It is easier to start data collection for decision-tree models than for folk taxonomies or cultural models, because they are more like an in-depth interview—you only need questions; you don't need stimuli. However, the analysis of decision-tree models is challenging and time-consuming. Multiple decisions related to a domain can take a lot of time for data collection and analysis. Aspects of a decision may be subconscious and initially difficult to draw out in interviews, necessitating that researchers skillfully probe for more information. However, accurate decision-tree models are important sources of information, particularly for policy makers, social marketers, and those who administer programs—all of whom frequently wish to change a group's behavior but first need to understand why they do what they do. Overall, cognitive anthropological approaches are ways to get at specific emic understandings and etic representations of those understandings that inform behavior in specific domains. This makes them particularly suitable for aiding agencies or organizations in understanding those they serve and making appropriate, optimal decisions about how to best engage them.

Try diagramming a decision you've made in the past where you had to make a choice between two options (this could have been a "yes/no" or "either/or" decision). First, list all the aspects you considered when making your decision. Then try to prioritize (based on your memory), identifying which aspects were considered first and which were considered later in your decision-making process. Finally, try to diagram your decision process using a flowchart. This will get you started with thinking about how to visually display decision making and help you identify steps or concepts related to decision-tree models that are confusing or unclear for you.

Pairing the Textbook and Workbook

In this chapter, you've learned three of the most commonly used methods for modeling cognition and cultural knowledge: folk taxonomies, cultural models, and ethnographic decision-tree models. Many students find these methods more challenging, both in terms of understanding the theory underlying the methods and in terms of successfully building valid models. Remember, these methods have very particular applications and work only for certain kinds of narrowly defined research questions. Trying to use these methods to think about your own interior life—the ways you navigate social spaces, learn, communicate, and make decisions—will help you build a level of comfort and confidence in thinking like a cognitive anthropologist. As you try these methods out, you'll find them more foreign than in-depth interviews, because they structure the interactions with your participants in odd ways designed to reveal frequently subconscious patterns in how your participants think. Keep working at it! These methods are extremely useful in applied anthropology, so as was the case with surveys, it's a good idea to work on mastering them. You'll get more comfortable with these methods with practice.

Reflective Prompts

1. Am I monitoring my understanding? Have I backed up to reread a section for better understanding?

2. Do I understand the different types of information gathered and presented through folk taxonomy, cultural modeling, and ethnographic decision-tree modeling study designs?

3. Though I know selecting a research study design is related to the research question, which of these types of study designs resonated most with me as a researcher? Why?

Case Study

Kronenfeld, David B. 2008. *Culture, Society, and Cognition: Collective Goals, Values, Action, and Knowledge.* Mouton Series in Pragmatics; 3. Berlin and New York: De Gruyter Mouton.

Kronenfeld, David B., John Kronenfeld, and Jerrold E. Kronenfeld. 1972. "The Cognition of Restaurant Interiors." *Institutions/Volume Feeding* (June 12): 38–44.

The Project

Collective shared cognitive structures are often open-ended, so it helps to begin your modeling with a quick "snapshot" of the most shared central core, whether you are looking at a snapshot of a city, or a building, or disciplines—all kinds of things. In one study, I had a bunch of students describe a high school, both in the United States and in Mexico, by drawing one—not a specific one, just whatever the words evoked. In the United States, I got quasi-functional buildings on a dispersed campus, and playing fields. In Mexico, people drew a two-story building, with a flagpole and some classrooms. The composite drawing based on items showing up in several drawings becomes a rough approximation of a default picture they share, and what the terms evoke, before you put other scenarios or contexts in the picture. If you're approaching a new problem, you want to get a lay of the land without investing a lot of money or time. You don't need a big sample for this stage, either. Ten people are enough to get a picture that is fairly stable. This work and many similar projects are detailed in my book on culture, society, and cognition.

How do cognitive methods flow into one another, and for what purposes? How do you pick a method?

One of my criteria is what is worth the investment of time and money to answer a research question. You have the quick and messy methods: free-listing, sketching, and so on. These are analytic games to get at patterns of relevant ideas in culture. But you need the research question, or the pattern isn't very meaningful. With a research question, this approach gives you an initial starting point for patterns showing up in the population. At some point, you might want to move to more closed-ended things to get a tighter picture of that initial pattern. I did that once with restaurants in my first publication, which was on restaurant interiors. A class of students gave me quick sketches based on the word *restaurant*, and I made a composite from the shared features of those sketches. Some did a floor plan, and others did perspective pictures. In each case, their picture was your sort of generic Denny's or IHOP type of restaurant. There are a lot variations on this kind of method, and you want to be flexible and creative in approaching the question. You have to ask: Am I getting what I want from this? Are the time and money necessary to do it worth the results I am getting?

In other studies, where you're getting at collective structures that are communicated between people, you elicit statements about attributes of items in the domain that has come to people's minds. Then you turn the sentences or phrases you've collected into questions. In these studies, you have research questions that are shared across a population, and you don't need a lot of

(Continued)

people to understand these patterns. In general, with that kind of process, when the next few people you ask the questions of don't change your picture of the domain, your picture of the domain is stable. You start with an exploratory work, and you end with a more closed-ended method. Just getting a simple list of concepts associated with a word is cheap and easy and gives a first approximation of the domain.

If you're really trying to pursue things more deeply, you have to talk to people. And here, you can move to frame eliciting, which is a careful way to work through questions. You're working in the informants' language, and you're asking them generic questions and letting them come up with relevant specific versions of these. And then you're putting these into some kind of semantic structure. Some use it as an ethnographic technique, and others use it as an analytic structure for relating concepts. So you move from generic to specific questions, and you use the questions to organize the domain space. I've done some both ways with the car universe, which is messy because you have taxonomic-like structures of manufacturers, brands, and model types; of features, price, and luxury levels; and so forth. Once you find out that there are these different types of cars, there are games you can play, depending on what you want to study. Do you want people's default understanding of cars? Do you want to know the reasons why people might want one kind or another—the constraints that shape purchases? Why they made the choices they did? The frame eliciting is where you want to get a detailed mapping out of the domain, and it's a bit like a combination of a data collection method and an analytic method. But frame eliciting is very expensive. Not in money, but in time. It doesn't

take a big sample, but it takes a tremendous amount of time in each informant. And it's hard on informants. It's a lot of work—work for them, work for you. If you do it carefully and don't take shortcuts, it's boring as hell.

Finally, once you've done this frame elicitation thing, let's say now you have all these types of cars. You'd like to know the actual distribution: How many people have this versus that type of the car? At that point, you do a survey.

What kinds of anthropological questions drive your research in kinship?

I like to observe things in casual experience, and this is partly my fascination with kinship. I can observe these things in my own culture and then compare my observations in meaningful ways with my observations among the Fanti. It's not all people and personalities in kinship; it is also structure. And at the same time, it's not just structure; kinship is individuals and their personalities and contexts. So playing exotic or esoteric knowledge against everyday knowledge is of inestimable value. The more I do this, and the older I get, the more a framework develops to understand and interpret the data I collected when I was much younger. It's all about understanding the world, and we understand it in different ways. The formal system is useful—and I'm a big fan of this—but it's only one piece of a puzzle.

What advice do you have about cognitive anthropology research, based on your research career, for beginning researchers?

I carefully collected very systematic data in Ghana, making sure I had data on each of the steps between problem and conclusion, which enabled a very careful and detailed analysis. The typical anthropological trajectory is you go out there for a year, and you write it up and then move on to something else. But my well-thought-out systematic data enabled fifteen years of subsequent analytic work. I still get new insights on Fanti kinship as I find new analytic perspectives. So my strategy is to work more intensively on analyzing the data over time. I myself am not doing introspective ethnography, though I think it too has a use. My own ideal study is to compare a native anthropologist's ethnography with an outsider's. They will attend to very different things. It's not that either is right or wrong, but a native anthropologist finds the ordinary stuff in culture boring. This is why kids are so fun, because they force you to see the familiar through fresh eyes. When they're four or five years old, it's a whole new world for them.

Case Study Reflections

1. Kronenfeld has worked extensively on kinship systems throughout his career (as well as numerous other domains). How does his work on kinship tie in to the bigger theoretical questions anthropologists ask?

2. Kronenfeld describes a way in which multiple methods in cognitive anthropology can work together to refine understanding of a domain over time. Chart the course of action he proposes, and then generate an example that could work for this progressive, iterative research model.

3. Why would starting with a survey in cognitive anthropology pose problems for the data's accuracy and usefulness?

4. How has Kronenfeld used his initial ethnographic data over the course of his career? How might this trajectory provide insights that are different from the kinds produced by research careers that pick up more varied topics, field sites, and projects?

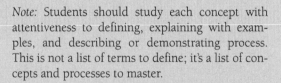

STUDY GUIDE

Note: Students should study each concept with attentiveness to defining, explaining with examples, and describing or demonstrating process. This is not a list of terms to define; it's a list of concepts and processes to master.

Cognitive anthropology

Ethnoscience

Model

Taxonomies

Folk taxonomies

Pile sorting

Frame elicitation

Lumpers and splitters

Cultural models

Schemas

Free-listing

Decision-tree models

Aspects

Constraints

Rules of thumb

Elimination by aspects

Consideration by aspects

Comparison frames

FOR FURTHER STUDY

Bernard, H. Russell. 2018. "Cognitive Anthropology I" and "Cognitive Anthropology II." In *Research Methods in Anthropology*, by H. Russell Bernard, 362–436. Lanham, MD: Rowman and Littlefield.

D'Andrade, Roy G. 1995. *The Development of Cognitive Anthropology*. Cambridge: Cambridge University Press.

Gladwin, Christina H. 1989. *Ethnographic Decision Tree Modeling*. Newbury Park, CA: SAGE.

Kronenfeld, David B. 2008. *Culture, Society, and Cognition: Collective Goals, Values, Action, and Knowledge*. Berlin and Boston: De Gruyter Mouton.

Pelto, Pertti J. 2013. "Free Lists: Getting an Inventory of Things in a Cultural Domain" and "Pile Sorting and Other Structured Interviews." In *Applied Ethnography: Guidelines for Field Research*, by Pertti J. Pelto, 169–98. Walnut Creek, CA: Left Coast Press.

Visit **study.sagepub.com/kirner** to help you accomplish your coursework goals in an easy-to-use learning environment.

CHAPTER 10

Indirect Observation

Orientation

So far, we've described methods of **direct observation**: methods that you use to directly participate in and observe people's behaviors or methods that ask them to describe their own thoughts, feelings, and behaviors. In this chapter, we'll cover a few methods of **indirect observation**, which use as data what is left over from human activity. You might think of indirect observation as the archaeology of human thoughts and behaviors, and, indeed, many of these methods are held in common with archaeologists. While this chapter provides the basics on these methods, archaeological training would greatly enhance your ability to use these methods effectively. In ethnography, indirect observation is most often useful when triangulated with other forms of data: that is, alongside interviews, surveys, or participant observation.

Visual and Material Culture

Anthropologists call the kinds of visual and material culture that we study **texts**. This doesn't mean that all texts are narratives or language-based (see Figure 10.1). In an anthropological sense, texts can include things such as photographs, artworks, and artifacts. Some texts are a combination of language-based data and visual data, such as memes on social media, flyers or signs, graffiti, and comics. Almost anything that human beings create can be considered a text for study. For example, an anthropologist might consider a **corpus** (collection) of graffiti, investigating not only the messages but also the images incorporated, the writing styles, and the locations the author-artist selected.

Chapter Learning Objectives

Students will be able to do the following:

10.1 Describe how to create study designs of visual and material culture

10.2 Explain how to collect and analyze visual and material culture data

10.3 Describe how to create study designs that incorporate diaries and explain how to collect and analyze diary data

10.4 Describe how to create study designs of archival materials and explain how to collect and analyze archival data

10.5 Explain how the original context of visual, material, and archival data is significant for interpretation

Figure 10.1 Types of Texts

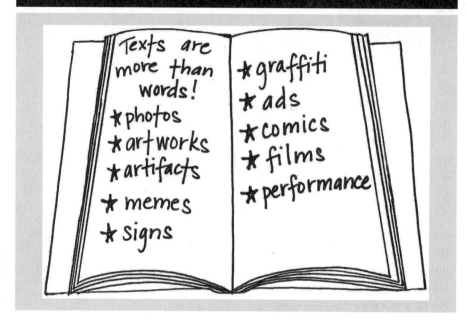

Texts are more than words!
* photos
* artworks
* artifacts
* memes
* signs
* graffiti
* ads
* comics
* films
* performance

Direct observation
Methods that directly observe or participate in people's behaviors or that ask them direct questions about their thoughts, feelings, and behaviors.

Indirect observation
Methods that analyze the materials left behind by human activities, such as material culture (artifacts, buildings), visual data (art, photos), and archives (written documents).

Texts A group of data for anthropological analysis (which does not have to be narrative or language-based).

Corpus A collection of texts.

An anthropologist may select a specific type of text in order to study how that particular form of expression conveys meaning, or they might select a wide range of texts related to a specific topic. In the case of studying graffiti, a researcher might be interested in who produces graffiti, what they are communicating, and whether they are using it as a means of artistic expression or merely to convey a functional meaning. Conversely, a researcher interested in how people are creating and sharing messages related to veganism might focus all the texts in their corpus on veganism or animal agriculture but may select many different types of texts, such as memes, social media narrative posts, advertisements, videos, signs, and even protest actions. For example, one such action conducted in 2008 by the People for the Ethical Treatment of Animals (PETA) in Seattle, Washington, involved models laying in pools of fake blood, wrapped in plastic packaging. Such actions are expressive in nature and can serve as one of the texts that inform an understanding of how people understand veganism and convey core messages about it to others.

The starting point for working with visual and material culture data is to translate whatever the information is to a photo that can be digitally cataloged. You'll want a consistent file-naming system, similar to what you did when naming files for interview data. In all cases of using such texts, you should be sure to record where, when, and how you got the data (see Figure 10.2 for an example). Where was the protest sign you have a photo of, at what protest, and when? Did you take a photograph of the sign, or did you acquire it from a newspaper? Second, you should record how the video, image, or item was used (its explicit use or meaning), if you know this information. Think back to analyzing data for manifest versus latent content. You'll want to record the manifest content

Figure 10.2 Example of a Record of Visual or Material
Culture Data

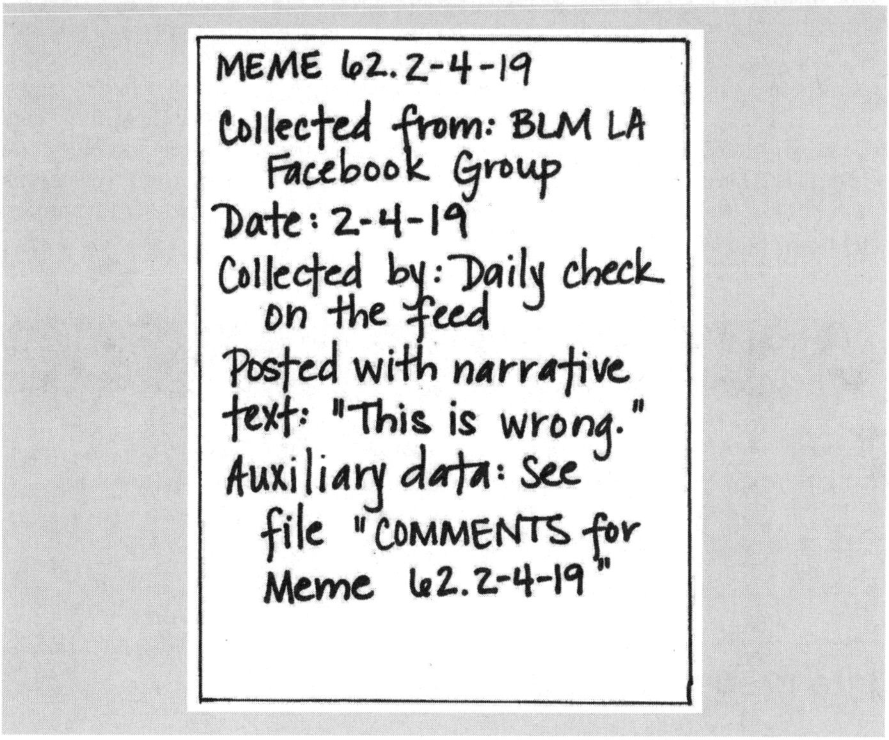

> MEME 62. 2-4-19
>
> Collected from: BLM LA
>   Facebook Group
> Date: 2-4-19
> Collected by: Daily check
>   on the feed
> Posted with narrative
> text: "This is wrong."
> Auxiliary data: See
>   file "COMMENTS for
>   Meme 62. 2-4-19"

of the data, if you have this information. In the example of the PETA protest action, the manifest content was an expressive piece protesting animal agriculture and meat-eating. But there could be latent content as well.

Finally, you should record any auxiliary data that give further insight into the piece's meaning. This could include interview notes from informants to whom you show the item or observed communications around you in the original setting where the item was. If you're observing the PETA protest action, and people around you are talking about it, it would be helpful to capture (through field jottings) what they say about it. This can be more helpful in some ways than interviewing people about it later (using photographs), because it provides insight into how other people interpret and receive the expressive piece in its original context. However, if you aren't able to observe people's reactions in the original context, and you are curious how the piece is received by others, you can provide people with video or photos of the data (whether a protest action, an artwork, or a meme) in interview or survey contexts. In this way, you can ask others what they think the piece means and how it makes them feel.

Remember that interpreting visual data of all kinds is very challenging. Frequently, there are multiple messages and multiple uses embedded in non-narrative data. Much of the time, visual data contain both manifest and latent content. For example, in the PETA protest piece, the organization used models who were young, white, and thin and who were presented nearly naked. While the manifest content of the piece was about animal agriculture, the latent content included messages about women's bodies. Additionally, visual data can be tricky because the text often relies on **symbols** to convey its message. Symbols frequently have **multivalent** and **dynamic** meanings, which enable them to generate meaning and emotion for many different people, but which also make them more challenging for anthropologists to decode. Because of these qualities of visual data, you must gather information about how others (your participants) create meaning of the visual data. This isn't as simple as looking for latent meanings; you have to engage people in the culture you are studying to understand their own meaning-making as a process and in terms of the meanings they generate.

Discussion

When you think about your research question you developed in Chapter 1, can you think of any visual or material culture data that would be significant to consider? Try making a list of the texts you would include based on your research topic. How might you collect these texts for study?

Interpreting Material Culture

There are many ways to approach interpreting material culture and visual data. As we just discussed, it's very important to gather participants' own ways of making meaning out of such data. Before attempting to analyze the data, you should generally think about how to gather data associated with the visual or material culture piece that provides insight into how participants in the culture make meaning of it. In some cases, such as many memes shared on social media, the visual data are accompanied by narrative data that provide context as to how the participant (who shared the meme) understands the visual data, creates meaning out of the information, and shares it with others (including why they share it). In other cases, such as images of the Virgin Mary, there may be no associated narrative data. In these cases, it is helpful to provide images you are analyzing to participants and ask them for their reactions. You can ask questions such as "So tell me about what this means. . ." or "How does this image make you feel, and why?"

Visual data can be very helpful for the study of cultural domains as well. For example, you could gather advertisements that show women doing various activities and ask participants to free-list associations with each of the advertisements. Conversely, you could ask participants (especially if you are working through an online medium) to pick three advertisements they think show what a "real woman" is and then to explain why they selected those. There are many ways to use visual and material culture data integrated with more direct forms of observation and questioning or triangulated with these more direct forms.

Symbols Things that stand for something else.

Multivalent The quality of symbols that allows them to have multiple meanings for different people.

Dynamic The quality of symbols that allows their meaning to change over time.

Once you've assembled not only your texts (your visual and material culture data) but also the auxiliary data you need, it's time to analyze the data! There are many ways you can approach analyzing the data. You can use grounded theory to look for common patterns in the visual data (or reactions to the data) itself. You can use content analysis to look for latent messages in the data. For example, if you have a body of texts that focus on "fitness," you might decide to investigate the texts for representations of gender, sexuality, age, and race, to locate any latent messages about who is considered fit (or who belongs in spaces and pursues activities dedicated to fitness). Similar to cultural modeling, you might look for patterns in frequency and use: Where and when does the image or material item show up? Finally, you might look for symbolic meaning, but you should do this very cautiously. Usually, you need participants' reactions and ways of making meaning of the image or artifact to adequately understand its symbolic meanings. This is because symbols are often tied to complex historical and cultural contexts that structure their meaning.

Discussion

Considering the texts that you thought would be helpful to examine for your research topic, how might you best approach analyzing them? Think first about the steps you might take to ensure you have data on how your participants make meaning of the data. Then think about how your research question might be best addressed through a specific analytical method.

Diary Studies

There are two primary types of narrative texts used for triangulation in ethnographic research: **diaries**, which participants can produce themselves and **archives**, which are narrative texts that already exist. Unlike archives, diaries are produced by participants based on guidance or instruction from a researcher. Diaries are often helpful for triangulating data, especially in the case of tracking behaviors that might be difficult to fully capture through interviews or surveys. For example, let's say you're interested in food habits among college students. While you will be able to get at some of their choices through surveys or interviews, it's likely that your participants will not accurately report what they're eating. Why? Think back to the things that can go awry in interview data. Your participants may report better eating habits than they actually have due to social shaming around eating fast food and snack food. Or perhaps your participants have forgotten what they ate over the course of the past week, which is highly likely because such information isn't something we usually have to remember. Collecting food diaries from your participants, in which they track what they eat, when, and where for a week, will enhance your data in multiple ways. You will have a better record of what people are

Diaries Narrative texts that participants produce, tracking their feelings, thoughts, or experiences.

Archives Narrative records that already exist, which can come from a wide range of sources (including historical documents and contemporary digital narratives).

actually eating, where and when, and potentially therefore why (such as noticing patterns of eating fast food when people have a long day on the college campus). But you'll also be able to see discrepancies between the way people remember and report their eating habits and what people are actually eating, which provides potentially interesting information about how college students understand their own foodways.

There are three types of diaries that are often useful for ethnographic research: regular-interval diaries, signal-entry diaries, and event-contingent diaries (see Figure 10.3). Each type of diary is suitable to different types of research questions. The **regular-interval diary** is a type in which people make entries at a regular period of time, such as daily or weekly. Regular-interval diaries are particularly helpful when the research question involves understanding people's ordinary patterns of life. For example, perhaps you'd like to better understand gender roles in the household and how they've changed over the generations. While you could interview people about their views on gender roles, you likely won't get the whole story. Many people don't calculate how they spend their time and the household tasks they do (as well as their frequency), so their views on gender roles may not match the way in which they spend their time and effort in the household. Asking people to keep a daily diary that tracks their tasks and the time they

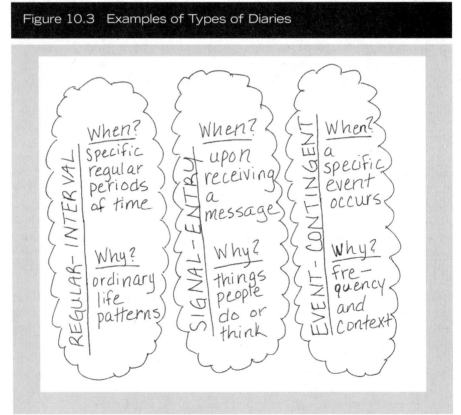

Figure 10.3   Examples of Types of Diaries

REGULAR-INTERVAL
When?
Specific regular periods of time

Why?
ordinary life patterns

SIGNAL-ENTRY
When?
upon receiving a message

Why?
things people do or think

EVENT-CONTINGENT
When?
a specific event occurs

Why?
frequency and context

Regular-interval diary A diary that people keep for a regular period of time, such as daily or weekly.

spend on them can provide valuable data on how people operationalize their gender roles into their daily lives.

A **signal-entry diary** relies on the researcher to send a message to the participant to write in their diary. Researchers using this diary method often program devices, such as apps on a smartphone, to periodically send such messages automatically. The prompt can be provided at random times during waking hours. Signal-entry diaries are particularly useful for understanding the ways in which people spend their time or the thoughts that they have. As you'll read about in Chapter 11, there are ways to address this question through direct observation, but it can be very invasive for participants. Signal-entry diaries accomplish producing a similar dataset without intruding so much on participants' lives.

Finally, an **event-contingent diary** instructs the participant to make entries when a particular event occurs. For example, let's return to our gender roles project. One way to approach this research question was to use a regular-interval diary, keeping track of the tasks that people of different genders (and in different household arrangements) do. Another way to approach the same research topic, but getting at different questions, is to ask about individuals' experience of stress and whether this is related at all to gender roles. An event-contingent diary would ask participants to make an entry each time they felt stressed, recording the date/time and the circumstances in which they felt the stress. The frequency of stress and the context around it would help the researcher determine whether gender roles and relationships in the household play a role in stress.

While diaries of all kinds used to be literal notebooks (and still can be), with the rise of the internet and smartphones, many researchers now use websites with logins or apps. The use of apps is particularly helpful in the contemporary developed world because people then nearly always have their diary with them in their phone. Entries, especially if they are customarily short, can easily be made anywhere and at any time. Apps can also be programmed to provide reminders to log in and make an entry, making it easier for the researcher to ensure that the participant maintains regular participation. Diaries in illiterate populations can be made by using colors or shapes to represent behaviors or feelings and tick marks for recording behaviors. There are many ways to work around participants' limitations in order to acquire the necessary data! While diaries are a form of indirect observation, remember that because you are having participants produce original data, you will need to collect informed consent. This should be collected using the same type of informed consent form that you used for interviews but should reflect the procedures used for the diary study.

Analyzing diaries is like analyzing other forms of narratives. You can use a variety of analytical methods, but a common one for diary-related studies is deductive content analysis. In this form of analysis, you create a framework for analyzing the data ahead of time that is related to your research question. Unlike latent content analysis, you're not looking for hidden meanings in the diaries. Instead, you're defining the purpose of the diaries ahead of time in order to clearly prompt the participants and then using the data you collect to answer those specific research questions. For example, if you're interested in what causes stress among college students, you'd analyze the diaries for patterns related to where the stress occurred (on campus, at home, at work), when (day of week, time of semester), and why (exam next week, work scheduled changed, had an argument with a friend). Your codebook, therefore, could change dynamically as you analyze the data but is structured ahead of time to speak directly to your research question and the kinds of information you are prompting participants to give you in their diaries.

Signal-entry diary
A diary that prompts participants to make an entry based on messages from the researcher (at structured or random times).

Event-contingent diary A diary in which participants make entries only when specific events occur.

Discussion

When you think about your research question you developed in Chapter 1, can you think of an aspect of this question that might benefit from diary data? What would that question be? What kind of diary would you use, and why?

Archival Studies and Digital Ethnography

Remember that archival studies analyze narrative data that already exist, usually in the form of a collection of historical or contemporary documents. These documents might be historical letters, company records and reports, blog posts, or discussions among fans on social media. There are many different kinds of archival documents, but what exists won't always match what you'd optimally use for your research. You can start from two different points in archival research: from your research question or from an archival collection that exists. In the case of starting from your research question, you would need to creatively

Figure 10.4 Methodology Combining Interviews and Archival Data

think of what documents may exist already that relate to your question and then attempt to locate these (see Figure 10.4). For example, one of your authors, Kimberly Kirner, was interested in comparing how people experienced environmental change over time and how it was characterized by land and water management agencies. In this case, she could collect interviews from elders about their memories of specific local places over the last fifty years and then compare their memories with the ways agencies described these places in official reports. By doing so, she could better understand critical differences in how organizations and local communities notice and understand environmental change, as well as the ways in which these might lead to conflict between the two groups.

The other starting point is to develop research questions that arise from a particularly compelling archival collection (see Figure 10.5). Kirner was doing an internship at a bioregenerative farm, phenomenologically approaching the issue of how adults learn to sustainably produce food. The farm asked all interns to write blog entries about their experiences during the internship. This blog formed an archive of current and past interns' learning processes, in their own words. Such an archive could inspire multiple research questions: What is most salient (noticeable) to people as they learn? What feelings does learning to farm elicit? How are people's feelings linked to their learning process? Does learning to farm change how people emotionally and spiritually relate to food and the land, and if so, how? Does learning to farm together change how people

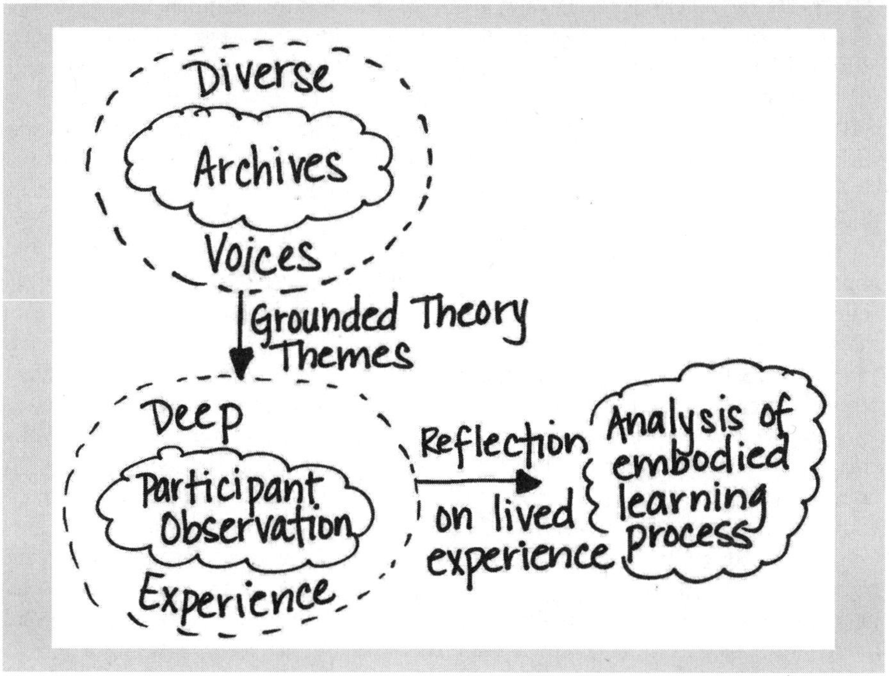

Figure 10.5 Methodology Combining Intensive Participant Observation and Archival Data

socially relate to each other? How do people choose to express their learning process? In this case, the value of the archival material is found not in comparing it to some other body of data (or even the researcher's own experience) but rather in providing a broader set of data from a more diverse group of interns, to pair with the researcher's deep interior experience of the learning process.

The advantage of archival data is that the information is completely nonreactive. Unlike interviews or participant observation, in which people around the researcher may change their responses or behavior based on the researcher's qualities, archival data are static and therefore nonreactive. These data can also be invaluable for studying cultural change over time, because you can select contemporary and historical archival sources that speak to the same issues. However, archival data are not without their disadvantages. The sources are sometimes not very accurate. The researcher must always remember that they're reading a human being's *interpretation* of events and processes, not an objective recording of exactly what occurred. This is true even if you are using sources that are supposed to be objective. Think back to Chapter 1. Remember how truth is always somewhat subjective, because reality is interpreted through human brains? This applies to archival data, even supposedly objective sources, as well. A government agency's report or a scientist's published findings may have the *intention* to be objective, but invariably there will be a certain amount of bias and interpretation that finds its way into the document. When we use archival sources, we have to remember that we are analyzing a variety of different documents, written for varied (and sometimes oppositional) purposes and audiences. It is important to use our understanding of the source's author, cultural and historical context, and intended purpose and audience in our analysis of the information we can extract from the archival material.

Finally, the other big challenge in archival research is that you may struggle to find sources that speak to your research question. Sometimes, as a researcher, you have a sense of what would be very helpful, but it may never have existed. Additionally, archival materials are unfortunately sometimes destroyed, because they can be expensive and space-consuming to maintain. Many museums, libraries, government agencies, and research institutions have to make difficult decisions about destroying documents that are deemed to have marginal research or historical value. Sometimes, we don't realize those documents have value until a researcher asks a new question. Other times, archival materials may exist but may be very difficult to locate. They might exist in small libraries or university collections that aren't readily available. They may exist in private collections, such as families' collections of their ancestors' letters and diaries. In many cases, through enough footwork and the social network that researchers build with one another, you'll be able to locate materials that enhance your research. However, in some cases, the archival materials that would assist you might never be found.

Ultimately, the types of archival documents that you select, and the ways in which you choose to analyze them, are dependent on your research question. For some types of research questions, a deductive content analysis approach is best. For example, in Kirner's work to compare local elders' accounts of environmental change with agencies' documents, a deductive codebook that coded the decade of change, type of environmental change, and assumed causal factors created continuity in approaching the different kinds of data, focusing the analysis in ways that would address the research question. Conversely, in coding intern farmer blogs, a grounded theory approach was best, because the interns expressed a wide range of information in their blogs, ranging from inspired poetry to detailed, pragmatic summaries of what they learned. You have to consider your research question and then skim over some of the archival materials you will analyze in order to also use an analytical method that speaks to the archival materials themselves: the sorts of expression they use, the information they contain, and how different or similar these might be.

For some anthropologists, their entire fieldwork, including participant observation, is online in virtual spaces. **Digital fieldwork** is ethnography with an online field site, such as discussion forums, social media sites, and blogs. The difference between digital ethnography and archival studies is that in digital fieldwork, much like in regular fieldwork, the anthropologist enters a space as a participant observer. Therefore, while archival studies may pull online documents for analysis, digital ethnography will engage the researcher in participating in online communities. It is this participation over time, in a virtual space that forms a social network or community of people interacting with one another, that is the difference between archival studies and digital ethnography. Digital ethnography can be very helpful, especially when paired with event-based or multi-sited research, to study research topics and populations that are not geographically boundaried. These might be studies of things such as fandom (of sports teams, authors/book series, films, or comics), minority religious traditions (especially new religious movements, such as Neo-Pagan traditions), and social and political movements (such as Black Lives Matter).

Remembering the Original Context

In all forms of indirect observation, it's important to remember the context around the data. With the exception of diary studies, which the researcher prompts, the materials being treated as data were not produced for the purpose of the study at hand. It's very important to capture the original context and consider it in our analysis. Whom was the original piece crafted for (the audience)? What circumstances, historical and cultural contexts, and events prompted the piece to be created? From what perspective was the creator of the piece operating? How was the creator of the piece positioned in their society, and how did this inform the piece's content and choices of expression? What were the creator's goals or agenda? How are we reinterpreting the piece outside of its original context? When collecting existing materials to study, never forget that these already existed for an audience and a purpose—and this context is necessary for fully analyzing the materials as data.

Digital fieldwork
Ethnography with an online field site.

You've learned three of the common ways researchers use indirect observation: studies of visual and material culture, studies of diaries, and studies of archival materials. We can consider these methods auxiliary to the core methods of participant observation, interviews, and surveys because they are relevant only to specific research questions and when the appropriate materials exist. Most students will find that the types of research questions or topics that interest them either lend themselves to one of these methods, or they don't. Some students also feel more drawn to studies of existing cultural data (photographs, artistic works, archival materials), while others feel intimidated or bored by such studies. The important thing is to be sure that the research questions you select will fit with the methods you will use. You can use your own life (or the lives of your friends and family) to consider the sorts of aspects of your life that would show up in materials that exist, such as your social media posts, your journals, or your photographs. As you try these methods out, you might find them comfortable and familiar (if you are used to reflecting on your own life through social media posting, keeping a diary, or creating art), or you might find them challenging. Don't forget to reflect, as you practice, on your own learning process and how your relative level of comfort and confidence is related to the ways in which you chronicle your own life.

Reflective Prompts

1. What strategies have been most helpful for me to learn concepts throughout this course?

2. Can I explain the different types of indirect observation?

3. Can I generate examples of research questions that would be suitable for a study that incorporates visual or material culture?

Case Study

Scheld, Suzanne. 2003. "The City in a Shoe: Redefining Urban Africa through Sebago Footwear Consumption." *City & Society* 15, no. 1: 109–30.

Scheld, Suzanne. 2007. "Youth Cosmopolitanism: Clothing, the City and Globalization in Dakar, Senegal." *City & Society* 19, no. 2: 232–53.

The Project

In my work in Dakar, my focus was on fashion and clothing and how these relate to self-representation. I used photography. I had students in Dakar tell me about their daily lives through photography of their neighborhoods. They also used photography to capture their view of current fashion styles and then wrote short stories about these styles and why they were important. I collected styles and youth perspectives on these fashions through engaging one middle-class and one poorer-class neighborhood in producing an informal fashion journal. I gave them disposable cameras, and then we looked at all these photos together, and they picked pictures that were meaningful to them. They wrote short stories about these photos, and then we did fashion magazines based on this work.

The less-than-middle-class group had many more traditional forms of clothing. They photographed their mothers and aunts more often, because they felt it was the right thing to do, and they had relationships with adults that required that. The middle-class group didn't have as much intervention from adults. Photography captured the meanings of the fashions, but the process of doing this work illuminated so much more of what young people's lives were about. The stories they wrote were great, and sometimes so funny. The students enjoyed this—the writing and talking with one another. It was a lot of fun, and I learned a lot of interesting things about the young people. And you're giving back, too, because they felt like they had a nice souvenir of their own cultural trends at the time. So we re-created the fashion magazine model—pretending to be fashion photographers—as a way to engage students and learn about their perspectives, while also having some legitimate photos of fashion at the time.

How have you integrated photographs with other forms of data collection in other studies?
In my focus of places with special meaning in a study of Walkway-Over-the-Hudson, a footbridge that is also a state park [discussed in the next chapter's case study], people took pictures of benches, the sky, a steeple, of people. Up to the mid-1990s, this was the remains of a burned-down train trestle sticking out over the Hudson River. Kids were hanging out on the tracks. The history is a whole other story, but a community group worked over a decade to turn this scary-looking, unsafe structure into a very interesting public park. Our participants were visitors to this park who were asked to take a picture of something that has special meaning and a picture that says "Poughkeepsie" or "New York": "Take a picture of something you like/don't like." Different kinds of prompts guided them. It wasn't like people were wandering around with an unstructured mission there. This was combined with transect walks of the park.

What challenges have you faced in using these methods?
There's a strong group of people who are still very attached, a type of "friends of the park" organization. They'd been volunteering a lot in research studies—not just ours, but very frequently, where researchers framed their involvement as community engagement. By the time we came around, they wanted to participate but were running out of steam from these prior studies. We were using iPads so we could have access to upload data right away and make it easier for these citizen researchers; we were trying to streamline things and move on to the next step. We were working with a community group, and they were also using iPads to interview people on the bridge. The challenge in the park study was getting photos on the move in a crowded place. We also wondered if some people would come back with the iPad they were using. It was awkward—you feel like you're

(Continued)

(Continued)

trailing and surveilling people, making them uncomfortable. Establishing rapport with expensive technology in certain contexts can be challenging. The debriefing process to interpret their photos was also challenging. It's easy to take a lot of photos, but debriefing can take a long time. People are there in a park to recreate, and interviewing them for a very long time is an imposition.

What advice do you have about using this method, based on your research career, for beginning researchers?

It's very important to contextualize the photos with the stories from people who take the photos. The photos do not stand on their own. They are there to prompt discourse. Photographs are not that meaningful unless they're contextualized and unless they're well documented. Who, what, where, and when this image was produced is important and tedious to track. So tracking the production of the photos is important as well as the context in which they're being taken. And then using them. You can use photographs to decorate something you're saying, but you can also use photographs to make a point. Not every photograph has to be included as evidence of something. Photographs can help you imagine a point you want to make. But you don't need all of them in a final report.

Case Study Reflections

1. Scheld's work highlights how visual data might be used alongside interview data. Why are these two forms of data necessary for the kinds of research questions she is asking?

2. How might photographs be especially useful for studying expressive culture or places?

3. Scheld encountered many challenges in her work in the park over the Hudson River. Pick one of these challenges and try to generate a potential solution.

4. Why is context so important for analyzing visual and material data? What should the contextual information include?

STUDY GUIDE •

Note: Students should study each concept with attentiveness to defining, explaining with examples, and describing or demonstrating process. This is not a list of terms to define; it's a list of concepts and processes to master.

Direct observation

Indirect observation

Texts

Corpus

Symbols

Multivalent

Dynamic

Diaries

Archives

Regular-interval diary

Signal-entry diary

Event-contingent diary

Digital fieldwork

FOR FURTHER STUDY

Bernard, H. Russell. 2018. "Direct and Indirect Observation." In *Research Methods in Anthropology*, by H. Russell Bernard, 323–53. Lanham, MD: Rowman and Littlefield.

Galman, Sally Campbell. 2013. "Analyzing and Understanding 'Other Kinds' of Data." In *The Good, the Bad, and the Data*, by Sally Campbell Galman, 68–78. Walnut Creek, CA: Left Coast Press.

Pelto, Pertti J. 2013. "Using Hypothetical Scenarios, Diaries, and Other Special Techniques." In *Applied Ethnography: Guidelines for Field Research*, by Pertti J. Pelto, 237–50. Walnut Creek, CA: Left Coast Press.

Visit **study.sagepub.com/kirner** to help you accomplish your coursework goals in an easy-to-use learning environment.

CHAPTER 11

Behavior and Context

Orientation

We'll close our introductory journey in qualitative methods by investigating two particular methods for understanding human behavior and context. We've already discussed in earlier chapters how people do not always report accurately about their own behavior for a variety of reasons, such as a feeling of social stigma or a failure to remember exactly what they did. Your participants may also struggle to answer questions related to *why* they behaved the way they did, because the reasoning behind our behavioral choices is not always conscious. While participant observation balances the self-reported and self-interpreted information you receive from interviews and surveys, there are times you may wish to only observe, rather than also engage as a participant. In this chapter, we'll discuss passive direct observation, a method for closely observing others' behavior and noticing patterns in it without participating yourself. We'll then move on to further investigate the ways in which the built and natural environments (places and pathways) shape human behavior. To do so, we'll explore two ethnographic methods for mapping behavior geographically.

Mapping Human Behavior

Many kinds of mapping are useful in ethnographic research. In general, mapping captures the activities that humans do, in the places they do it. Mapping can also capture how humans think about the landscape: the places people feel are significant and the pathways between those places. Maps are useful for all kinds of different things. **Census mapping** can help a

Chapter Learning Objectives

Students will be able to do the following:

11.1 Describe how to construct designs for mapping studies and explain how to collect and analyze participatory mapping and mobility mapping data

11.2 Define *passive direct observation* and describe its advantages and disadvantages

11.3 Describe how to construct designs for continuous monitoring studies and explain how to collect and analyze continuous monitoring data, including how to construct an ethogram

11.4 Describe how spot sampling data are collected and how this method differs from continuous monitoring

11.5 Explain how behavioral data may be described and interpreted in ethnographic narratives

researcher build collaboration and rapport when they first enter a community, mapping out who is in each household. Census mapping is very useful in remote, smaller villages that may have no map or records of who lives where. In many rural communities, especially in the developing world, it is challenging to conduct a random or stratified sample because there are no census data or consistent form of contact (telephone, recorded address). Census mapping rectifies this situation and also orients the researcher to the place in which they're living and conducting research. It builds rapport by allowing the researcher an opportunity to introduce themselves (and their research) to everyone. (See Figure 11.1 for an example of a census map.)

Mapping has many research question–related uses as well. Maps can help researchers understand the built environment, the places and pathways built by humans. **Built environment analysis** is a methodological process to engage key social issues or problems that integrate with these human-created places. Such issues or problems could include questions such as these: How do people with disabilities navigate a neighborhood? How are diet and health disparities linked to food availability? How do different cultural groups view the family/household, manage economic resources, and navigate regulations on persons per housing unit? How do farmers manage land and rotate crops over time in response to weather, environmental change, or regulatory change? In all these cases, interview data get you only so far. Participant observation gets you farther, because you experience a landscape. But mapping the resources and changes over

Census mapping A type of mapping in which fieldwork generates a map of households in the field site and who lives in each one.

Built environment analysis A method that focuses on understanding and responding to problems related to human-created places and pathways.

Figure 11.1 Example of Census Map

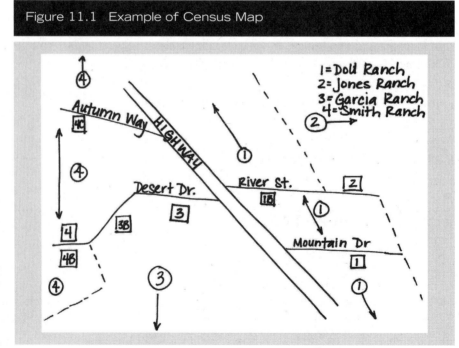

time will help you gain a broader and wider perspective and will allow you to clearly represent spatial problems to others. A good example of this is to consider food deserts. Food deserts are places that have no readily available healthy food nearby. In many poor urban areas (and many rural places) in the United States, there are no grocery stores in a reasonable vicinity. People may find that their only nearby options for buying food are convenience stores and fast-food restaurants. This can contribute to poor diets and negative health impacts. While you could interview people on food choices and availability, it would be difficult to see how people are affected by food deserts unless you map out where people can acquire food and compare food deserts to areas that have better resources (see Figure 11.2 for an example). The maps help verify that people's behaviors are informed by resource availability geographically, not choices they are making without being constrained by the place they are in.

Maps can help us understand **social and organizational networks** by showing linkages between different individuals or organizations (see Figure 11.3 for an example). Researchers can make maps that show the movement of ideas and objects, that visually diagram patterns in resource procurement, or that show how people's environments have changed over time. Our identities, communities, and behaviors are informed by places. Mapping helps us understand how people conceptualize themselves, their communities, and their senses of place, as well as capture socially held memory and knowledge.

Figure 11.2 Food Desert Map

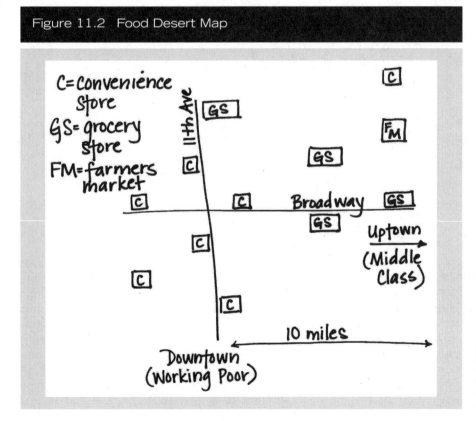

Social and organizational networks The relationships between individuals or organizations, usually depicted spatially in a web-like map that shows who interacts with whom.

Figure 11.3 Organizational Network

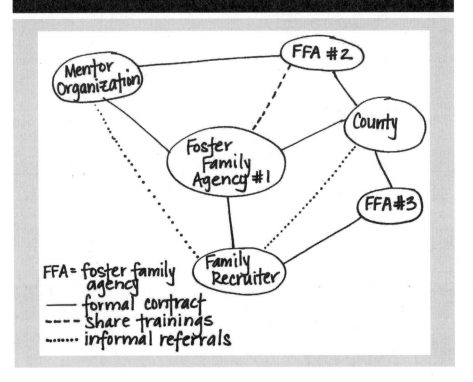

Various kinds of **cultural knowledge** can be mapped in order to represent and retain them in the ways they are usually structured culturally and cognitively. These can also be used to help teach and maintain such knowledge in communities, such as place names and stories (including myths, legends, and historical events), traditional/local ecological knowledge (where resources are at what time of year, stories, uses), traditional lands and movements across land (ownership, use-rights, pilgrimages), and cultural models of places (high schools, a neighborhood, public transit).

Mapping, in terms of the technique required to accomplish the production of maps, can be done with varying levels of technology. Participatory mapping can be as simple as having a community draw maps in the dirt with a stick and taking a picture to replicate later. Alternatively, mapping can be as complex as GIS-enhanced surveys that provide easy means of geostatistical analysis or participatory map websites where people can click on a location (such as Google Maps) and enter information they want the project researchers to know about. Researchers should consider their technical and financial capacity when making these choices, as well as how their choice affects their ability to answer their research questions. Another key question to consider is whom you will ask to answer your questions. Like interviewing, participatory mapping can use a random sample of persons of a given population or key informants. Selecting one or the other is very similar to the decision you would make about interviewing: Is the research trying to involve everyone, such as for a community needs assessment, so that it also is reaching out about potential changes? Is the

Cultural knowledge
Knowledge held in a social group, shared and maintained collectively (which may be related to places).

research asking for information about what ordinary people do or know? Is the research asking for information that only a few people would know or that certain people would be much better at pointing out? For example, mapping where people shop for food in an urban area could (and should) be answered by many different people. However, mapping where people harvest traditionally used medicinal plants may best be answered by key informants whose specialty is in using those plants to heal people in their communities.

There are many different mapping methods, but two primary ones are worth discussing in an introductory fashion here: **participatory mapping**, in which your participants construct maps (individually or collectively, hand-drawn or online), and the more specific method of **mobility mapping**, in which you use participatory mapping to study the movements of individuals or social groups. Both of these mapping methods can be very easily done by students with minimal technology for basic research questions. In participatory mapping, you can give a small group of people (three or four folks) large blank sheets of paper and markers. You can start them with a few main roads of a place and instructions on what to map to help get them going; as they fill in the map, you can add requests for increasing detail. (See Figure 11.4 for an example.) You should write down their comments as they do this, capturing the conversation that the task produces.

Figure 11.4   Example of Participatory Map

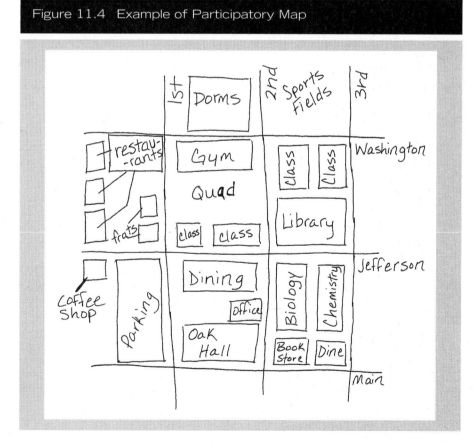

Participatory mapping A mapping method in which participants draw maps based on your research question and prompts.

Mobility mapping A mapping method in which participants engage in participatory mapping to generate data about the movement of individuals or social groups.

One of your authors, Kimberly Kirner, used participatory mapping to capture how elders in several different cultural groups in California rural communities remembered the past landscape and recognized specific places that had changed, as well as the reasons elders gave for why those changes happened. In her project, she drove elders to places they said had changed and used a Global Positioning System unit, or **GPS unit**, to capture the location, took photos of the place, and wrote down their observations of how the place had changed over time and why. In this way, she was able to construct an understanding of what kinds of places were significant in people's memories, the way they believed these places had changed over time, and why these changes occurred. This was helpful to understand how local people experienced long-term environmental change (over the course of fifty years). A student, alternatively, could have started a similar project with low-technology requirements, by having elders draw significant places on a map and explain what they felt had changed and why. Kirner's method was likely to produce more accurate results, because the places could be mapped with specific coordinates, and people often remember places better if they're there when they describe the past. But much could be gained from even the most basic, low-tech exploration of the research topic through participatory mapping.

In mobility mapping, you might sit down with a small group of people with Google Maps on a laptop or tablet. You can toggle between satellite view, which shows an aerial photographic view, and street-map view, which shows major roads. You can then ask your participants to point out places they visit for certain purposes, places they drive to each day, or everywhere they went in the last week (see Figure 11.5 for an example).

Alternatively, you can take a GPS unit with you and drive or walk with someone as they show you significant places based on your research question. At each significant place, you can write down the relevant information and the GPS coordinates, so that you can locate the place on a map later. For example, let's say you're interested in understanding how people with mobility disabilities (such as people who need to use wheelchairs or scooters) navigate a suburban area, and how this compares to people without such disabilities, so that you can report to the city about challenges people with disabilities face in transportation and parking. You might ask people in a quota sample (people of varied socioeconomic status, with or without disabilities) to sit with you and point out on Google Maps the places they usually go each week and how they get there, places where they face challenges, and places they don't go to because they lack appropriate design to meet mobility-challenged people's needs.

Mapping can be a process for data collection, or it can be used for data analysis. Some kinds of research questions are inherently geographic in nature, as we've described. Mapping places related to such research questions can help researchers visualize answers. While anthropologists can team up with geographers to conduct geostatistical analysis to answer complex questions, such as how people might behave in a pandemic event or how different neighborhoods in varying climate zones cope with increased heat islands from climate change, many students' research questions can be answered using very basic techniques. Participatory maps, hand-drawn as described earlier, are both a process that you can study and a product that can be

GPS unit A handheld device that gives you precise longitude and latitude coordinates of where you are located.

Figure 11.5 Example of a Mobility Map

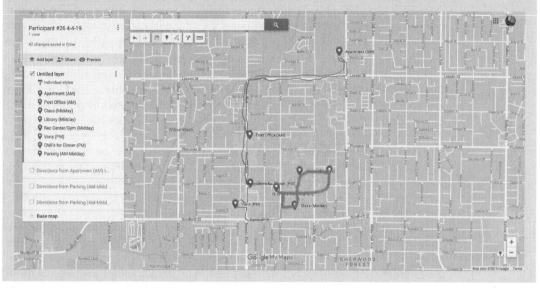

Source: http://www.google.com/maps/d/edit?hl=en&mid=1QEN-tzdfqGdTDD9uz9JLl1mE9jOPs41k&ll=34.243612661
4951%2C-118.53301877777096&z=15/.

analyzed (and then reproduced to help describe your findings). The process in which participants produce the map, and the conversations they have while doing so, can be very informative in the way that focus groups are. You have not only the visual and geographic data the map provides but also information about how participants share geographic information with one another and think through issues around place. These kinds of processes can speak to broadly interesting and grand (BIG) questions in anthropology, such as how humans form memories of places, how they share cultural knowledge about places with one another, and how their sense of self is informed by place.

Discussion

When you think about your research question you developed in Chapter 1, are any aspects of that question related to geography or social networks? What would that sub-question be? Which type of mapping would you do, and why?

Passive Direct Observation

Passive direct observation is when you watch people and record their behavior in the moment it occurs. Unlike participant observation, you do not participant in the behavior that other people are doing. Additionally, while you begin this method with detailed jottings, you use these to create a tool with which you can tally others' behaviors in future field sessions without resorting to written jottings again. In this way, passive direct observation is particularly useful for generating a relatively short list of specific behaviors and the contexts or circumstances in which people (or animals) perform them. This method is used not only in the study of human behavior but also in **primatology** and in animal behavior studies more generally. In direct observation, you can be blatant (**reactive**) or unobtrusive (**nonreactive**). In reactive direct observation, people know they are being observed; in nonreactive observation, they are not aware that you are observing them.

Direct observation is useful because you will acquire more accurate results than you would by merely using interviews or surveys that inquire about behavior. This method also allows you to study things that you otherwise couldn't, because people aren't consciously aware of all their behaviors and the contexts around them. For example, some anthropologists have studied the subtleties of body language–based communication, such as interpersonal spacing (how much space we're culturally conditioned to feel comfortable with between ourselves and another person). Most people, unless they've traveled a lot to visit other cultures and thoughtfully reflected on their level of comfort in crowds, do not realize that people in different cultures are conditioned for different amounts of interpersonal space. Because people aren't aware of this, it'd be difficult to get this information through interviews and surveys. While you might notice this information through participant observation, by inserting yourself into the circumstances, you are likely to shift the behavior you observe. By passively observing, you could study interpersonal spacing without affecting others' behaviors.

Such direct observation is a cost-effective and productive way to tackle problems that specifically deal with patterned behaviors in specific circumstances. This can be very helpful when attempting to solve certain kinds of social or environmental problems. Direct observation can be used, for example, to find patterns in behavior in company meetings—and figure out what generates productive versus unproductive behaviors in employees. You might also use this method to figure out what circumstances lead people to litter in parks. There are many ways in which this method can be applied to solve practical problems by discovering the patterns of behavior and the context around them. Direct observation is also useful for triangulating with interview and survey data, as a method to produce data that can challenge emic understandings or that can illuminate reasons for discrepancies between ideal and real culture. The method isn't without its disadvantages, however. Researchers may be biased by expectations of what they are looking for, leading to **confirmation bias**. It's also very common, especially in the beginning, for researchers to feel quite socially awkward as they observe others, tallying behavior on a clipboard. The method is often tedious, requiring many hours of being at a location watching others. Of course, it is often paired with other methods, such as interviews or surveys, because the method expressly does not capture emic meaning (because you aren't interacting with anyone). In fact, the entire point of the method is to emerge with a better understanding of the patterns of the behaviors themselves, which rarely explains how the actors understand and make meaning of their own behavior. It is imperative that the researcher remembers the method's limits and does not assign

Passive direct observation A method that involves watching people and recording their behavior in the moment it occurs, without participating in it.

Primatology The study of primates.

Reactive A term used to describe a situation where participants are aware they are being observed.

Nonreactive A term used to describe a situation where participants are not aware they are being observed.

Confirmation bias A tendency to look for (and therefore be more aware of) evidence that confirms your preexisting hypothesis or belief.

Figure 11.6 Advantages and Disadvantages of Passive Direct Observation

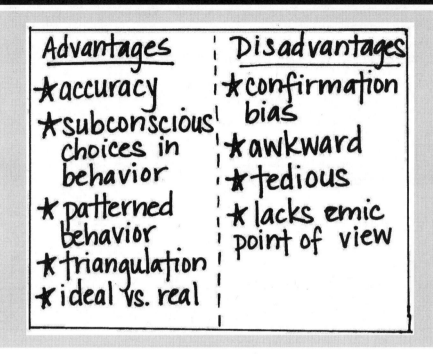

Advantages
- ★ accuracy
- ★ subconscious choices in behavior
- ★ patterned behavior
- ★ triangulation
- ★ ideal vs. real

Disadvantages
- ★ confirmation bias
- ★ awkward
- ★ tedious
- ★ lacks emic point of view

meaning to the behaviors without the data to do so. See Figure 11.6 for a summary of the advantages and disadvantages of passive direct observation.

Continuous Monitoring

The most common direct observation method is **continuous monitoring**, also called **focal follows**. In this form of direct observation, you watch people and record their behavior. This method is used extensively in studies of human and animal interactions. The end result of continuous monitoring is an **ethogram**, a list of behaviors for the species being studied. Obviously, especially in a species as complex as humans, this would be a larger project than any beginning researcher could do! In general, creating ethograms that adequately reflect the variety of behaviors a species displays is very challenging and involves complex coding schemes. Even assistant researchers who conduct continuous monitoring using already developed ethograms frequently have months of training on how to accurately and efficiently score behaviors, especially given that the researcher is often observing many individuals at once. However, this method can be scaled down to involve behaviors that arise only in a specific context, which keeps the project manageable and feasible. (See Figure 11.7 for an example of an ethogram.)

Continuous monitoring A method of direct observation in which you watch people (or animals) and record their behavior. Also called *focal follows.*

Focal follows *See* Continuous monitoring.

Ethogram A list of behaviors for a specific species.

Figure 11.7 Example of an Ethogram

Researcher: _____

Date: _____ Class: _____ # of Students (Estimate): _____

_____ Time (in Fifteen-Minute Intervals)

Faculty–Student Interaction						
Direct Interaction (#)						
Indirect Interaction (#)						
Eye Contact (#)						
Body Language (#)						

Student–Student Interaction						
Direct Interaction (#)						
Indirect Interaction (#)						
Eye Contact (#)						
Body Language (#)						

Operational Definitions	
Faculty–Student Interaction	
Direct Interaction (#)	Professor and student interact through speaking to one another.
Indirect Interaction (#)	Professor and student interact through a means such as a clicker, an instant message or chat function, TopHat Monocle, or another technology-assisted or indirect method.
Eye Contact (#)	Professor and student interaction includes shared eye contact.
Body Language (#)	Professor and student interaction includes reliance on body language (student and/or professor seems to look at the other person for cues toward feeling/thought, gestures that indicate reassurance or encouragement, etc.).
Student–Student Interaction	
Direct Interaction (#)	Students interact through speaking to one another. (Count the number of groups/partner pairs, not individual interactions, for this measurement.)
Indirect Interaction (#)	Students interact through a means such as a clicker, an instant message or chat function, TopHat Monocle, or another technology-assisted or indirect method. (Count the number of groups/partner pairs, not individual interactions, for this measurement.)
Eye Contact (#)	Student interaction includes shared eye contact. (Count the number of groups/partner pairs, not individual interactions, for this measurement.)
Body Language (#)	Student interaction includes reliance on body language (student seems to look at the other person for cues toward feeling/thought, gestures that indicate reassurance or encouragement, etc.). (Count the number of individual interactions observed.)

The starting point for continuous monitoring is direct observation without yet having an ethogram. This involves taking jottings during iterative fieldwork sessions until most of the behaviors that you might encounter have been entered into your field notes. After you've constructed an ethogram, you'll use it for many field observational sessions in order to collect enough data to be able to confidently describe behavioral patterns accurately. At first, you may find that your ethogram doesn't work quite as well as you'd like it to. You can refine your ethogram several times, testing each iteration in the field, before settling on one that you consistently use. When you've collected enough observational data by using the ethogram to experience a high level of repetition, and to see patterns in the behavioral data begin to emerge, you can begin writing up your findings.

Alternatively, if you are very familiar with the context in which the behaviors are being performed, and if you have very specific, targeted research questions (often of an applied nature), you might begin by reflecting on your prior knowledge of those behaviors to build the ethogram. In either case, the second step in the process is to develop an ethogram. An ethogram provides a list of behaviors that may occur in the specific context and is organized in a table format so that the researcher, when conducting further continuous monitoring, need only mark behaviors as they occur (sometimes paired with specific circumstances around the behavior and/or the time the behavior occurred). For example, in a study conducted at California State University, Northridge, by Drs. Von Mayerhauser and Kirner, faculty teamed up with graduate students to study students' behaviors in classes as part of a university-wide campaign to introduce tablet-based activities. These specific "tablet-enhanced" classes prompted concerns about potential problematic behaviors, ranging from technology failures to students using the tablets to get on social media. By first creating an ethogram of potential positive and negative behaviors, based on prior knowledge of classroom management and behavior, and then conducting continuous monitoring in tablet-enhanced classrooms, the team was able to inform the university about the effects of using tablets intensively in the classroom.

Spot Sampling

The other direct observation method, **spot sampling** (also called **time allocation**), differs from continuous monitoring because of its periodic (rather than continual) nature. In spot sampling, you show up at randomly selected places and times and record what people are doing. This represents an accurate portrayal of how a population spends its time. This can be particularly helpful in cases in which ideal culture is quite different from real culture. Most students will be familiar with this problem if they observe student study habits. Most students understand the need for time dedicated to studying and working on class assignments and will schedule time for this activity. However, this doesn't mean that the time they schedule for studying is spent entirely on studying. Students may write in their calendar that they will study for three hours, but this time may also involve various distractions in the form of other activities, such as conversing with a roommate who just got home, answering phone calls and texts that interrupt the work, getting on social media, and eating food. If you ask a student how they spent this three-hour block, the odds are they will say, "Studying." This is what they scheduled the time for, and it's probably what they thought they spent most of their time doing. But did they spend most of their time studying? Spot sampling of student "study times" might show

Spot sampling A direct observation method in which you show up at randomly selected places and times to record what people are doing. Also called *time allocation*.

Time allocation *See* Spot sampling.

otherwise! This can help us understand disconnections between students' understanding of how they spend their time and what they're really doing with it—which can lead to better advisement on study habits (such as to turn one's phone to silent and put it away and to build structured break times that are time-limited).

Spot sampling can be rather intrusive, because researchers come and go at various times and days. As was described in the previous chapter, signal-entry diaries are a way around this problem. They can be used for **experience sampling**, in which the researcher asks participants to answer prompts at automated times (often by using smartphone apps) to chart their behavior, rather than showing up to record it themselves. Spot sampling can be quite demanding for the researcher, and it poses unique challenges, such as sampling questions that reach well beyond the usual considerations: Where should the researcher show up? When? Should the researcher show up at night? How often should they show up, and for how long? What happens if the person is doing multiple behaviors, such as cooking dinner while talking on the phone? Or answering e-mail while also minding a small child? Spot sampling, therefore, takes a lot of careful planning—and a lot of patience with the process, which can be both demanding and awkward!

You might have already thought that direct observation, especially when it is nonreactive, seems a little bit like spying on people. In fact, many beginning researchers *do* feel like they're spying on people when they first directly observe them without announcing their presence. While there are good ethical reasons why there are contexts in which you should conduct reactive direct observation, and good research-related reasons why you might need to conduct nonreactive direct observation, neither of these methods is actively deceptive. That is, in both reactive and nonreactive direct observation, your starting point is typically public behavior (continuous monitoring is often in public spaces or spaces in which it isn't unusual for people to be observed) or people who know they're being observed (often, this is the case in spot sampling, especially if you're entering private spaces). **Disguised field observation** is when you pretend to be part of a group and secretly record your data. It relies on *active* deception, which is basically lying to participants. Disguised field observation has obvious ethical dilemmas inherent in it but depends somewhat on the place of observation (public vs. private—public observation is usually less ethically problematic) and topic (sensitive vs. not—sensitive topics are more problematic). Sometimes, such deception is the only way to get an inside story. However, it's very ethically problematic. **Passive deception**, on the other hand, does not manipulate participants. The anthropologist shows up to public spaces and acts like they are doing some appropriate activity while observing others.

Experience sampling Sampling in which the researcher asks participants to answer prompts at automated times to chart their behavior.

Disguised field observation A form of active deception in which the fieldworker pretends to not be a researcher and gains access to more private spaces or groups based on this pretense.

Passive deception A form of deception that does not seek to manipulate participants and instead is primarily practiced in public spaces, where the researcher doesn't try to hide their activities but also doesn't announce them.

Discussion

When you think about your research question you developed in Chapter 1, what are some behavioral aspects of your research that might benefit from passive direct observation? Why? What method might you use, and why would this method be suitable? How could the data you acquire be paired with interviews or surveys to achieve both emic and etic points of view?

Describing Behavior and Context in Ethnographic Narratives

In all studies of behavior and its context, it is helpful to remember that discrepancies may exist between real (actual) behavior and self-reported data. This is why direct observation and mapping actual movements (by tagging along with participants) can be very helpful when your research question is dependent on understanding what people are really doing (as opposed to how they remember what they're doing). However, it's important to remember that not all research questions depend on procuring accurate behavioral data. In some cases, we're more interested in how people *think* about or *remember* their own behavior or that of others. In the case of mapping, sometimes we are asking how people remember places or construct complex mental maps that guide their lives. It's important to consider what your research question is asking—and therefore what kinds of data it requires.

It's also important to consider how to communicate your findings from direct observation or mapping studies in ethnographic narratives. In many cases, pictures are worth a thousand words, as the folk saying goes. It can be very helpful, for example, to use line drawings or photos to illustrate ethograms. This way, the reader does not erroneously assume that certain words describing behaviors mean specific observed qualities. Instead, the combination of the researcher's description of the behavior and a visual demonstration of it helps the reader understand exactly what is being observed. Similarly, the use of maps to communicate geographic data—even just to orient the reader to where you are when you're in the field—helps communicate place-based findings more clearly. However, don't make the mistake in thinking that a visual (whether a photograph, line drawing, or map) means that you don't need descriptive writing to get your points across. Some students mistakenly *replace* ethnographic, descriptive narrative with visuals—and this is not helpful to the reader. You must always explain and narrate your maps, photographs, and line drawings, as well as fully integrate these data with other forms, such as informant quotes. In this way, you can write a robust narrative that provides the reader with a rich and clear depiction of the behavior you're discussing and its context.

Pairing the Textbook and Workbook

In this chapter, you've learned two specific ways of approaching questions around behavior and context. To understand geographically shaped behavior, you can use mapping. There are various types of mapping, and you learned about two of the most common mapping methods: participatory mapping and mobility mapping. You might consider, as you practice these methods, the ways in which your own life is shaped by geography: the built environment, pathways and roadways, and your memories of place. This will help you think about the kinds of

(Continued)

(Continued)

research questions that fit with mapping methods. Continuous monitoring (and passive direct observation as a whole) is also a method that fits only specific kinds of research questions, most often studies of behavior in specific contexts. You might try continuous monitoring not only with human participants (as the workbook guides you to do) but also with other animals, such as dogs, cats, or even animals you visit in a zoo or animal park. This is especially important to practice if you plan to move into a research program in primatology. Many students will find using mapping methods or continuous monitoring somewhat challenging, because we don't usually do these types of inquiry in our everyday life. As always, practice will help you develop confidence and competence in using such methods. Congratulations! You've finished the content for your introduction to qualitative methods! The last chapter in this book will explain how to use self-assessment and peer review to hone your methodological skills over time, as well as how these methods can be used in significant projects to demonstrate your skills comprehensively. Hopefully, as you try out these final auxiliary methods in the workbook, you feel a sense of accomplishment in beginning to demonstrate competency in a wide range of skills!

Reflective Prompts

1. Do I need to ask clarifying questions?

2. Can I compare and contrast participatory and mobility mapping?

3. Can I describe what types of data can be gathered using continuous monitoring and this method's advantages for answering certain kinds of research questions?

Case Study

Low, Setha M., Dana Taplin, and Suzanne Scheld. 2005. *Rethinking Urban Parks: Public Space & Cultural Diversity*. Austin: University of Texas Press.

Taplin, Dana, Suzanne Scheld, and Setha M. Low. 2019. "Conservation and the People's Views: Ethnographic Perspectives from Jones Beach State Park." In *Human-Centered Built Environment Heritage Preservation: Theory and Evidence-Based Practice*, edited by Jeremy C. Wells and Barry Stiefel, 143–56. New York: Routledge.

The Project

With the Public Space Research Group, directed by Setha Low at the Graduate Center (CUNY), I worked with Setha and Dana Taplin on a bunch of studies of big urban parks and beaches. We used a battery of methods that we derived from REAP (Rapid Ethnographic Assessment Procedures); we did participant observation, key informant and constituent interviews, and focus group and group interviews. We also did neighborhood group interviews, like going into barbershops in Jersey City, bars, churches, libraries—the neighborhood institutions. After hearing about broader neighborhoods or parks, we'd try to map out these cultural resources. These maps were pretty similar to the kinds that nongovernmental organizations use in development studies, where you get the community together and they draw maps of, say, where all the wells are in the community. We call them cultural resource maps. We produced those as part of the products that we gave to clients so they'd have a sense of how people view these spaces. People can then visualize this information as a map.

We also did a lot of transect walks. This is interviewing someone while moving through a space and learning about their view of the symbols of the space, or learning how certain spaces are imbued with memory and meaning. People pause and tell stories by particular views, scenic views and places—what comes to mind, memories, and so on. It can be done while walking, on bikes, or driving. This is what I've wanted students to do. Take car rides with people on their commutes on the 405 [a Los Angeles freeway] or something, or bus rides around Los Angeles, and look at the landscape and discuss it with others. We did this with cameras in Walkway over the Hudson, which was formerly a train trestle that was turned into a footbridge and public park. The transect walk is moving through space and giving people a chance to talk about the experience. And sometimes it's just the experience of moving that evokes meaning. There is a lot of literature, such as Tim Ingold's work, on the meaning of walking—how much you learn ethnographically by taking walks. There is a wide discussion in anthropology on structured and unstructured walking.

How did you decide to use mapping as a method, and why?

When talking about space, mapping brings to life or illuminates for audiences important facets of space that people don't see, appreciate, or realize. I think mapping is a really excellent tool for sensitizing people to the cultural dimensions of space. You can talk about space in an abstract way, but it's always good to illustrate what you mean. Mapping is about capturing and representing relationships in space. So we're looking for ways to find the cultural dimensions in space and then illuminating them so people can become aware of them.

Can you describe your method for mapping?

In our approach to studying space, we always felt it was important to triangulate information and data, because we were often doing applied projects that were very rapid (REAP). You don't have a lot of time; people need answers. Mapping helped us figure out which spaces were robust in terms of human interaction or offered the best possibility to answer the park managers' questions. Cultural resource mapping is an end product, but physical trace mapping and transects, as well as participant observation, helped build the data themselves—the physical space itself and the human interactions with aspects of it.

We've also done other types of things, like behavioral mapping, where you watch what people do in space. You can trace how people move through space. Take bird's-eye-view maps of the space, and then trace the trajectories people follow, and this tells you something. You can break these behavioral maps into categories, such as comparing the movement of genders, the movement of couples versus individual people, the movement of people on scooters versus walking, the movement of people plugged into headphones or with coffee cups. You can decide if and what any of these viewpoints tell you about space. There's a lot of environmental psychology that foregrounds physical space, such as studies of the design of physical urban spaces. We were informed by this approach, but we tried to examine with thicker description, in a more anthropological way, what those spaces actually mean to people.

(Continued)

(Continued)

How did you analyze your mapping data? What made you select those methods for analysis?

It's important to triangulate information and see the patterns, seeing themes that reemerge through interviews, surveys, participant observation, and mapping. Analyzing these things in groups of researchers is also important in REAP. It's useful to have a group, because you see if the pattern or code is something multiple people see or not. Sifting, comparing viewpoints among the researchers themselves, helps everyone come to better interpretations.

What advice do you have about using mapping, based on your research career, for beginning researchers?

Actually making the map itself is challenging. You have to find a base image. I end up asking geographers for help. Actual mapping skills, beyond the stick-figure mapping method, is difficult. The boundaries of the map are difficult to determine; the baseline image can be difficult to select. Jones Beach, which is huge, was very hard to map. We looked at the ends of the beach, and particular areas with reputations for certain kinds of activities. You have to show a beach in a context, too, or you're just showing space. Whereas if you're in Philadelphia looking at Independence Hall (another space that we studied), you have clear streets and buildings. Having a technique to do this is hard. In the early days before Geographic Information Systems (GIS) software, trying to draw Pelham Bay Park in the context of the Bronx in my kitchen, using pencils, was incredibly difficult. But I've also seen maps students have made that are way too technical, and they don't communicate effectively. You have to figure out the map's message, and then figure out how to execute that. Who is the audience? What is the message, and how can you convey it?

Case Study Reflections

1. Why is mapping particularly important for work on space and place, such as the type that Scheld does? How is it tied to applications for park managers and other stakeholder groups?

2. Why is it particularly important to triangulate data and researchers' analyses when using Rapid Ethnographic Assessment Procedures (REAP)?

3. How does ethnographic mapping go beyond what is done by other mapping methods to allow people to understand the meanings places have for people?

4. Why is it particularly important to identify the map's message and audience before producing the map itself?

STUDY GUIDE ●

Note: Students should study each concept with attentiveness to defining, explaining with examples, and describing or demonstrating process. This is not a list of terms to define; it's a list of concepts and processes to master.

Census mapping

Built environment analysis

Social and organizational networks

Cultural knowledge

Participatory mapping

Mobility mapping

GPS unit

Passive direct observation

Primatology

Reactive

Nonreactive

Confirmation bias

Continuous monitoring

Focal follows

Ethogram

Spot sampling

Time allocation

Experience sampling

Disguised field observation

Passive deception

FOR FURTHER STUDY

Bernard, H. Russell. 2018. "Direct and Indirect Observation." In *Research Methods in Anthropology*, by H. Russell Bernard, 323–53. Lanham, MD: Rowman and Littlefield.

Pelto, Pertti J. 2013. "Structured Observation of Behaviors and Events" and "Mapping: A Powerful Tool in Ethnographic Research." In *Applied Ethnography: Guidelines for Field Research*, by Pertti J. Pelto, 217–50. Walnut Creek, CA: Left Coast Press.

Visit **study.sagepub.com/kirner** to help you accomplish your coursework goals in an easy-to-use learning environment.

CHAPTER

12

Conclusion

Putting It All Together

Orientation

We've come to the end of our adventure in qualitative methods. We hope you feel accomplished in what you've learned! While this text is only an introduction, you've acquired quite a range of concepts and skills. You've learned the process of research design, including how research questions are tied to selecting specific methods and sampling plans. You've considered the ethics of conducting various types of research with different populations. You've explored your own research question through all three of the fundamental qualitative research methods (participant observation, interviews, and surveys) and through some of the more specialized ones. At this point, you've gotten significant experience in trying out a wide range of methods for data collection and analysis, as well as brief samples of ethnographic writing. In this concluding chapter, we'll discuss the process of improving yourself as a researcher.

Self-Assessment and Refinement

If you've used the companion workbook along with this textbook, you've noticed that we've offered self-assessments for each of your major research activities. Self-assessment is a key skill in research and ethnographic writing, and it's one you should practice developing as you make your way through your degree. **Self-assessment** helps you periodically review your own work against standards you've selected. You might use **rubrics** like the ones in the workbook (you can also find rubrics online for many different skills or types of writing), which help you evaluate your work against standards others have agreed on. Or you might have a looser form of

Chapter Learning Objectives

Students will be able to do the following:

12.1 Describe the importance of self-assessment

12.2 Explain the ways in which peer review helps researchers refine their work

12.3 Describe major products that can be constructed by a beginning researcher

self-assessment, in which you reflect carefully on whether your work has achieved your goals and where you could improve.

The purpose of all self-assessment is **continuous improvement**, which is a concept that is often applied to interventions and programs but can also be applied to ourselves. In this kind of model, you recognize that there is always room to get better and commit yourself to constantly assessing yourself, with an eye toward how you can grow and develop your skills. For example, you might assess your first set of ten interviews and find that while you took excellent interview notes, you often failed to ask follow-up or probing questions. After you notice this, you'll want to figure out why you didn't do this, so that you can come up with a plan for improvement. Do you forget to ask follow-up questions? You might insert a prompt into your interview guide. Do you feel anxious about asking questions impromptu? You might generate sample probing or follow-up questions based on an anticipated range of answers that you put into your interview guide. You could combine this with using your everyday social conversations as opportunities to practice the skill of asking impromptu questions of others so that you become more comfortable with it. In committing yourself to continuous improvement, you recognize that professional research is a learning process that never ends. No one ever reaches the finish line and becomes the perfect researcher or writer. You can always get better!

Discussion

Can you think of an instance in which you did self-assessment, either formally or informally? What did you do to assess yourself? What do you feel the value is in assessing your own work?

Self-assessment A process by which you periodically review your own work against standards you select.

Rubrics Sets of standards that help you evaluate your work by giving it a score on different qualities, based on commonly agreed-on goals and indicators.

Continuous improvement A broad goal in which you want to continually get better at your skills.

Collegial Relationships and Peer Review

The other big way to improve, which you've also practiced if you've completed the workbook, is to use feedback from colleagues (your peers). Academic research is based on forming collegial relationships with our peers. This includes not only activities such as reviewing one another's work, brainstorming together, and working as research teams but also more informal activities. These less formal activities might include venting frustrations to one another and providing encouragement. The research process can be stressful, challenging, and isolating. It's easy for people to fall into a mental pattern called *imposter syndrome*, a psychological pattern that is quite common in academia but can cause a lot of distress.

When you experience imposter syndrome, you worry that you don't really know what you're doing and that your work is a fraud. It's natural in the beginning for us to doubt our work and skills (after all, this is a good assumption to make—we're still learning!). But later, when you're fully trained and your skills have been endorsed by a graduate degree, a successful career, and peer-reviewed publication, it's less reasonable to consider yourself incompetent. Yet, somehow, this happens to many academic researchers. Both of your authors have faced it. It's especially common among researchers who are women, who are from minority ethnic groups, or who entered college with lower socioeconomic status. In part, this is because our life experiences and values are often less valued in the university than those of white middle-class-or-higher men. Having good colleagues who genuinely support you and will encourage you when you develop these self-doubts is essential. They help remind you, from a peer's vantage point, that your work is worthwhile and well done, and that while you can always improve, you are a competent researcher.

Our relationships with colleagues are also essential for the **peer review** process. The peer review process is fundamental to scholarly publication, by having several academics review ethnographic writing (usually "blind," that is, without the reviewers knowing who the author is). Reviewers have several functions. Editors usually help the author catch grammatical mistakes and make suggestions about organization, length, and other key elements of writing, as well as determine whether the proposed work is appropriate for the publisher or journal. If the editor finds that the work is appropriate for their publication and of sufficient writing quality, it is sent out to peer review. Peer reviewers examine the quality of the literature review (background literature the author uses to make their case), methodology (how the work was done), data collection, and data analysis. Peer reviewers determine whether the data and findings are of high enough quality to publish, and they often make suggestions to the author for additional literature or points of analysis to include. Peer review is used not only for publication but also for allocating grants from private sources (such as the Wenner-Gren Foundation) and public sources (such as the National Science Foundation). Similar to peer review for publication, reviewers will determine whether or not the grant proposal should be funded, and they also provide the author with feedback on how to improve the proposal if it is not funded (including points for clarification or elaboration and suggestions for improving the methodology).

Discussion

What kinds of collegial relationships could you build with fellow students right now? How could you help one another with feelings of imposter syndrome? How could you help one another with refining your work, through something like a peer review process?

Culminating Experiences

At the master's or doctoral level, the thesis or dissertation (a long body of work based on many months or even years of research) is the culminating experience: the product that demonstrates mastery of all the skills involved in research (design, collection, analysis, and writing). But at the undergraduate level, you can still demonstrate your skills in a

Peer review
A process for research and writing in which your colleagues review your work for methodological soundness and writing quality.

number of ways that qualify as culminating experiences. Some of these products can be very useful for applying for graduate school or for building independent research skills that are useful in practicing careers in your discipline. We'll broadly discuss two types: research design experiences and research reporting experiences (see Figure 12.1).

Research design culminating experiences include different types of formal proposals that you write to acquire approval of a research project. One of these types of proposals is an institutional review board (IRB) protocol, the document you submit to an IRB to have your research reviewed for ethics. Another of these proposals is a grant proposal, which persuasively outlines your research question, methodology, and reasons for your research. While IRB proposals seek to use peers to help you conduct research ethically and effectively anticipate and manage risk, grant proposals seek to convince your peers to provide you with funding to complete your research project. In both cases, clear and concise detail is imperative. It is only through clear and detailed writing that your colleagues will understand your research plans and be able to make determinations about it.

Undergraduate students who plan to apply to graduate school and those at the very beginning of their master's program should strongly consider working with their professors to prepare early for writing grants for their graduate research (particularly the National Science Foundation Graduate Research Fellowship Program). Even if a student isn't competitive for the program, grants are good to think with. That is, in writing a short grant proposal, you'll think more carefully about your research question, its significance, and how you plan to do your research. Furthermore, grant writing is a valuable skill in both academic and applied/practicing sectors. Many nonprofit organizations, local governments, and tribal governments need grant writers who can articulate a research or intervention design and justify why the proposed project is important and ought to be funded. Grant writing is not only a skill in itself but also a skill that can become a career of its own (or can significantly enhance an academic career), so it is a good idea for students to try their hand at it early and often.

Figure 12.1 Culminating Experiences

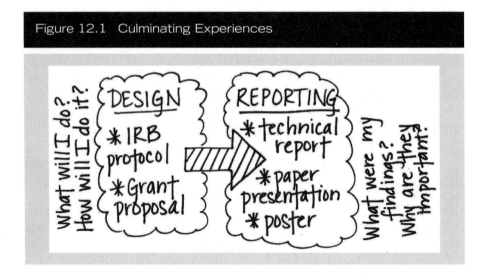

Research reporting experiences include a few different forms of reporting for different kinds of audiences. While the formal, academic article–length paper or mini-ethnography (as many master's thesis projects are written) is beyond the reach of beginning students, other academic products, including technical reports, paper presentations, and poster presentations, are not. A technical report is an expository form of writing that describes the research question, methodology, data, and analysis and interpretation (the findings or discussion). Technical reports can weave together multiple kinds of data in order to address the research question, as well as describing "next steps"—what the researcher plans to do to push their work on the research question forward in the future. Paper presentations, often given at academic conferences, are a short form of technical reporting. Usually ten to twenty minutes in length, depending on the conference, the paper presentation describes the research question and the methodology very briefly, then spends most of the time discussing the data and analysis in an integrated fashion.

Much like writing an ethnographic narrative, the presentation will select only a few key themes or points to make, interweaving original analytical commentary with data (quotes from participants, statistics, photographs, and maps). The paper presentation, unlike the technical report, is usually delivered to an audience using PowerPoint or another visual aid. Key skills in producing a paper presentation include not only those used in writing but also skills in selecting or producing appropriate graphics to pair with text, organizing the PowerPoint presentation with an optimal mix of meaningful text and visuals, and public speaking. Many students have a fear of public speaking, but it's an essential skill in social science. Paper presentations provide another opportunity to be collegial to your classmates and practice together, so that you not only improve your public speaking ability but also reduce your fear about the activity.

Poster presentations are a bit like paper presentations, but all delivered at once and without any formal public speaking! Usually, a poster is created that is very much like a paper presentation: with a mix of text (covering the same points) and graphics. Rather than presenting the research through a single talk to an audience, the student stands with their poster and answers questions that audience members ask. The audience freely roams around the poster exhibition, looking at the research that seems interesting or relevant to them and interacting with researchers when they wish. For some students, this much more informal way of interacting with other researchers is a good first step, especially if they are very nervous about speaking in front of a group. However, creating a good poster is not easy. It takes considerably more planning for conciseness and visual displays (including layout) than a PowerPoint presentation requires. However, it is another set of skills that can be very marketable and helpful in future careers.

Whatever way of reporting your findings you select (or is selected for you), in all cases, it is important to be clear, detailed, and engaging with your audience. Whether written or spoken, your research presentation needs to clearly explain your core research questions, what you did, how you did it, and what you learned. You should consider, as you create your research report or presentation, who your audience is. Is the audience fellow social scientists, educated laypersons, or the public at large? Are they busy decision makers, or do they have lots of time? What do they need and want to hear about your research? How can you make your research engaging and interesting for them?

If you've collected data for the research question you've been developing for the entirety of the book, how do you think you'd want to present it? To whom? Why did you select the format for presenting your work that you did? What are your future plans with your research? Do you plan to continue with this research question or generate a new one? Can you see yourself drafting an IRB protocol or grant proposal in the future? Why or why not?

Pairing the Textbook and Workbook

You've practiced a wide range of skills so far: research design, different methods for data collection and analysis, and ethnographic writing. It's time to bring all these skills to bear to produce one or more culminating projects: products that unite your skills and challenge you to articulate them in integrated, cohesive ways. Your instructor (or you) might select one or more of the culminating experiences in the workbook for you to demonstrate your skills (the activities in Chapter 12 of the workbook). As you work on your culminating experience, remember that much of the content and process has already been completed in a draft form in other chapters of the workbook. Research is a process that builds on the stages of work you've done before. Don't hesitate to use those past workbook activities and the feedback you received from your colleagues and instructor to refine and improve your work, without reinventing it. Remember, too, that if you wish to go on to graduate school or a career in research, you should keep practicing all these skills after your class ends! Research is a lifelong learning process that can be deeply rewarding and enjoyable, even if it is also challenging!

Reflective Prompts

1. Did I ask myself questions throughout Chapter 12 to ensure that I understand how these various concepts weave together?

2. Do I have any lingering questions about any key concepts from the course that I need to ask to improve my understanding?

STUDY GUIDE

Note: Students should study each concept with attentiveness to defining, explaining with examples, and describing or demonstrating process. This is not a list of terms to define; it's a list of concepts and processes to master.

Self-assessment

Rubrics

Continuous improvement

Peer review

Visit **study.sagepub.com/kirner** to help you accomplish your coursework goals in an easy-to-use learning environment.

Glossary

Activism: The idea that the researcher is in service to a cause.

Aggregate: To combine the data from multiple units.

Analysis: Detailed examination of the elements or structure of your data, typically as a basis for interpretation and drawing conclusions.

Analytical memos: Extended field note entries in which you reflect on a number of asides and commentaries.

Archives: Narrative records that already exist, which can come from a wide range of sources (including historical documents and contemporary digital narratives).

Asides: Brief analytical comments in the margins, related to specific short bits of field notes.

Aspects: Specific characteristics important to the decision maker.

Audience: The people who will be the primary consumers of your writing.

Audit trail: A record of the researcher's procedures and thoughts while conducting research.

Autoethnography: A combination of ethnography and autobiography, connecting personal experiences with cultural ones.

Average: A calculation in which you add (sum) all responses, then divide by the number of respondents. This is meant to be a measurement that helps you understand how the most common person would respond, but it should be analyzed with comparison to the median and mode.

Back translation: A process for reliable translation that involves two different translators to ensure that the translation asks the questions you really mean to ask.

Built environment analysis: A method that focuses on understanding and responding to problems related to human-created places and pathways.

Case studies: Small projects that have limited generalizability but offer significant preliminary or localized findings.

Causality: A statistically significant relationship between two variables, in which one variable is the cause of another variable changing.

Census mapping: A type of mapping in which fieldwork generates a map of households in the field site and who lives in each one.

Closed-ended questions: Questions that offer a list of options from which participants select their response.

Cluster sampling: Using geographic space as a way of dividing people into subpopulations and then using geographically defined spaces and places as a sampling frame.

Codebook: An organized record of your codes and their definitions.

Coding: An analytical process by which you identify important bits of information that recur in your data and keep systematic notes on what these are.

Cognitive anthropology: The study of the relationship between human society and human thought.

Commentaries: Longer analytical comments (one or more paragraphs) related to a particular episode, sketch, or entry in your field notes.

Comparison frames: An interview technique in which the researcher presents sets of alternatives as a prompt.

Completion rate: The rate at which respondents complete a survey (some respondents may open the survey and begin it but give up partway through taking it).

Conceptual definitions: Abstractions that facilitate understanding.

Confirmation bias: A tendency to look for (and therefore be more aware of) evidence that confirms your preexisting hypothesis or belief.

Confirmatory research: The stage of research that develops a research design to further refine initial findings through developing hypotheses and ways to test them with further data collection and analysis.

Connected integration: Integration of the data by generating only one type of data at a time, with the first dataset informing the formation of the second dataset.

Consideration by aspects: The second stage of decision making, in which a person consciously weighs options based on a variety of aspects.

Constraints: Specific limitations a decision maker is under that affect their decision.

Content analysis: An analytical method that looks for patterns in the meanings of documents, communications, or media.

Continuous improvement: A broad goal in which you want to continually get better at your skills.

Continuous monitoring: A method of direct observation in which you watch people (or animals) and record their behavior. Also called *focal follows*.

Convenience sample: A sample that engages anyone willing to participate, usually starting with people the researcher knows.

Corpus: A collection of texts.

Correlation: A statistically significant relationship between two variables, such that when one changes, the other is affected.

Cultural knowledge: Knowledge held in a social group, shared and maintained collectively (which may be related to places).

Cultural models: Models that organize knowledge that is used to plan for or understand actions—that is, how to act or think.

Cultural relativism: The idea that the researcher first seeks to understand a practice or belief within its own historical and cultural context, without judgment, but may later take a stand.

Culture shock: Depression or other emotional discomfort that people experience when they enter a culture that is unfamiliar to them.

Debrief: A period of time in which you communicate to your participants and field site community that you are leaving soon, answer any questions they have, give back in meaningful ways, and make plans for how and when to return to the site in the future with your analysis and conclusions.

Decision-tree models: Models that organize the use of knowledge in which people must choose between two or more options with constraints.

Deduction: A way of conducting research that begins with selecting a theory, then creates hypotheses to test theory, and finally conducts research that generates observations to support or refute the hypotheses.

Deductive coding: Coding in which you start with your theoretical lens, create labels or categories that make

sense for using this theory, and then attach labels to your field notes in appropriate places.

Deference: When the interviewee tells you what they think you want to know or hear (rather than answering truthfully).

Demographic questions: Questions that establish the attributes of individuals in a population.

Dependent variables: Variables that are affected by independent variables.

Diaries: Narrative texts that participants produce, tracking their feelings, thoughts, or experiences.

Digital fieldwork: Ethnography with an online field site.

Direct observation: Methods that directly observe or participate in people's behaviors or that ask them direct questions about their thoughts, feelings, and behaviors.

Disguised field observation: A form of active deception in which the fieldworker pretends to not be a researcher and gains access to more private spaces or groups based on this pretense.

Disproportionate sampling: Actively over-recruiting and accepting more participants from a particular subpopulation due to the subpopulation being underrepresented otherwise.

Dynamic: The quality of symbols that allows their meaning to change over time.

Elimination by aspects: The first stage of decision making, in which a person subconsciously eliminates options deemed illogical or impossible by virtue of their cultural models, taxonomies, or other cultural knowledge.

Embedded integration: Integration of the findings from primary and secondary questions by framing the secondary question findings within the overarching research question.

Emic: Insider (i.e., in the cultural group under study).

Episodes: Portions of narrative that are dedicated to describing sequences of actions.

Epistemology: The study of how we know things.

Ethical codes: Documents that provide agreed-on guidelines and standards for a profession in order to consistently minimize harm and maximize benefits during the course of the professional's work.

Ethics: Standards of what we ought to do in terms of right and wrong actions.

Ethnography: Writing about a specific culture at a specific place and time.

Ethnology: General theoretical discussions that seek to account for human behavior across many cultural groups and geographic locations.

Ethnoscience: The study of the ways in which people classify and understand the world around them.

Ethogram: A list of behaviors for a specific species.

Event-contingent diary: A diary in which participants make entries only when specific events occur.

Expectancy: When an interviewer gets a response they expected because they shaped the response.

Experience sampling: Sampling in which the researcher asks participants to answer prompts at automated times to chart their behavior.

Explicit awareness: Mindfulness about what you are doing and experiencing.

Exploratory research: The stage of research that explores a research topic through collecting data and using those observations to (1) refine the research question and (2) select and build on relevant theory.

Field notes: Narrative descriptions of your observations and reflections that are used as a dataset to analyze.

Fieldworkers: Paid workers who help collect data.

Fieldwork roles: Ways in which we are positioned relative to our participants (whether in-group or as an outsider).

First person: The point of view in which writer tells the story with themselves inserted in it as the storyteller.

Focal follows: *See* Continuous monitoring.

Focused coding: A form of coding that looks specifically for data that relate to pre-identified themes.

Focus groups: A type of interview that is specifically designed, through both selection of the participants and construction of the interview guide, to elicit dynamic conversations among a small group of people on a narrowly defined topic.

Folk taxonomies: Informal (non-Western science) knowledge structures that organize information about specific domains.

Frame elicitation: A data collection method that uses a structured interview to collect folk taxonomic information on a specific domain.

Free-listing: A method of data collection for building cultural models in which a participant is provided with a set of stimuli and then, through a structured interview or survey, directed to spontaneously list a small number of words or phrases in response to the stimuli.

Generalizability: How broadly applicable a study's findings are to interpreting or predicting human behavior elsewhere (aside from the study site and participants).

GPS unit: A handheld device that gives you precise longitude and latitude coordinates of where you are located.

Grounded theory: An approach in which you develop theory from the data, rather than selecting specific theories to apply to the data.

Group interviews: A type of interview in which more than one person participates in the interview process at once.

Human subjects: A common formal term that means the people whom you study (your participants).

Hypothetico-deductive model: A two-stage process that combines inductive research (as the first exploratory stage) and deductive research (as the second confirmatory stage).

Ideal culture: The behavioral patterns that people view as ideal or optimal.

Identifying information: Information that identifies participants and allows them to be tracked in the real world.

Immersion: The process of living in our study participants' communities and participating and observing in their everyday lives.

Imposter syndrome: A state when you feel that you aren't qualified to do what you are supposed to do, even though you actually are qualified.

Independent variables: Variables that exist on their own, unaffected by the others.

In-depth interviews: A type of semi-structured interview that is designed to gather a lot of information in great detail on a narrowly defined subject area.

Indicators: One or more measurements for a variable.

Indirect observation: Methods that analyze the materials left behind by human activities, such as material culture (artifacts, buildings), visual data (art, photos), and archives (written documents).

Induction: A way of conducting research that begins with collecting data on a topic, then generates hypotheses based on the data, and finally uses hypotheses to build or discuss relevant theory.

Inductive coding: Coding in which you start with your data, create labels that make sense for important pieces of information in your field notes, and then pile those labels into larger categories that make sense.

Informed consent: A process that informs potential participants about the project's purpose, what it entails, and any risks they might face before they begin participating in the project.

Institutional review board (IRB): A board or process that reviews and approves all research involving human and animal subjects.

Intellectual property: Creations of the mind, which may be held individually or collectively.

Interview guide: A list of open-ended questions or prompts that guides a semi-structured interview.

Interview schedule: The highly structured guide to introductory and follow-up questions for a structured interview.

Jottings: Brief phrases or photos that help you remember what happened during participant observation so that you can write longer descriptive narratives (field notes) later.

Key informants: People who know a lot about their culture and are willing to participate in your study.

Latent content: The underlying meaning behind the surface content of a communication.

Likert scale questions: Questions that ask you how strongly you agree with a statement, on a scale of 1 to 5.

Lumpers and splitters: A problem inherent to building group taxonomic systems in which some people tend to see fewer larger, inclusive categories and other people tend to see many smaller, diverse categories.

Manifest content: The tangible or concrete surface content (data).

Median: The number that is the midway point in your entire set of responses for a question. If there is an even number of responses, you take the average (mean) of the middle two numbers to find the median. If there is an odd number of responses, the median is the middle number of the dataset.

Merged integration: Integration of the findings of separate qualitative and quantitative data, after these forms of data have already been analyzed.

Methods: The researcher's approach to collecting and analyzing data; this includes epistemology, strategic methods, and techniques.

Mixed methods: The combination of qualitative and quantitative approaches.

Mobility mapping: A mapping method in which participants engage in participatory mapping to generate data about the movement of individuals or social groups.

Mode: The most common response. You count the number of times each response is used, and the mode is the response with the largest number of respondents.

Models: Representations of emergent culturally constructed, shared, and transmitted patterns.

Moral relativism: The idea that no one can judge another culture's practices, because morals are relative to their historical and cultural context.

Multidimensional: A term describing a variable that has multiple aspects to it and factors that lead to it—and can therefore have multiple values for each case.

Multivalent: The quality of symbols that allows them to have multiple meanings for different people.

Nonprobability samples: Samples that collect cultural data, so they can use a small number of participants who represent the whole population of study.

Nonreactive: A term used to describe a situation where participants are not aware they are being observed.

Objectivity: Descriptions of human behavior that include reflections on one's own biases, assumptions, and responses so that the researcher is clear about what they are bringing into their observation and interpretation.

Observing participant: A researcher studying a group to which they already belong.

Open coding: A form of coding that assigns codes to every part of the data that seems significant, without yet looking for specific themes or frameworks to apply to the data.

Open-ended questions: Questions that allow participants to respond in their own words.

Operational definitions: Definitions that provide specific instructions for how to measure variables.

Oral histories: A type of semi-structured interview that is designed to help a participant tell their life story in detail.

Orientation: What the researcher is attentive to.

Outliers: As a concept (rather than a calculation), an outlier is a response that is quite different from most or all of the rest.

Paradigms: Theoretical perspectives that provide broad ways of looking at the world and define the major issues with which the researcher is concerned.

Participant observation: Collecting data through spending many hours with the people you are studying, participating in their activities and observing them in their ordinary lives.

Participating observer: A researcher who begins as an outsider to the group they study and enters the group in order to conduct the study.

Participatory mapping: A mapping method in which participants draw maps based on your research question and prompts.

Participatory research: Research in which the researcher and the community or population being studied work more intensely and equally together to define the purpose, methods, and outcomes of the research.

Passive deception: A form of deception that does not seek to manipulate participants and instead is primarily practiced in public spaces, where the researcher doesn't try to hide their activities but also doesn't announce them.

Passive direct observation: A method that involves watching people and recording their behavior in the moment it occurs, without participating in it.

Peer review: A process for research and writing in which your colleagues review your work for methodological soundness and writing quality.

Phenomenology: Treating the subjective, lived, and embodied experience of the researcher as data to analyze.

Pile sorting: A method for data collection that uses a set of stimuli that the researcher provides in order to understand how people categorize items in a domain.

Pilot studies: Studies conducted before larger studies on the same question or topic.

Point of view: Your position as the writer in relationship to the story being told.

Polyvocality: Inserting a variety of participants' voices into field notes and the final manuscript.

Positionality: How facets of our identity are positioned vis-à-vis our participants, usually based on class, ethnicity, and other attributes that describe how we are alike or different.

Presentation: The analytical process through which the writer chooses how to present information, including writing style and point of view.

Pretest: A process of administering a survey to a very small sample while you are present, so that they can express areas that need clarity and improvement.

Primatology: The study of primates.

Privilege: A way of describing the additional, special benefits and advantages that some groups receive in a diverse society.

Probability samples: Samples in which every unit (whether individual, household, or another unit of analysis) should have an equal chance of being drawn into the study sample.

Probing: Interview techniques that stimulate further detail or conversation without leading the participant.

Protocol: A detailed plan that presents the significance of the research and plans for dissemination, the sampling and methods, an assessment of risk to participants, and how the researcher will minimize risk.

Purposive (judgment) sampling: Sampling that includes all willing participants, so long as they meet the purpose of your sample.

Qualitative questions: Questions that produce narrative text.

Quantitative questions: Questions that produce numerical data.

Quota sampling: A stratified sample based on certain categories of participants, in which the categories are assumed to matter for answering the research question.

Rapport: Trust between a researcher and their participants, such that participants feel that they can be open and honest.

Reactive: A term used to describe a situation where participants are aware they are being observed.

Reactivity: People changing their behavior because they know they are being studied or in response to characteristics of the researcher.

Real culture: The behavioral patterns that people demonstrate under usual conditions.

Reciprocal ethnography: A methodological process in which the researcher collaborates with research participants to review the findings and address conflicts between the researcher's interpretations and those of their participants.

Reflexivity: Turning the critical gaze back on one's own experiences, feelings, and thoughts to investigate one's own biases and assumptions.

Regular-interval diary: A diary that people keep for a regular period of time, such as daily or weekly.

Reliability: The determination of whether study results are consistent over time and reasonably complete representations of the population at hand.

Replicable: The condition that similar results should appear in similar settings when the study is repeated.

Representative sample: A sample that has the same demographic profile as your study population.

Resocialization: Training the researcher in a new culture and social structure during immersion.

Response effects: Differences in the responses of people being interviewed based on the characteristics of the interviewer.

Response rate: The rate at which targeted people open and respond to your survey (e.g., if you send the survey to one thousand people and seven hundred of them respond, you have a 70 percent response rate).

Reverse culture shock: Feelings of disorientation or depression when you return home and reenter your own culture.

Rubrics: Sets of standards that help you evaluate your work by giving it a score on different qualities, based on commonly agreed-on goals and indicators.

Rules of thumb: Generally agreed-on principles or guides based on the collective experiences in a cultural group.

Sample: A smaller population of participants in your research study that represents the larger population you are studying.

Sample accuracy: The condition that the sample isn't biased; every unit in the population has the same chance of being selected for participation.

Sample precision: The condition that the sample really represents the population being studied, and your results really would be how people in your study population would respond.

Sampling frame: A list of units of analysis from which you'll take the sample and to which you'll generalize.

Sampling grid: A table that outlines the variables you want to compare and how many participants you need in each of the resulting categories.

Schemas: Subcomponents of cultural models that are themselves models of more narrowly defined domains that are nested within the larger domain.

Selection: The analytical process through which the writer decides what to write about and what to leave out.

Self-administration: A form of survey distribution through the mail or online, where participants take the survey without any assistance or guidance from the researcher.

Self-assessment: A process by which you periodically review your own work against standards you select.

Semi-structured interviews: Logically structured but relatively open-ended interviews that schedule a time and location for each interview in advance.

Signal-entry diary: A diary that prompts participants to make an entry based on messages from the researcher (at structured or random times).

Simple random sample: A sample in which the sampling frame is queried based on randomly drawing participants on a numbered interval; every person (or unit) theoretically has an equal chance of being selected.

Sketches: Highly descriptive portions of narrative that contextualize your recorded observations.

Snowball (respondent-driven) sample: A sample drawn from the social (referral) networks of only a few people whom the researcher knows, who fit the category of participant needed.

Social and organizational networks: The relationships between individuals or organizations, usually depicted spatially in a web-like map that shows who interacts with whom.

Social desirability: When the interviewee tells you what they think will increase their social standing or status.

Specialized informants: Key informants with expert, specialized knowledge in a specific domain of the culture you are studying.

Spot sampling: A direct observation method in which you show up at randomly selected places and times to record what people are doing. Also called *time allocation*.

Strategic methods: How data are collected and/or analyzed.

Stratified random sample: A sample in which the sampling frame is divided into subpopulations based on key variables, prior to randomly drawing participants on a numbered interval.

Structured interviews: A highly structured type of interview in which people respond to a set of stimuli that is presented as identically as possible to each participant.

Surveys: Structured interviews that are often delivered online or via mail, rather than in person; also known as *questionnaires*.

Symbols: Things that stand for something else.

Taxonomies: Models that organize the relationships of entities within a domain.

Techniques: The details of how a researcher chooses to do what they choose to do.

Texts: A group of data for anthropological analysis (which does not have to be narrative or language-based).

Themes: Categorizations that articulate how the most significant patterns in your data fit into answering the research question.

Third-party effects: When the presence of a third person during an interview changes how the interviewee responds, usually due to issues of social desirability.

Third person: The point of view in which the writer tells the story as if they're a camera recording events around them.

Time allocation: *See* Spot sampling.

Total sample: A sample that includes all willing people from the larger population you are studying as your participants.

Triangulation: The search for agreement among multiple, different sources of information.

Unidimensional: A term describing a variable that has only a single value for each case.

Unstructured interviews: The type of interview most like a normal conversation, which happens anywhere and at any time, without prior scheduling, but focuses on the research question.

Validity: The determination of whether research measures what it is claiming to measure.

Value neutrality: A condition where the researcher would have no biases or values of their own and would be entirely neutral as an observer.

Values: The specific options an indicator can take.

Variables: Aspects of a research question that can take on more than one value.

Vulnerable populations: Groups within a society who face greater risk in their ordinary lives than the rest of the population.

Index

Interaction focused episode, 95
Internal states:
    assigning, 99
    variable, 6
Internal v. external behavior, 15
Interpretation, field note writing and, 90
Interval level of measurement, 12
Interview guide, 114–115, 248
Interview(s):
    archival data and, 210
    body language and, 122, 165
    culture and, 122
    data inaccuracies in, pressures that produce, 124
    deference and, 123
    diary v., 208
    discussion, 116, 124
    echoing, confirmation and, 120–121
    expectancy and, 123
    facilitating conversation, reflection, 122
    focus group, 115–116
    "grand tour" questions, 121
    group, 114–115
    guided questions, 114
    I don't know answers, probe meaning of, 121
    in-depth, 114
    nonverbal responses, 121–122
    open-ended prompts, 114
    oral histories, 114
    probing respondent, 120
    response effects, 123
    semi-structured, 114, 116–119
    silence, culture, conversation and, 120
    social desirability and, 123
    structured, 114
    third-party effects and, 123
    truth and, 122–124
    types of, 115
    unstructured, 113–114
    writing questions for, 120
Interview schedule, 114, 248
Introduction:
    ethnographic story and, 145
    interviewing and, 118
IRB. See Internal review board (IRB)

Jargon, 75
Jottings:
    continuous monitoring and, 228
    convert to field notes, 96–97
    defined, 248
    discussion, practice, 97
    field notes and, 79–83
    visual/material culture data collection, 205
    See also Field notes; Writing field notes
Journaling, 93, 103
Journal of Folklore Research, 173
Judgment, suspending, 74

Key informant:
    choosing, 58–59
    defined, 32, 248
    See also Informants
Knowledge:
    cognitive anthropology and, 177–178
    cultural, 177–178
    emergent patterns and, 185
    expert, 34
    mapping cultural, 222
    qualitative research and, 1–2
Kronenfeld, David B. (case study), 64–67, 199
Kronenfeld, Jerrold E., 199
Kronenfeld, John, 199

Language:
    skills, participant observation and, 74–75
    wording survey questions, 161
Latent content:
    analysis, 133–134
    defined, 133, 248
Latent meanings, symbols, 206
Leading question:
    avoiding, 162
    example, 163
    framing, 117
Letters, 210
Levels of measurement:
    types of, 12
    units of analysis, 11–13. See also Units of analysis
Likert scale questions, survey, 157–159, 190, 248
Limitations:
    case study, 11
    decision-making and, 192
    emergent, responding to, 37
    logistical, sampling, 53
    participant, 209
    resource, 167
    student researcher and, 21, 22, 64
    time, research and, 79